Rereading
Nadine Gordimer

Kathrin Wagner

INDIANA UNIVERSITY
PRESS
Bloomington and Indianapolis

© Maskew Miller Longman (Pty) Ltd and Witwatersrand University Press, 1994

First published and manufactured in South Africa by
Maskew Miller Longman in collaboration with
Witwatersrand University Press and Indiana University Press in 1994.

Library of Congress Cataloging-in-Publication Data

Wagner, Kathrin
        Rereading Nadine Gordimer
    Kathrin Wagner.
        p.   cm.
    Includes bibliographical references.
    ISBN 0-253-36303-9 (cloth)
    1. Gordimer, Nadine—Political and social views. 2. Feminism and literature—South Africa—History—20th century. 3. Literature and society—South Africa—History—20th century. 4. Women and literature—South Africa—History—20th century. 5. Race relations in literature. 6. South Africa—In literature. 7. Blacks in literature. I. Title.
    PR9369.3.G6Z96   1994
    823—dc20   93-44183

1 2 3 4 5 99 98 97 96 95 94

Set in 10 on 12 point Sabon
Typeset by Beverley Visser
Imagesetting by Castle Graphics
Printed by CTP Book Printers

Epigraphs

It is not in apartheid or protest against apartheid practices that our literature has gained its truly original note, but rather in the unique degree to which the cultural desert has penetrated its inner being, establishing a certain quality of nullity (whether found in a shop-window display or dismal post-war suburb) that is the deepest source of their work. There are a host of writers who simply, helplessly, reiterate the most mundane of empirical realities in all their triviality, reproducing the imaginative flatness of their subject unimaginatively, whether they be hymning the South African institution of the corner cafe or the Sunday braai-vleis at the Vaal Dam. But there are also a few who can render this cultural flatness so as to suggest something other than its own impoverishment, who are able to extract from flatness itself a uniquely haunting note.

Stephen Watson (1)

Never trust the artist. Trust the tale. The proper function of a critic is to save the tale from the artist who created it.

D.H. Lawrence (2)

Contents

Preface

*For while objectively a social reality, the work of art is, in its
genesis, a projection of a deeply personal process, and any
approach that ignores the personal at the expense of the social
is necessarily incomplete . . . The artist is no freer than the
society in which he lives.*

Ralph Ellison[1]

*Reading is never innocent; its deepest concealed reserves are a
will to authorise certain views of texts and suppress others;
even a certain 'blindness' in the interpretation owes not a little
to attempts to evade, misjudge, and mispronounce; to clear
space, so to speak, for certain texts in such a way that they
may unfurl their wings undisturbed in a terrain full of the
alarming noise of struggle, where voices are sounded only as
countervoices to others.*

Lewis Nkosi[2]

This book grew out of an investigation of landscape iconography
in South African fiction which was originally intended to examine the extent to which descriptions of place in the novels of three
major South African writers, André Brink, Nadine Gordimer and
J.M. Coetzee, not only reinforce these novelists' thematic concerns but also seem to encode a characteristically settler or colonial consciousness of Africa-as-not-Europe.[3] The extent to which
the vision of these writers appears to be directed (often unconsciously) by a Eurocentric perspective seemed to me to set up
an interesting tension between their subjective emotional orientation and their overtly anti-colonialist political commitments.
That some of these tensions have been endemic in white English-
language South African fiction since its beginnings has been
convincingly demonstrated in J.M. Coetzee's 1988 study of early
poetry, fiction and travel writing, *White Writing*, but no parallel
analysis of the issues raised by such tensions in more recent white

English-language writing has yet appeared. My own growing interest in tracing the implications of such perceptions across the range of Gordimer's writing in particular led to a conviction that a reassessment of her work within such a framework would not only prove fruitful but should take precedence over the investigation originally planned.

In consequence, this study now moves beyond a narrow focus on landscape to offer a rereading of Gordimer's novels at several levels, with a particular focus on areas of her work which have to date received little critical attention. A brief consideration of Gordimer as a political writer is followed by an examination of the subtextual survival and prevalence of cultural and ethnic stereotypes in her novels. These often conflict considerably with the overt ideological thrust of the fiction, and at times establish a subtextual field of reference which qualifies her political project as an *engagé* writer in significant ways. An analysis of both the credibility and significance of her denial of a feminist perspective in her work, an examination of the stereotypes which she inherits and develops in her construction of the figure of the black South African in her fiction, and an investigation of the extent to which landscape iconography is shaped by colonialist paradigms form the subjects of further chapters.

These readings are centred upon an attempt to establish Gordimer's relative strengths and weaknesses as both an interpreter and a recorder of the South African experience, an enquiry initially prompted by my deep-seated discomfort with the claim that she should be seen as *the* spokesperson for white South Africa. In particular, the assumption embedded in such a description, that her fiction may function as a transparent mirror of her society, 'innocent' of ideological bias, is queried; instead, I argue that her work is of necessity marked at every level by her enmeshment in a specific historical situation whose primary characteristics of conflict and division are not only the novels' overt subject matter but also work internally to complicate and qualify her project. The ambiguities which arise from such tensions shape the works in interesting and often contradictory ways, and an examination of the many ways in which they manifest themselves in the novels, in particular, forms the core of this study.

The novels are not dealt with chronologically since it is the continuities of concern that will be illuminated in Gordimer's work, rather than her development as a writer or political activist: the interfiliations between history and Gordimer's fiction have in any case already been impressively dealt with in Stephen Clingman's study,[4] and need not be investigated in any detail here. The short stories have been excluded from consideration for several reasons. Firstly, the complexity of development made possible by the longer novel form allows contradictions and gaps in Gordimer's work to emerge more clearly there than in the more compressed, highly polished and carefully controlled short stories. Secondly, it is in the novel form that Gordimer may be seen to develop most fully her moral agenda as an artist in a society which she perceives as being in need of both guidance and enlightenment. Both her commitment to narrative realism and her sense of what the role of the artist in society should be were powerfully influenced by the nineteenth century novels she read so voraciously in her youth, and the legacy of form and philosophy this left her with needs to be more carefully examined. Thirdly, both the repetitive patterns of response and the thematic continuities which pervade the broad body of Gordimer's work, and which have received little critical attention to date, emerge with a useful clarity from a study of the longer works. In addition, we should note Gordimer's own attitudes to the longer form. Relatively early in her career, in 1965, she spoke somewhat wistfully of her attraction to the novel as a medium, saying that 'I really do want to write novels . . . I have written a few stories that satisfy me but I've not written a novel that comes anywhere near doing so.'[5] By 1984 her commitment to the longer form was fully established: 'I am finding life more and more complex,' she said in an interview, 'and it occurs to me as something less episodic; able to be explored better in larger works'.[6] Such statements encourage us to move away from the focus upon the short stories which has been so prevalent in many Gordimer studies to date, and to consider the nature and extent of her achievement in those 'larger works'.

This study was largely written before January 1991, and concentrates upon the nine novels written between 1953 and 1987; Gordimer's tenth and most recent novel, *My Son's Story*, published late in 1990, is discussed only in the conclusion. Several other works which will be essential to future Gordimer studies were either unobtainable in South Africa at the time or became available too late to reshape my original argument, while a subsequent eighteen months of academic travel outside South Africa have made any extensive later revision of this work impossible. It is, however, in the nature of academic research that work remains always 'in progress', and it is within that framework that these readings are offered.

The doctoral dissertation on which this book is based was accepted by the University of the Witwatersrand in Johannesburg, South Africa, in 1991.[7] I am particularly indebted to the University and its English Department for supporting me in paper presentations at two conferences in Germany and England which enabled me to test and refine my ideas within an international forum.* The original study could not have been completed without the patient and consistent advice, encouragement and support of a number of colleagues and friends: my warmest thanks are due to Brian Cheadle, Anthony Woodward, Martin Trump and Cherry Clayton; to Dennis Radford; and to Gillian Solomon, Mairead Helfrich, and Alice Tshuma, for their constant support at many levels over the years this project swallowed up. In Vancouver, thanks are particularly due to Herbert Rosengarten, Head of the English Department at the University of British Columbia, and to Renate Feuchtwanger and Kathy Brett, who both in their own ways greatly facilitated the final revision process. My son, Tom, was most affected during its creation and was perhaps the one most delighted upon its completion: it is dedicated to him, as a young South African.

Kathrin Wagner
University of British Columbia
June 1993

---

* I am also grateful to the Human Sciences Research Council, without whose financial support I could not have attended the ACLALS Triennial Conference at the University of Kent, England, in August 1989.

Chapter 1

Introduction:
South Africa's Conscience

Perhaps some Western writers are longing for subjects pro-
vided by spasms of historical change, but . . . we . . . perceive
History as a curse and prefer to restore to literature its
autonomy, dignity, and independence from social pressures.

Czeslaw Milosz[1]

[We] know that by openly fighting tradition we perpetuate it,
that revolutionary literature is a filial impulse, and that matu-
rity is the assimilation of the features of every ancestor.

Derek Walcott[2]

When Nadine Gordimer was awarded the Nobel Prize for literature in 1991, her achievements both as a short story writer and as
a novelist were given resounding international recognition. She
had, however, consistently attracted serious critical attention
both within and outside South Africa since the late 1950s. Both a
growing number of substantial scholarly articles and six
booklength studies have appeared in the last sixteen years, the
most recent contributions being Stephen Clingman's influential
analysis of the relationship between the novels, their historical
context and Gordimer's political development, and Judie
Newman's monograph dealing with Gordimer's response to the
imperatives of feminist and political ideologies.[3] Gordimer's
work has been particularly enthusiastically received in recent
years in America and Europe: an international readership
anxious to learn more about the complexities of the South African experience has found in her work what has seemed to be an
accessible, thoughtful and subtle reflection of what it might be
understood to have been 'really' like to have lived under South
Africa's apartheid régime over the past forty years. Indeed, given
the very small number of works of imaginative fiction emanating

from white South Africa over these decades, it is not surprising that Gordimer should by now be regarded as '*the* interpreter of the South African experience to the outside world', and, given her life-long articulate opposition to white supremacist politics, quite simply as 'South Africa's conscience'.[4]

Such assessments not only implicitly endorse her particular rendering of the South African experience, raising her representation of it to the status of an all-embracing 'Truth', but also give assent to Gordimer's own claim that her vision is in some way especially privileged by virtue of her status as artist-observer in her society. She herself clearly sees her work as going some way toward filling the gap identified in her 1965 comment that 'Africa needs an articulated consciousness other than that of newspaper headlines and political speeches',[5] and critics who have located the value of her work primarily in its political and historical dimensions have responded enthusiastically to the idea that 'Africa' may be endowed with such a consciousness through her writings. Stephen Clingman, for example, has characterised her work as 'history from the inside',[6] and tells us that 'if we are searching for an inner pathway to guide us through South African history over the past forty or so years, there are few better places to look for it than in her novels'.

Yet, despite growing international acclaim, Gordimer's work has been relatively unpopular within South Africa. Sales of her work to the general public have been, according to her publishers, 'really very low', and the response 'very limited',[8] while her status in the black community – with the aspirations of which she has identified herself – has in the past been equally uncertain.[9] Not only has she struggled to attract a popular readership at home; academic response within South Africa has also, and often overwhelmingly, expressed critical dissatisfaction with a number of aspects of her work. Early New Critical readings, deploying the Leavisite criteria current in university English Departments at the time, recognised her skills both as a social commentator and as a sensitive recorder of the particularities of place in all its sensory and emotional texturings, but attacked her for a hollowness of content,[10] finding the early novels in particular banal, sentimental, melodramatic and narcissistic, shot through not only with 'vulgarity' but also with cultural and sexual 'snobbery', and limited by what was dismissively termed a 'women's-magazine level' of sensibility. One critic concluded his sharp essay in 1961 with the caustic comment that 'she is a marvellous, vivacious observer, with nothing very subtle to say, and with an ever-growing facility for saying it',[11] while Dennis Brutus complained in a now widely-known remark that 'she lacks warmth, lacks feeling, but can observe with the detachment, with the coldness, of a machine'.[12] He laid the blame on the dehumanising impact of apartheid upon white and black alike, and was thus among the first to suggest that Gordimer may be understood best as a writer trapped within the historical situation her vision seeks to transcend.

As Gordimer's work became more sharply focused upon an examination of the manifold ways in which private lives are invaded by public realities in South Africa, criticism shifted to an attack upon the adequacy of her grasp of the political and ideological issues at stake: South African critics who were themselves firmly anti-apartheid responded at times with considerable irritation to the political vision embedded in the works. In 1983 Heribert Adam attempted to demonstrate that her widely read article entitled 'Living in the Interregnum', which was published in *The New York Review of Books* in that year, was based on misleading stereotypes and false assumptions about the course history was taking in South Africa.[13] It was a view which implicitly underpinned Morphet's claim the following year that Gordimer's analysis of the South African situation was both class and gender bound, being limited to what he termed 'the suburban kitsch of revolutionary politics'.[14] In 1989 Parker went further in suggesting that Gordimer's work unwittingly endorses 'a hegemony, not of class, but of colour, white'; and he dismissively characterised Gordimer's 'notion' in *A Sport of Nature* that only a 'spontaneous mutation' could save white South Africans in the coming New Age as one that simply 'will not do'.[15]

These assessments find themselves in a certain harmony with the more radical claim that Gordimer's achievement as an artist has in some respects been compromised rather than strengthened by her commitment to a specific political position. In 1984 Enright drily suggested that 'Nadine Gordimer survives as a writer of distinction by virtue less of her themes than of her distinction as a writer',[16] a view taken up in Maclennan's complaint in 1989 that 'it is ideology that demands her characters be emptied of all life except what is demanded by ideology. It is ideology that gives Gordimer's work its feeling of emptiness, futility and powerlessness'.[17] Indeed, Gordimer's increasingly single-minded commitment to exploring issues of race and colour in her fiction has led to the accusation that in effect she presents South Africa as a 'single-issue society'. Critical irritation with the limitations of this perspective has expressed itself both in Cooper's recent claim that Gordimer has been misled by such commitments '[to underplay] the realities of social class and [to compromise] on issues of gender',[18] and in Haugh's caustic observation in 1974 that 'if race is the only story worthy of the sustained attention of the South African novelist, then we must offer him our sympathy'.[19]

Such responses may be seen as a symptom of something more than an expression of the residual but still pervasive prejudice against the allegedly second-rate quality of indigenous fiction so often characteristic of colonial societies, which was a factor to be reckoned with in the recent past. Nor is this necessarily another case of a prophet's voice being unwelcome in her own country.[20] Claims such as these – however intemperate we may feel some of them to be – express such radical reservations among Gordimer's peers as to the value of her particular vision of the extraordinarily complex, multilayered and multifaceted world her fiction inhabits and emanates from, and contrast so sharply with the international acclaim her work has attracted, that they cannot simply be discounted, particularly as they isolate for critical rejection precisely those overtly political elements to which her anti-apartheid international readership has been most strongly attracted. In essence, they have in common an unease with the quality of Gordimer's vision, a sense by her compatriots that there is something fundamentally unsatisfying and even misleading about her interpretation of the South African experience.

We will come closer to the roots of that unease when we move away from the focus on politics to the ambiguities and contradictions inherent in Gordimer's position in her society. When Morphet tells us that much of her work is 'skewed' by her 'personal drama',[21] or Clingman argues that she is caught in a 'split position',[22] they alert us to those complex limitations and qualifications upon her vision touched upon in the self-directed irony of Gordimer's own admission that '[her] consciousness is of necessity the same colour as [her] face'.[23] The writer glimpsed here is indeed a far more interesting figure than the one stereotyped as the 'conscience' of South Africa or excoriated as merely banal in her interpretations. Here instead we have the shadowy outlines of an imagination not only personally but also to an unusual degree socially and historically compromised by the crippling limitations of life in a divided and compartmentalised society. Gordimer's work is in fact worthy of our sustained critical attention not merely because of its choice of subject matter but because of its fascinating revelation of a consciousness of necessity permeated, shaped and bounded by precisely those extraordinary and irresolvable tensions and contradictions characteristic of South Africa under apartheid which the narrative stance of the fiction implicitly claims to have transcended. Instead of simply tracing the outlines of the history offered, we need to query the concept of 'history' at work in the fiction; we need to ask what aspects of that 'history' she has been witness to, how restricted her sense of it has been and what subjectivities colour her representation of it. What indeed is the nature of the 'split position' in which Gordimer finds herself, and to what extent may she herself be seen to be entrapped in that Hegelian state of disintegrated consciousness which she has so incisively defined as the condition of white South Africans 'living in the interregnum'?[24]

Such an enquiry will illuminate the extent to which Gordimer's position is beset by paradox.[25] In her writings she implicitly and explicitly urges onward a historical process whose revolutionary phase must destroy the comfortable contexts within which she writes. She identifies herself with the political aspirations of a black community in which, as a white writer, she can have only observer status: one from which she is excluded not only by apartheid legislation but also by significant linguistic and cultural barriers. Her courageous and essentially idealistic expression of sympathy with the oppressed must balance uneasily between her attraction to what her imagination makes of that black world and the implications of her base in precisely that class of wealthy, leisured, white South Africans whose comforts are assured by the continuance of the régime she condemns. Her fiction not only reflects a consciousness which has been as fully shaped by the inner tensions of the white culture she rejects as by the resistance ideologies she has come to embrace more fully; it is also at times undermined by precisely those terms which it tries to suppress. An examination of the novels in depth will reveal the many ways in which they reinscribe and valorise at a subtextual level some of those pervasive racial and cultural myths submerged in South Africa's psychic life which continue to survive considerable social, economic and political change in the country. Indeed, despite her engagement with the issues of a post-colonial reality in such novels as *A Guest of Honour* and *A Sport of Nature*, Gordimer remains in essence enmeshed and entrapped in some archetypal colonialist paradigms in her deepest psychic responses to the world she attempts to reflect.

Chapter 2

Liberalism, Ideology and Commitment

In respect of any art one takes seriously one has to make value-judgements, since a real response entails this; it entails forming an implicit critical sense of the human significance of the art in question, and the demand of the intelligence is that one should bring one's sense to conscious definition.

F.R. Leavis[1]

All white African literature is the literature of exile, not from Europe, but from Africa.

Doris Lessing[2]

'a romantic struggling with reality'

Gordimer's first novel appeared in 1953, only a few years after the Nationalist government took power in 1948 and began to entrench its policies of racial division; her most recent novel was published in 1990, even as the De Klerk government moved to release Nelson Mandela and took its first substantive steps towards dismantling the apartheid state. During these forty years apartheid became the all-consuming single internal issue at the core of the country's psychic and intellectual life, while South Africa's international image increasingly became, in the words of one critic, that of 'a rather small hole of howling white savagery'.[3] More particularly, the urgent philosophical and moral problems apartheid threw up on a daily basis inevitably drew writers of conscience into an increasing focus on an anti-apartheid polemic in their work, giving rise to what Morphet has called a 'solidarity constitution' in the literature of the time, or, more simply, the 'culture of apartheid'.[4]

Gordimer's position as, in effect, one of the founders of this

'culture' is not a simple one. Firstly, there is the problem of
audience already touched upon in the previous chapter. The gap
between her reputation as a writer outside South Africa and that
within, suggests something of the extent to which her work has
been valued internationally not only for its literary qualities but
also for the sheer amount of information she appears to be able
to offer outsiders about the actual conditions of life within the
country. However, her typical internal readership of politically
well-informed peers has demanded of her a vision which goes
beyond a mere record or reflection of conditions all too distress-
ingly familiar.[5] However fresh and informative her depiction of
these conditions may appear to be to outsiders, it seems clear that
those readers who are subject to such conditions on a daily basis
often find her depictions tired or clichéd. There has also been
some resistance to the prescriptive tone of her statement in 1984
that 'the white writer's task as cultural worker is to raise the consciousness of white people', a stance in any case somewhat at
odds with her comment in the same year to Robert Boyers that 'I
myself don't write for any audience . . . while I'm writing I have
this crazy illusion that it's only for me'.[6]

Secondly, as a number of critics have pointed out in discussing
Gordimer's work, her position as a white South African
problematises her status as a post-colonial writer. Although she
has embraced the post-colonial future South Africa is headed towards whole-heartedly, her work continues to be seen as limited
by its origins in a white 'settler' perspective, despite her whole-
hearted alignment of herself with the forces of change. There is
considerable inherent irony in Brennan's observation that, although Gordimer and Coetzee both clearly play 'a mediating
role, [they] are probably better placed in some category of the
European novel of Empire because of their compromised positions of segregated privilege within colonial settler states'.[7] The
difficulties critics have experienced in politically 'placing' her
work is reflected in the fact that Gordimer's name does not appear in the index to Ashcroft, Griffiths and Tiffin's influential
1989 contribution to post-colonial literary theory, *The Empire
Writes Back*, nor is her work included for discussion in recent
studies of 'African writing' or 'African women's writing'. Lewis

Nkosi has remarked that Gordimer and others of her generation 'were never classified under the rubric of the "new" [literatures in English] . . . their subject matter may have been considered somewhat "exotic", but no one thought of them as anything but continuers of a metropolitan tradition of English literature'.[8] In addition, the narrative realism of the novels, which many South African writers felt was required by the times, marginalised Gordimer's work in a period of radical technical innovation and experimentation in mainstream English-language literature. In effect, her fiction may be said to have fallen between the gaps in contemporary literary theory.

Thirdly, Gordimer's enmeshment in private and characteristically colonial dilemmas, and in particular her struggle to find ways to connect with her African inheritance and to separate herself from aspects of her settler origins, expresses itself in a network of ambiguous and complex responses to the imperatives of her position which problematises her work considerably. On the one hand, her need to discover or construct a genuinely *African* identity for herself is one shared by many of her white South African readers, and it is this submerged aspect of her work, still largely unrecognised in critical commentaries, which may eventually be of most enduring interest to a future audience. However, the extent to which this search underlies and informs the overt political commitments of the fiction also throws into question the claim that the value of Gordimer's work should be seen to lie simply in its investigation of the impact of apartheid on individual lives. On the other hand, the fiction does not, in fact, offer us as straightforward and unequivocal an articulation of political commitment as it appears to do. The tensions between the conflicting claims of liberalism and radicalism in Gordimer's life, of passivity and activism, escape and engagement, individualism and the collective imperative, pervade and infuse every aspect of the fiction, and contribute a subtext of ambiguity and contradiction which runs below the surface of all of the novels. Examination of these tensions will reveal something of the complex connections in both work and life between private experience and public action, and will illuminate some of the lesser known origins of her particular and complex body of work.

'an unbeliever living in the midst of a fanatical cult'

The maintenance of a delicate balance between continuity of concern and ambivalence of response is, as we shall see, the hallmark of Gordimer's fiction when it is understood in its entirety, beyond the overt certainties of its moralist stance in relationship to the impact of apartheid on South African lives. Whereas we find the clearest and most unequivocal statements of the personal ideology which sustains such certainties in the non-fiction, it is in the fiction that a contrary emphasis on ambiguity, ambivalence and contradiction is revealed which simultaneously contextualises and interrogates the moralist's thrust; it is only here that Gordimer fully develops her sense of the acute tensions between the private world of subjective experience and the felt need to engage with the public political demands of the day which lie at the core of her work. Ambivalence resists closure; and the extent to which she herself has recognised the irresolvable nature of the personal dilemmas with which the fiction is concerned is frequently brought to the fore in the novels, as when Bray in *A Guest of Honour* emphasises complexity as a fundamental condition of life in musing that 'one could never hope to be free of doubt, of contradictions within . . . this was the state in which one lived – the state of life itself – and no action could be free of it' (487).

The constraints of doubt and contradiction have clearly affected Gordimer's own development. The characteristic emphasis in the novels on the invasive impact that the environment of institutionalised racism has on the individual's moral and emotional development is already apparent in Gordimer's perception of the stages of growth she herself experienced. In particular, her occasional and scattered accounts of her own childhood are illuminatingly paralleled in her analysis of Helen's development in *The Lying Days*. For instance, like herself, Helen rejects in late adolescence the narrow contexts of the mining world into which she has been born for *personal* rather than for political reasons, an emphasis which reveals the extent to which Gordimer's own later overt opposition to the ideological framework of life in apartheid South Africa began initially as simply an expression of her disaffection with that style of colonial life into which she was born, and to which apartheid was as natural as the air she breathed. Her early education in the ways of the world in a childhood framed by the stable conservatism of an East Rand mining town, where the existence of the black underclass was scarcely noticed, was counterbalanced by the deep influence upon her of the liberal humanism she absorbed through her voracious reading of the classics of both the English and the Continental tradition, making of her, in Tom's words as he muses on the changes in Jessie at the end of *Occasion for Loving*, 'an unbeliever living in the midst of a fanatical cult' (285).

Although she was relatively well socialised into the mining community in which she grew up, her almost exclusively Eurocentric literary education, pursued largely in privacy outside the framework of family, friends and the daily routine, provided her with those liberal values which were to set her at odds with the apartheid ideology of her society. Her personal rebelliousness was atypical, but her willingness to look to Europe for models by which to shape her experience alerts us to the extent to which she may be understood as, nevertheless, a typical product of colonialism, suffering from its characteristic sense of both cultural insecurity and marginalisation.

That she was beset by both is implicit in the many autobiographical details she has offered in those of her essays which chart the extent of her early disaffection with colonial culture before her opposition to apartheid came to the fore in her work. For example, in 1964, Gordimer detailed for the English readers of *The Times Literary Supplement* the formative influence the writers of Leavis's 'Great Tradition' had had upon her emotional and philosophical development.[9] Although she notes on the one hand how fortunate she had been to be able to internalise the substance of this literature without being 'coerced in [her tastes] by the kind of education, libraries, journals, conversation, class distinction, and even ancient buildings which surround a literature in the country and among the people of its origin', she simultaneously characterises her South African childhood contexts (in contrast to the metropolitan contexts of her reading) without affection as 'mealy-mouthed, genteelly hypocritical and petty respectable – the whole smug suet of white provincialism that covered my seventeen years, swaddling and shroud in one'.[10]

This world was not only 'something to kick flying'[11] through forays into the world of student intellectuals, of liberal professionals and of the black townships, but also lay behind her initial and apolitical urge to 'escape' South Africa's isolation by 'fleeing' to metropolitan Europe. It is an urge which surfaces again and again in the novels, tempting characters from the *The Lying Days* to *A Sport of Nature* to abandon South Africa's complexities for brighter shores. Although Gordimer herself, unlike other colonial writers such as Pringle, Schreiner and Mansfield, did not succumb to this impulse to escape, the fact that so typical a colonial urge surfaces repeatedly in the fiction is perhaps as significant as its defeat, and the vividness with which the temptation is presented frequently stands in sharp contrast to the often perfunctorily presented and obscurely motivated decisions to remain or return with which a number of the novels unsatisfactorily conclude.

Moreover, it is important to realise that such impulses express a wish to escape not only *to* Europe but also *from* the tensions of the South African political context. Gordimer's writings in effect clearly show that her political development has been dogged by a struggle to *deny* or evade that imperative so often felt by aware South Africans to engage in action, to join a group, to 'do something' about the injustices of the régime: in a 1959 essay significantly entitled 'Where Do Whites Fit In?', she wrote – in the present tense – that

> some of us in South Africa want to leave . . . I myself fluctuate between the desire to be gone – to find a society where my white skin will have no bearing on my place in the community – and a terrible, obstinate and fearful desire to stay. I feel the one desire with my head and the other with my guts . . . If one will always have to feel white first and African second, it would be better not to stay on in Africa. It would not be worth it for this. Yet, although I claim no mystique about Africa, I fear that . . . I might, dumped somewhere else and kindly treated, continually plod blindly back to where I came from.[12]

Such passages suggest how deeply Gordimer has felt herself to be exiled from that spiritual and philosophical metropolis whose values seemed to survive only in debased and corrupted forms in the colonial context. At the same time she also experienced herself as being in 'internal exile' in the land of her birth: not only because she was opposed to the dominant apartheid ideology of her time but arguably also because, for a considerable period, she resisted the felt imperative to 'join up'. The fiction reflects this sense of multiple exile. Novel after novel investigates the feasibility of various escape routes both from the physical context and the pressure to 'be committed', presenting us with characters in flight not only from their backgrounds but also from the ideological imperative itself.

Within such a context, Gordimer's choice of metaphor in her comment (in 1963) upon the growth in her sensitivity to the political issues of her own country is revealing: 'The "problems" of my country did not set me writing; on the contrary, it was learning to write that sent me falling, falling, falling through the surface of "the South African way of life".'[13] It is a fall into a hellish Conradian 'heart of darkness' which is fiercely resisted, both explicitly in Gordimer's repeated insistence upon the writer's need to maintain her autonomy and political independence, and implicitly in the emphasis she gives to her characters' reluctance to sacrifice their lives to a cause, despite the repeated charting in the novels of the defeat of such impulses to resist the imperatives of historical process.[14] We may also speculate that Gordimer's particular sympathy for the positions of the Black Consciousness Movement in the early 1970s expressed not only an acceptance of its claim that white contributions to the new Azania (which was taking on an ideological identity at the time) were redundant, but also, perhaps, a submerged element of relief at finding the uncomfortable option of acting on behalf of the oppressed masses to be no longer a valid one.

That such tensions underlie the fiction's increasingly overt commitment to the need for political engagement as the only solution to the compromised position of white South Africans is revealed in the ambivalence of Gordimer's responses, not only to a liberalism presented as debased, paralysed and impotent, but also to the only viable alternative offered, radical political activism. On the one hand, the marked impulse both to escape small-town South African bigotry, and at the same time to avoid the destructive vortex of political commitment, is assigned in the fiction to precisely that class of well-to-do English-speaking whites whose superficial 'liberalism' of outlook becomes the target of her most devastating critique.[15] Yet, in so far as Gordimer may be understood to 'know' the particular dilemmas of these individuals from the inside, her ultimate rejection of their attitudes is of necessity qualified both by her sense of the complexity of their position and by an inherent element of conservatism in her own perspectives which have as yet received too little critical attention. The debate mounted in the novels between 'liberalism' and its radical alternatives is, in fact, more complex than at first appears.

There are three distinct groups of liberals who are under attack to a greater or lesser degree in the fiction. Firstly, there is a large group made up of those who do little more than embrace alternative attitudes and lifestyles which incorporate a disapproval of apartheid and an awareness of and respect for the idea of fundamental human rights for all. But progressive and even radical opinions fail to impel such individuals to meaningful action other than, for example, the writing of academic papers, and their liberalism expresses itself chiefly in no more than the self-flattering and only occasionally discomfiting development of instructive friendships and liaisons across the colour bar. Gordimer's condemnation of this group throughout the novels expresses reservations widely felt about liberalism within South Africa during the last four decades. Es'kia Mphahlele, for example, spoke for dissident South Africans in general in saying in 1983 that 'there is something sinister about white liberalism in this country . . . [it] constantly pleads that the law be obeyed, and that the political morality of the rulers can only be subverted when the same rulers experience a change of heart'.[16] In so far as liberals were seen to insist on respect for the laws of even an unjust regime, they were accused of collaboration with apartheid, as Mehring is in Gordimer's subtle analysis of the relationship between liberalism, capitalism and apartheid in *The Conservationist* (1974).[17] As early as *The Lying Days* we have the beginnings of a critique of the passivity, self-deception and ego-centricity attributed to such circles in Gordimer's depiction of Helen's disillusionment with the group of trendy young Johannesburg intellectuals which Joel introduces her to, a group which will reappear in various guises in the novels to come. What repels Helen is also what repels Toby, Jessie, Elizabeth and many of Gordimer's other protagonists: the stultifying imprisonment of this group within the ideological clichés to which complex ideas are reduced, and which finds expression in a concentration on petty appearances rather than on meaningful action. Frequently an initial idealism is reduced to an obsession with trivial details which easily slides into a form of hypocrisy. Helen's opinion of Jenny, for example, changes radically when she realises that Jenny accepts the fact that she is 'not allowed' to wear a hat by her husband because to do so would be labelled 'bourgeois' (*The Lying Days*, 214). Her disillusionment becomes full-blown when Jenny and her family nevertheless move with many excuses into the comfortable 'bourgeois' suburb of 'Parkcrest' as soon as they can afford to do so. The hypocrisy of Antonia in *The Conservationist* is not very different. She gratefully accepts an exit permit acquired through the help of lawyers paid for by her lover, the arch-capitalist Mehring, whose political stance and economic connections she professes to despise, rather than go to prison for her liberal beliefs and radical friendships. In *Occasion for Loving* Jessie laments the element of posturing in such circles, and the felt need to create and maintain an image, when she complains that

> the whole way we live becomes a political gesture above every-
> thing else . . . there's no room to develop as a person because any
> change in yourself might appear to be a defection. And yet if you
> can't change . . . how can you be ready for some new demand?
> (243-44)

In this novel the extent to which a mere academic interest in Africa and its history and affairs, however worthy, marginalises its devotees is suggested in the contrast set up between Tom Stilwell's and Boaz Davis's liberal but safe pursuits, and the sense of acute danger which overwhelms Gideon and Ann when their affair changes from being a mere diversion into what appears to be a genuine commitment to each other. Maureen's paralysis of will in *July's People* is a logical extension of Tom's well-meaning passivity, while Hillela in *A Sport of Nature*, mourning Whaila's assassination, bitterly blames the liberals 'who let it happen' (267) in a characteristic castigation of the inexcusable impotence of liberalism in the face of violent aggression. Gordimer gives this group short shrift throughout her fiction.

Anna Louw in *A World of Strangers* belongs to what may loosely be identified as a second, loosely-knit group of white liberals, one which gains an increasing prominence as Gordimer's work develops, and which may be identified as made up of those who attempt to involve themselves directly in some sort of anti-apartheid activism: civil rights lawyers such as Anna Louw, Lionel Burger and his friends and associates in *Burger's Daughter*, human rights activists such as Toby's parents in *A World of Strangers*, and earnest workers for a cause in general such as Colonel Evelyn Bray in *A Guest of Honour* and Pauline's circle in *A Sport of Nature*. It is this class which Gordimer herself perhaps knows best, towards which she feels most ambivalent, and which at times becomes the target of her sharpest irony.

On the one hand, the element of enthusiastic, generous and romantic idealism which inspires the commitment of these individuals is presented as, of course, having its own value, a value most articulately and persuasively defended by Sasha in his meditation in *A Sport of Nature*:

> The dynamic of real change is always utopian. The original impetus may get modified – even messed up in the result, but it has to be there no matter how far from utopia that result may be.
>
> Utopia is unattainable; without aiming for it taking a chance! – you can never hope even to fall far short of it . . . Without utopia – the idea of utopia – there's a failure of the imagination – and that's a failure to know how to go on living. (187)

But so unequivocal an affirmation comes only late in Gordimer's career, and in the bulk of her work she not only sketches in the undeniable virtues of this group of 'do-gooders', but also highlights with considerable sharpness their inadequacies and failures as both activists and individuals. Their tendency, for example, to betray a self-righteous and insensitive rigidity of attitude is fiercely resisted by Gordimer's favoured protagonists. In *A World of Strangers*, Toby remembers with anger that his parents took away from him his grandfather's sword, which he found as a boy and wanted to hang up on display in the hall; they also refused 'to display his grandfather's citation for Boer War bravery in a home where Imperialism was deplored' (33). The child's natural attachment to this romantic element in family history is violated and denied in the service of ideological cliché, with the result that Toby sees his parents' world suddenly as one in which

> the atmosphere of ideological flux which I had breathed all my
> life . . . seemed terrifyingly thin . . . My mother and father gave
> up a great many small, unworthy things that, together, consti-
> tuted a workable framework of living, but what did they have to
> offer in their place? Freedom, an empty international plain where
> a wind turns over torn newspapers printed in languages you don't
> understand. (34)

Gordimer's fundamental criticism of this brand of liberalism seems to be that although the impulse to such well-meaning action constitutes an understandable response to the dilemma the apartheid régime poses for decent citizens, it is essentially ineffec-tual: it cannot make enough of a difference in the struggle and offers no more than a personal path to a private absolution for individual whites. Self-delusion, vanity and irresponsibility are frequently defined as its failings, and Gordimer indeed suggests repeatedly in other passages that the activist impulse among such 'liberals' is sometimes no more than a form of self-aggrandise-ment. In *The Lying Days*, when Paul's friend, Edna, fails to find her name on the list of those restricted under the Suppression of Communism Act, Helen comments that 'she was dis-appointed . . . distinctly peeved' at being 'denied martyrdom' (289); while in *Occasion for Loving* Jessie tells us of

> a white woman who had just been charged with incitement and
> was out on bail [who] was dressed [at the party] as if for a diplo-
> matic reception, in a midnight-blue velvet coat and antique gold
> earrings. Someone said: 'How she enjoys it all!' (287)

Similarly, in *A World of Strangers*, Toby comments that the Left is peppered with people 'who had failed to secure attention in other ways; by identifying with Africans they were able to feel the lime-light on their faces for the first time' (169). For such people a spell in prison is not at all a catastrophe – it promises to provide them with the right credentials with very little risk supposed for themselves. In its most extreme variation, this group is seen as psychologically 'sick'. Thus Anna Louw tells Toby that the group of well-meaning 'activists' to which she belongs is largely made up of people who are simply inadequate in their own sphere:

> We want to change things because we haven't got the divine selfishness of really healthy beings; we're not *enough* to our-selves. (211)

Such an emphatic and consistent dismissal of typical white South African 'liberals' as hypocritical, prone to posturing and thoroughly ineffectual, would lead us to expect an affirmation of truly radical responses in the fiction, but suprisingly this is not the case. Instead, Gordimer's third group of white liberals, a small one made up of those who eventually clumsily risk life itself for their beliefs, is rejected for its very willingness to further change through violent action. Such extremism is, on the whole, perceived negatively in the novels, and with its rejection the whole range of radical resistance politics is thrown into question. Gordimer's ambiguous treatment of violence as a valid means of forcing change upon the country lies at the heart of her ambiva-lence towards this group. It seems that, despite her overtly revo-lutionary sympathies, she herself has never fully overcome her instinctive revulsion against violence as a mode of forcing change. At times she attempts to resolve the dilemma by casting violence in a romantic glow as in an early essay in which she approvingly quotes Graham Greene's claim that 'violence can be the expression of love, indifference never. One is an imperfection of charity, the other the perfection of egoism'.[18] But, on the whole, she treats the option of violence with extreme caution, both in the complex and ambiguous response offered in *The Late Bourgeois World* to Max van der Sandt's planting of the station bomb, and in the later novels. A debate on the use of violence in *A Sport of Nature* ends with the italicised words, unequivocal in their implications, that 'Killing is killing. Violence is pain and death' (70), despite the necessity acknowledged elsewhere in the novel that violence must be seen to be an unavoidable tool of the struggle. It seems that, for Gordimer, violence comes uncomfort-ably close to an anarchy which is anathema to the liberal sensibil-ity: by definition it operates outside the safe frameworks of both public and moral law. The fact that activism in general always

implies the ultimate possibility of complicity in violence may explain why Gordimer's characters are unwilling to do more than
defend 'human rights' in that traditionally liberal 'grey' area
where they are still within generally accepted moral law, even
though they may be transgressing the unjust laws of the apartheid state.

Although Gordimer's protagonists typically attempt to maintain an independent stance outside the three groups of liberals
delineated above – unwilling to 'join up' and acutely aware of
the extent to which public commitment overwhelms and betrays
private needs and responsibilities – their sympathies and identifications rank them as liberals nevertheless, even as they find themselves radicalised and inexorably drawn into 'the struggle'. At the
same time the force with which their suspicions of the emotional
and moral pitfalls of commitment are articulated operates as a
powerful counterbalance in the fiction to the imperatives to
which they succumb. Thus, although *A World of Strangers* sets a
pattern in the fiction by charting the process whereby Toby is, in
a sense, returned to his parents' fold (as Rosa Burger will be after
him), the force with which his disillusionment with their world is
given expression echoes through the novel, and within this
framework his choice of an apolitical human connection with
Steven Sitole over, for instance, the possibilities of a relationship
with Anna Louw, becomes fully significant:

> I've always thought that there are two kinds of people, people
> with public lives, and people with private lives. The people with
> public lives are concerned with a collective fate, the private livers
> with an individual one. But – roughly since the Kaiser's war, I
> suppose – the private livers have become hunted people. Hunted
> and defamed. You must join. You must be a Communist or Anti-
> Communist, Nationalist or Kaffirboetie . . . You must protest,
> defy, non-co-operate. And all these things you *must* do; you can't
> leave it all in the infinitely more capable hands of the public
> livers . . .
>
> The private livers, the selfish man, the shirker, as you think him
> – he's a rebel. He's a rebel against rebellion. On the side, he's got
> a private revolution of his own; it's waged for himself, but quite a
> lot of other people may benefit. I think that about Steven. He
> won't troop along with your Congress, or get himself arrested in

the public library, but, in spite of everything the white man does
to knock the spirit out of him, he remains very much alive . . .
He's alive, in defiance of everything that would attempt to make
him half-alive. (122-24)

It is, predictably, only through his grief and shock at the loss of
his *personal* relationship with Steven that he can be brought to a
point where he begins to be able to identify in a general way with
'the world of dispossession' (265) of which Steven was a victim,
and thus at least potentially to enter the political struggle.

In Toby, in fact, as in others of Gordimer's protagonists, a
positive activism emerges only when he experiences injustice as a
personal violation of his own emotional connections and moral
integrity. Indeed, as we shall see, until the private is inescapably
invaded by the public, the demand to be *engagé* is consistently
resisted by Gordimer's characters throughout the fiction. Toby's
protest here articulates the problem most of Gordimer's characters will have to confront and resolve sooner or later: they will be
brought to discover that simple 'aliveness' is not enough, and
that only by responding fully to the implications of their commitments to others, and by realising their complicity in the distortions history has made these relationships subject to, can they lay
claim to living morally responsible lives. A 'concern with human
dignity', writes Gordimer in *Occasion for Loving*, 'as a common
possession that, lost by individuals, is lost by all' (262) is *the* central value of whose fundamental importance she seeks to convince us in the fiction. As Helen says to Joel in *The Lying Days*,
'although you may come to a compromise with your own personal life, you can't compromise about the larger things ringed
outside it' (358); for, ultimately, as Jessie discovers in *Occasion
for Loving*, there is no escape, for 'nothing [is] innocent' (259).
There can be no refuge from the ramifications of injustice and
thus no escape for the morally responsible individual from the
imperative to confront.

The extent to which disinterested action for the general good
is rooted in an implicit valorisation of subjectivity and individualism, as outlined above, makes it clear that although Gordimer felt
she had made an early break with the 'English' liberal tradition
and 'range[d] further',[19] her work remains firmly based in a

strongly internalised liberal-humanist perspective. Visser's useful definition of the characteristics of what he terms 'liberal narrative' (in an attempt to distinguish between this and 'radical fiction') further illuminates the fundamentally liberal character of Gordimer's stance:

> Liberal narrative . . . is marked by the way it privileges the individual consciousness, focusing on the autonomy and self-realisation of the individual character. At the core of liberal narrative is the assumption that the individual, as the origin of meaning and value, comes to a knowledge of 'truth' or 'reality' through experience and introspection. By way of corollary to its emphasis on consciousness, liberal narrative systematically translates social, political, and economic categories into moral, ethical, and experiential terms. Broader material and social forces are measured in their relation to the conscious subject and take on significance in so far as they give coherence to individual experience . . . [Such] methodological individualism is inconsistent with certain kinds of political commitments.[20]

It is Gordimer's perception of the extent to which the fundamental tenets of liberal humanism have been corrupted and violated in the name of that humanism itself which repels her and which gives her voice that marked coldness of tone which has so often been commented upon. Although she contemptuously dismisses the *pretensions* to liberalism of her white protagonists, the values in terms of which those characters are measured and found wanting may be seen to be at root themselves shaped and formed by an essentially liberal philosophy. This becomes particularly clear if we bear in mind recent non-invidious definitions of liberalism as originally meaning 'to be free from narrow prejudice or bigotry' and 'from unreasonable prejudice in favour of traditional opinions or established institutions', and as then coming to embrace the additional idea of being 'open to the reception of new ideas or proposals for reform' and of being determined to live in accordance with the dictates of conscience.[21] It is clear that Gordimer's own convictions are rooted in a liberalism understood within these parameters, and that her much-discussed 'critique of liberalism' grows out of her sense of the extent to which liberal values have been debased and corrupted by white South

African smugness, hypocrisy, and greed. In essence she mourns in the fiction the failure of liberalism to triumph, rather than rejecting its fundamental precepts – precepts which continue to inform her responses.

This may well be one of the grounds of Gordimer's popularity outside South Africa. As Brennan has pointed out:

> What we are seeing [in post-colonial literature] is a process whereby Western reviewers are selecting as the interpreters and authentic public voices of the Third World, writers who, in a sense, have allowed a flirtation with change that ensures continuity, a familiar strangeness, a trauma by inches. Alien to the public that reads them . . . they are also like that public in tastes, training, repertoire of anecdotes, current habitation.[22]

The suggestion is that Gordimer, while writing for the metropolis, simultaneously appeals to a shared set of Western values opposed to apartheid ideology. It is an appeal which makes her very much 'one of us' – the lone voice of an isolated Western conscience raised in a distant wilderness for her fellows 'at home' to hear. Indeed, when seen in this Foucauldian light, the phenomenon of her international popularity neatly illustrates his point that works acquire meaning and status via the nature of their answers to questions about 'where does it come from?'. In Gordimer's case, the very familiarity of her values and the solid predictability of her moral vision has ensured her a much wider audience overseas than the merely 'exotic' character of her subject-matter could have attracted alone.

These fundamental values are established in broad outline at the start of her career, in her early novels, and remain essentially unchanged throughout the remainder of the fiction. The goal of her characters' moral development remains their acceptance of a particular kind of responsibility for the evil of apartheid, which eventually must express itself within the pragmatic framework of a political commitment to resistance in some form. In other words, in Gordimer's world the morally responsible person – as distinct from the merely morally aware – cannot indefinitely avoid the imperative of ideological alignment. It is an emphasis which has been paralleled in the author's own development; she too has been drawn increasingly into an alignment with explicit politically and ideologically determined positions, notwithstanding her early description of herself, in a well-known passage published in 1965, that

> I have no religion, no political dogma – only plenty of doubt about everything except my conviction that the colour bar is wrong and utterly indefensible.[23]

Yet, despite her increasingly conscious alignments in both life and works, Gordimer has not been read as a 'novelist of ideas'. Recent critical responses to her work have noted the extent to which her representation of the issues of the day in the fiction remains relatively unsophisticated, little more than a simple sketching in of the outlines of the ongoing debates of each consecutive phase of 'the struggle'. Her fundamentally conservative liberal-humanist values have not only inevitably allied her with the forces ranged against the apartheid state, but have also paradoxically ensured that her perspectives should soon take on the colouring of the ideological positions of the anti-apartheid radical Left, as these have developed over time. The underlying political assumptions of the works quickly came to be clearly responsive to and often a mirror of the changing fashions in left-wing thinking, despite Gordimer's ongoing resistance to 'joining up' (she is, however, now officially a member of the unbanned African National Congress).

Such encoding of what amounts to ideological clichés at the heart of her work has attracted some negative comment:[24] Cooper, for example, points out that

> the repressive laws, the bannings, the bombings, the torture, underground activity and guerilla warfare, encompass Gordimer's South African history entirely, rather than consisting of one aspect of it.[25]

In fact, as we shall see, Gordimer's inscription of the various modes of racist oppression extant in her society is not as comprehensive as Cooper suggests, while her allegiance to more extreme left-wing positions is strongly qualified by the essential moral conservatism of her perspectives – despite her insistence by the mid-70s that she should be seen to be a 'white South African radical' and not a liberal.[26] Her fundamental values remain more

closely aligned to basic Christian and traditional liberal values
than to the frequently extreme Marxist radicalism current in
South African intellectual circles in recent years. This becomes
clear in her perceptive analysis in 1985 of the ambivalence and
ambiguity associated for her with the concept of radicalism:

> I think that we do live in a time that we all experience as a time of
> crisis, as a time in which much has been destroyed and much has
> been lost, and we experience the demand on us as writers, and I
> think also – and why not – as human beings, to be both a radical
> demand and a conservative demand. It's radical because we want
> to help change what is evil in our society and bring to birth some-
> thing that will help assist in the correction of certain fundamental
> wrongs and injustices. And we are conservative, because we
> know that in this process so much is being destroyed that we
> cherish and that we value.[27]

Gordimer has said of herself that she is an atheist, and I use the
label 'Christian' here to indicate not a religious commitment but
an affiliation to a Western historico-cultural matrix which is uneasy with extreme Marxist positions. In fact, her deployment of
the terms 'radical' and 'liberal' should be understood within the
very particular historical and contemporary contexts of South
African society within the years in which she has been writing; as
we have seen, in these contexts 'liberalism' quickly came to be
associated with ideas of impotence and hypocrisy, and was
rejected for its failure to effectively halt the apartheid machine
despite its 'fine sentiments'. As early as 1962 Mphahlele defined
the liberal

> in an African context [as] a white man who believes in redressing
> political wrongs by constitutional means. More often than not he
> accommodates himself in the legislative machinery in the hope
> that he can use the concessions by which he has come to occupy a
> certain position within the machinery to persuade the oppressor
> to change heart . . . the trouble with liberals in South Africa, of
> course, is that they spend two thirds of their energy trying to
> avert a revolution, and one third to verbal protest against repres-
> sive legislation. Their attraction for a certain class of the non-
> white elite fits in with their anti-socialist sentiments.[28]

In Gordimer's case, her later explicit rejection of liberalism is clearly linked to her sense of the changing meaning of the term within South Africa. In 1987 she told Anthony Sampson that 'liberalism used to mean, to whites and blacks, that blacks should be allowed into the existing white structure, legal and governmental . . . the definition of liberal, now, is one who believes in incremental reform'.[29] Although so narrow, historically specific and limited a definition of liberalism clearly makes it an untenable position for Gordimer, her use of the term 'radicalism' is as restricted by contemporary contexts. It signifies little more than a commitment to active and overt opposition aimed at achieving a genuine restructuring of society in terms of non-racial, egalitarian ideals.

Thus I would argue that, although Gordimer allies herself with what right-wing South Africans consider to be radical positions, her personal sympathies are rooted in what are essentially liberal and in the widest sense conservative (neither innovative nor original) convictions: that is to say, her identification with South African political radicalism arises from her perception of its dependence on those moral ideals which it shares with fundamental Christian perspectives (here we might usefully note the role of the churches and of churchmen in the history of the resistance to apartheid). Indeed, that Gordimer's interpretation of these terms is not at all idiosyncratic is suggested by an interesting comment made by her contemporary, Doris Lessing, in a 1985 interview, in which the link between liberalism, Christianity and 'Communist' affiliations among young radicals in the decades of the fifties and sixties is perceptively laid bare. She reminds her readers that

> Marxism didn't create these ideas of harmony and happiness and equality. It [*sic*] comes from religion. Utopias long predate Marxism . . . So Marxism is in fact structured like Christianity, with Heaven and Hell – Hell being capitalism, and Paradise, the suffering redeeming you. It's exactly the same structure. And the idea of paradise in the classless society. It predates even Christianity. It's the old Golden Age theme.[30]

Gordimer's depiction of the ideals informing political activism in South Africa in the era with which she deals not only does not contradict but rather fleshes out this perspective more fully. For

example, her critically distanced interpretation of Communism
as we find it in *Burger's Daughter* (1979) examines the extent to
which it appealed to the latent *religious* yearnings of her protagonists.[31] Rosa tells us that Lionel Burger was drawn to the
Communist party of the day because it was the only non-racial
political party available to idealists and humanists like himself. In
essence, he understands and practises Communism almost
exclusively within the framework of mainstream Christianity's
command that one be one's brother's keeper (172). Such an interpretation of 'communism' was a natural consequence of the
government's insistence on indiscriminately lumping together
Marxist-Leninist initiatives and general anti-apartheid activism:
the Suppression of Communism Bill passed in 1950 had extended
the definition of communism to include

> 'any related form of that doctrine' which sought to establish the
> dictatorship of the proletariat, or to bring about 'any political,
> industrial, social or economic change within the Union by the
> promotion of disturbances or disorder', whether in association
> with a 'foreign government' or not, or by encouraging hostility
> between Europeans and non-Europeans.[32]

Gordimer's 'radicalism' has not, in fact, included support for
Russian Communism as such. Her later explicit rejection of it as
a viable political doctrine in itself[33] is foreshadowed in her
conventionally superficial rejection of communism in her 1958
novel, *A World of Strangers*. Anna Louw is depicted as disillu-
sioned by a visit to Russia in 1950, but, as Toby comments with
sharp approval, 'unlike most Communists' she did not 'remain in
[that] state of spiritual convalescence which [is] as far as [disap-
pointed Communists seem] able to recover from the loss of faith'
(183).

Within this framework, Gordimer's attempt to resolve the
tension between the public and the private realms by causing her
characters to move from what they come to perceive as an alienated private life to that promise of emotional integration which
the novels present as the corollary to and the reward of a commitment to the collective good remains a problematic aspect of the
novels. The emotional power of her writing more frequently (and
perhaps unconsciously) valorises the pull of the individual and

the private over the imperatives of the collective. As a result, the novels often fail to achieve a convincing emotional closure. The sense of relief and release attributed to the characters at the end of many of the novels as they make their cautious commitments to being 'African' and to 'the struggle'[34] often strikes the reader as insufficiently motivated, artificial and unpersuasive. A pervasive scenario of frustrated hopes and impotent ideals contributes instead to a certain bleakness in the endings; affirmation, where it occurs, carries with it a note of despairing defiance of the insuperable odds against true integration into black Africa, and the reader at times is left chiefly with a growing sense of Gordimer's own alienation, not only from apartheid society as such but from her characters' solutions to their dilemmas as well.

Despite her commitment to the idea of public responsibility and to the need for radical resolutions, in fact, Gordimer's protagonists remain reluctant revolutionaries throughout.[35] This is hardly surprising: given her acute perception of the difficulties of maintaining a morally respectable stance within the framework of the terrifying power of the apartheid state to suppress dissent (particularly from the sixties onwards), it is to be expected that her characters will frequently be merely uneasily disaffected and see only extremely limited choices available to them. Apartheid laws may be defied by attempts at relationships of love and friendship across the colour bar (in which the personal is essentially pitted against the political), but any activism which may lead to imprisonment or exile is approached with extreme caution. Of course, neither personal nor political commitments can thrive in such a context. Gordimer finds none of the available options particularly comfortable or comforting, and within the constraints of so few and such unsatisfactory choices her characters find their residual human impulses to decency frequently blocked both by political marginalisation and by personal inadequacies. Thus a certain impotence and paralysis of the will are presented as a norm and, despite Gordimer's unequivocal anti-apartheid stance, the protagonists of the novels are in general allowed little more than having their hearts in the right place. Her characters are good at sympathy, friendship and moral support, but political action is confined to the extreme margins of the radical Left and remains mostly tentative, putative and potential rather than actual. The only central figure who can be considered an activist in his own right, Max van der Sandt of *The Late Bourgeois World*, is presented in so morally ambiguous a light that the final effect is as much one of condemnation as of a validation of his act. Gordimer's often self-deluded, hypocritical, but always idealistic liberals are in essence offered no alternative to their untenable position. On the one hand, activism is too dangerous and, in so far as it eventually in its extreme form must incorporate violent action, too morally ambiguous in its consequences to be embraced wholeheartedly. Flight, on the other hand, represents an unacceptable abrogation of moral responsibility. At best her characters are forced to content themselves with the private decencies of a personal and often ineffectual witness. Within such a framework, the observer rather than the actor is the characteristic protagonist in the novels.

Indeed, Gordimer herself has not been politically active other than as a writer and as a champion of the concerns of writers. Although she has been an eloquent opponent of censorship and of the banning of the works of those listed under the Suppression of Communism Act, she has not involved herself in radical political activity outside the bounds of her concern as a writer in South Africa. In her 1987 interview with Anthony Sampson she gave her reason for these choices: 'I don't have the courage – still don't – to be a complete revolutionary,' she said, 'to face the possibility of jail for life.'[36] It is a position eloquently reflected in the words of a peripheral character in *A Guest of Honour*: 'I'm not a revolutionary. I haven't the courage to risk prison. But I can't let them get away with it unwitnessed. I have to stay and oppose in my mind' (199). It has, however, not been a comfortable position to rest in. The rise of the Black Consciousness Movement in the early 1970s as a political force made the unsung heroism of simply bearing witness and 'opposing in the mind' even less of a viable alternative to flight than it had been before.

'politics is character, in South Africa'

Not only Gordimer's response to liberalism but also her relationship to ideology as such is a problematic one. To begin with, her deployment of the term in various statements suggests that she understands it simply as a label for the clearly articulated pro-grammes of particular groups with specific social, political and economic agendas. At this level her stance is essentially anti-ideological. For example, in 1980 she wrote that

> as a novelist I am not interested in 'reconciling' political ideolo-gies; only in writing about human beings and representing through my characters as faithfully as possible their beliefs and concerns as, living among them, I observe these.[37]

However, such a claim is problematic for two reasons. Firstly, it is directly contradicted by numerous other statements which arti-culate Gordimer's strong commitment to a particular political position: thus in 1984 she said of herself that she has

> strong political convictions in the country where I live. I am par-tisan, yes. Sometimes when I'm writing there will be a character who belongs to 'my' side, the side of radical opposition to apart-heid.[38]

Secondly, Gordimer's stance fails to take into account contempo-rary definitions of ideology such as, for example, that offered by Althusser, who wrote in 1966 that ideology slides into all human activity . . . It is identical with the 'lived experience' of human existence itself: that is why the form in which we are 'made to see' ideology in great novels has as its contents the 'lived experience' of individuals.[39]

Gordimer's rejection of 'political ideologies' is in fact mislead-ing, as she is neither apolitical nor a moral relativist. As we have seen, the novels characteristically concentrate upon charting the many ways in which the individual consciousness is brought to a personal and private grasp of the significance of the ramifications of apartheid as they invade the innermost recesses of daily life. In so far as this is so, each of the novels may be said to constitute not only a *Tendenzroman* but also an *Erziehungsroman*. Her charac-ters find that, in a process analogous to that which Gordimer writes she herself experienced, growth is a 'clumsy battle to chip [one's] way out of shell after shell of readymade concepts and make [one's] own sense of life'.[40] Growth is only possible through a process of breaking out of cocoon after cocoon towards a final 're-birth' as a human being among other human beings.[41] 'First,

you know,' says Gordimer, 'you leave your mother's house and
then you leave the house of the white race.'[42] Although such
growth is also understood to have as its corollary a process of
incremental disillusionment, its bitter fruit paradoxically not
only informs a fundamental sense of alienation, but also makes
possible a series of rebirths. 'Young South Africans,' she wrote in
1975, 'are born twice: the second time when, through situations
that differ with each individual, they emerge from their trappings
of colour consciousness'.[43]

Ideas of metamorphosis and revelation are inherent in these
images of cocoon and the sloughing off of outgrown perspectives; they alert us not only to Gordimer's positive conception of
growth, but also to the submerged but powerful element of didacticism which infuses the works. It is a didacticism given particular impetus by Gordimer's belief that the artist's special gifts
of insight and eloquence bring with them a unique responsibility
to act as society's moral guide and guardian. Already in 1961 she
argued that the role of the writer in South Africa is to provide a
dull readership with the means to self-knowledge:

> In South Africa, in Africa generally, the reader knows perilously
> little about himself or his feelings. We have a great deal to learn
> about ourselves, and the novelist, along with the poet, play-
> wright, composer and painter, must teach us. We look to them to
> give us the background of self-knowledge that we may be able to
> take for granted.[44]

Although critics have found such implicitly dismissive assessments of the average South African reader as either un-
enlightened or morally corrupt to be disturbing,[45] Gordimer,
however, continues to claim superior insight and vision for the
writer: for example, in 1975 she argued that the writer possesses

> powers of observation heightened beyond the normal [which]
> imply extraordinary disinvolvement, or rather the double pro-
> cess, excessive preoccupation and identification with the lives of
> others, and at the same time a monstrous detachment . . . The
> tension between standing apart and being fully involved; that is
> what makes a writer . . . The validity of this dialectic is the syn-
> thesis of revelation; our achievement of, or even attempt at this is
> the moral the human justification for what we do.[46]

In this Wordsworthian conflation of the moral and the human, in the use made of the concept of revelation, and in the emphasis on the writer's faculties as being in some way superior to those of the 'ordinary' man (claims repeated later in her assertion that writers 'have at least some faculties of supra-observation and hyper-perception not known to others'),[47] we find the roots of Gordimer's implicit didacticism and of her ideological alignment. In 1982 she defended the right of society 'to impose responsibility upon writers' and suggested that morally aware artists should ask 'to what we are bidden . . . [and] what is expected of us, by the dynamic of collective conscience and the will to liberty'.[48] Her repeated denials that her own fiction responds to such imperatives, such as in her comment to Diana Cooper-Clark a year later that 'the writer shouldn't be pressed into any kind of orthodoxy . . . you must give yourself the freedom to write as if you were dead',[49] merely reinforces JanMohamed's definition of ideology as 'a subtext embedded within the text . . . never selfevidently apparent, [and having to be] (re)constructed after the fact'.[50]

The conflict between the need to defend an abstract ideal of the writer's freedom, on the one hand, and the imperative to be a politically *engagé* individual within the particular historical circumstances of contemporary South Africa on the other, continues to be reflected in Gordimer's ongoing attempts to disentangle the contradictions between the two positions. In 1975 she argued in a well-known passage that

> in a certain sense a writer is 'selected' by his subject – his subject being *the consciousness* of his own era. How he deals with this is, to me, the fundament of commitment, although 'commitment' is usually understood as the reverse process: a writer's selection of a subject in conformity with the rationalisation of his own ideological and/or political beliefs.[51]

Buried within this implicit distinction between art and propaganda is a conception of 'Truth' as both ideologically neutral and accessible. The writer's vision is presented as one which transcends narrow ideology, in contrast to the post-modernist perspective which persuasively suggests that both the perception of an era's 'consciousness' and the way in which it is articulated in writing are of necessity shaped and directed by the ideological

assumptions which inform each individual's vision; ways of seeing cannot be innocent. Gordimer recognises that the work of
necessity responds to and records the 'political aspects' of its
time, but avoids the implications of the corollary of this perception, that at a deeper level the writer herself is immersed in,
shaped by, and subject to the flux and flow of ideology. Her grasp
of the extent to which 'politics' imbue everyday life in South
Africa merely encourages her to draw a distinction between the
morally passive eye of the recording artist and the morally active
commitment of the decent citizen. Thus in a 1985 interview with
Susan Sontag she explains that

> the political aspect is something that came into my work impli-
> citly, because the life around me was imbued with it, even the
> most private aspects of life were penetrated by the effects of poli-
> tics . . . [But] the day when it's more important for me to be more
> than a writer in the public sense, in the sense of being answerable
> to some political or social problem, in which I may be involved as
> a citizen: the day that becomes more important than being a
> writer, I think I'm discounted in the world.[52]

There is a revealing contradiction here, for a growing perception
of the extent to which 'even the most private aspects of life [are]
penetrated by the effects of politics' leaves little room for the distinction Gordimer nevertheless attempts to draw between her
commitments as a citizen and those she is subject to as a writer.
Her disclaimers are perhaps best read as embodying at a
subtextual level that distrust of 'politics' so frequently characteristic of the liberal stance,[53] and they thus function (somewhat
ironically) as a further pointer to the extent to which she does not
abandon the liberalism into which she initially educated herself.

'what is the life of man?'

Gordimer's ambivalence towards the influence of politics and
ideology upon her work of necessity problematises the connections between the private and the public realms, the personal and
the political, in her world. On the one hand, she has repeatedly
emphasised the extent to which the individual in South Africa is
inescapably entrapped in the socio-political processes of his time

and compromised by his acquiescence in the imposition of apartheid on the black majority; thus in 1975 she commented again that

> all that is and has been written by South Africans is profoundly influenced, at the deepest and least controllable level of consciousness, by the politics of race . . . There is no country in the Western world where the creative imagination, whatever it seizes upon, finds the focus of even the most private events set in the overall social determination of race laws.[54]

Gordimer's third novel, *Occasion for Loving* (1963), demonstrates the invasion of the world of private emotion by the public political realities of the time particularly clearly; the love affair between Ann Davis and Gideon Shibalo is shown to be irremediably corrupted by the grip of the apartheid state:

> A line in a statute book has more authority than the claims of one man's love or another's. All claims of natural feeling are overridden alike by a line in a statute book that takes no account of humanness, that recognises neither love nor respect nor jealousy nor rivalry nor compassion nor hate – nor any human attitude whatsoever where there are black and white together. (216)

But the opposition between the public and private worlds in the novels is not always as explicitly dealt with as it is here. The apartheid background is on the whole simply assumed, its details only lightly sketched in where necessary: that a crass racism will repeatedly violate the sanctities of private life at their deepest level is an inescapable 'given' for Gordimer, 'deeply implicit', as she explained in 1965, 'in whatever I write, since it is *there*: part of the substance of life within which my instinct as a writer must struggle'.[55] She therefore expends little energy on detailing the depredations of racism or the precise ramifications of oppression in the novels, contenting herself with those general references which will serve to sufficiently orientate the moderately well-informed reader within the broad parameters of the system: apartheid exists simply as context and backdrop of the action.[56] 'I don't write about apartheid,' Gordimer said to Boyers in 1984; 'I write about people who happen to live under that system'.[57] Thus the novels concentrate instead on the central problem which confronts every well-meaning white protagonist who attempts to retain a degree of moral respectability in the fiction: how is one to live under such a régime and yet retain one's humanity?

In exploring possible responses to this question, Gordimer finds no easy answers to the conflicting temptations of retreat and engagement. For her, the contrary claims of the public and private realms are caught in a relationship of irresolvable tension, as made clear in her 1982 confession that

> there are two absolutes in my life. One is that racism is evil – human damnation, in the Old Testament sense, and no compromises as well as sacrifices, should be too great in the fight against it. The other is that a writer is a being in whose sensibility is fused what Lukacs called "the duality of inwardness and the outside world", and he must never be asked to sunder this union. The co-existence of these absolutes often seems irreconcilable within one life, for me.[58]

The convoluted intensity of this declaration suggests something of the earnestness which Gordimer brings to her perceived task as a crusader against the evils of racism in a world conceived of as caught between the two poles of Old Testament moral absolutism, on the one hand, and the consuming flux of subjective and emotional response on the other. In 1985 Gordimer characterised these two poles as the inner and the outer landscape, arguing that

> it's [been] shown that it's possible for the inner landscape and the outer landscape to become one, to be melded together in the same work. In other words, the inner landscape, which is really the subjective novel, the techniques, the sensibilities, the perceptions even the technical side of it, the method – can be fused with the outer landscape, the subject.[59]

In effect, however, the two landscapes remain, for the most part, in uncomfortable opposition to one another. In the novels, the tension between them expresses itself in the uneasy balance Gordimer maintains as a writer between the felt imperative to engage with the political realities of the day, and an opposing pull towards the private world of subjective experience. As a young girl, Gordimer was deeply attracted to the writings of both D.H. Lawrence and

Proust, and their impact on her imagination expresses itself in her early work in a strongly marked inscription of both a Lawrentian sensuality and a Proustian sensitivity towards the minute shifts of consciousness out of which new worlds of subjective significance are constructed.[60] While the 'outer landscape' encourages her to respond to the dominant political debates of each succeeding decade, the 'inner landscape' fuels that drift towards the tentative, inconclusive, evasive and subjective life of the feelings into which the novels' protagonists repeatedly sink.

These oppositions are communicated in part by Gordimer's representation of the private realm as primarily the site of love, of the internal, the passive, the domestic, the individual, the passionately sensual and sexual and of the politically non-subversive (love affairs in the novels are never directed by or serve political ends). The public realm, on the other hand, is presented as the site of conflict, the external, the active, the political, the collective – and of the potentially politically subversive. The novels chart the various ways in which the individual is persuaded to move from the relative safety of the one to a reluctant embracing of the imperatives of the other: that is, from the marginalities of private life to the mainstream of public political commitment. In so far as commitment to public action is conceived of as rooted in and originating from private subjectivities, however, the former remains inextricably bound up with the emotional ramifications of the latter. What this emphasises most strongly is Gordimer's implicit conviction that abstract theory and imposed ideologies have no necessary power over the imagination: they will fail as spurs to action if not given form and substance by the force of personal experience, without which they cannot penetrate beyond the fringes of consciousness. This controlling idea is already articulated in the earliest of the novels, *The Lying Days,* in which Helen tells us that

> the mine was unreal, a world which substituted rules for the pull and stress of human conflict which are the true conditions of life; and in another way, the University was unreal too: it gave one the respect for doubt, the capacity for logical analysis, and the choice of ideas on which this equipment could be used to decide one's own values – but all this remained in one's hand like a shining new instrument that has not been put to its purpose. (240)

Helen goes on to claim that intellectuals belong 'only to the crust, below which the real life lay' (240). 'Reality' in South Africa is the private suffering of its oppressed peoples, and it can only be apprehended through a personal involvement at an emotional and experiential level which will make the abstractions of theory and ideology become individually meaningful.

This route to commitment seems to reflect the pattern of Gordimer's own growth to a full political awareness. The emphasis in her first novel, *The Lying Days*, on the undercurrents of anti-Semitism common in the mining communities of the East Rand should be set against her awareness of her own part-Jewish heritage;[61] her identification with the marginalised, the oppressed and the excluded may be understood to have originated not in any intellectual analysis of the magnitude of black oppression in South Africa but in her own early experience of *difference* on a variety of levels. In *The Lying Days*, the failure of Helen and Joel, as Gentile and Jew, to break through the invisible but powerfully internalised and intensely felt prejudices which blight the potential of their relationship at the end of the novel becomes paradigmatic of later failures in the fiction to cross the barriers of race and colour successfully. The intensity of both the attraction and of the regret felt at the 'impossibility' of a true consummation remains a powerful component of such attempts until *A Sport of Nature* breaks the mould.

For Gordimer, then, the only route to a public and political commitment is via the intensity of a private epiphany. Within such a framework, it is clear that what occurs in the sphere of the private will determine the shape and direction of public action throughout the fiction. Gordimer makes no gender distinctions here. The origins of political action in private subjectivities are as apparent in Max van der Sandt's ultimate decision to plant a bomb as in Maureen's inchoate impulse to take flight towards the helicopter at the end of *July's People*; and as fundamental to Hillela's metamorphosis into an internationally respected anti-apartheid activist in *A Sport of Nature* as to Bray's involvement in the new post-colonial Africa. In *A Guest of Honour* Rebecca, Bray's mistress, reveals the emotional wellspring of his commitment to the independent state headed by his old friend, Mweta, and threatened with civil war by another, now dissident, comrade, Shinza, in her prediction that Bray *will* 'interfere' in the feud between the two men because, as she says:

> You love that man, that's the trouble . . . You are tied to someone, it goes on working itself out, like a marriage . . . You'll forget what people say, what it looks like, what you think of yourself. You simply do what you have to do to go on living. (262)

Bray's emotional commitments ultimately cause him to be partly responsible for the chain of events which will lead to his not so accidental and publicly misinterpreted death. In the same novel, the battle of wills between Mweta and Shinza is also represented as being rooted not in ideological differences but in Mweta's resentment of Shinza's insistence upon continuing to play the role of mentor even after Mweta has become President. 'He made up his mind he had to watch the rest of us the way he used to watch *them*,' Mweta complains to his old confidante, Bray, in his only unguarded outburst in the entire novel:

> He found out things I hadn't noticed, often he was right, he could warn you . . . I went to him as I always did, you understand – he was my father, my brother – he listens with a smile on his face and his eyes closed . . . 'I hadn't understood the issue properly.' 'Did I realise who I was dealing with?' – With his eyes closed. To smell me out. (173)

It is not so much that heart will overrule head, but that head will find a way to justify and ratify the decisions of the heart – will indeed come into operation only when the heart's responses shock it into action. Throughout the novels Gordimer presents us with the phenomenon of individuals politicised not by the persuasive power of ideological rhetoric but by their love of others who act upon the conscious and deliberate political commitments which they themselves as yet lack.

Oppression thus becomes emotionally meaningful to Gordimer's characters only when they are brought face to face with its effects on others or upon themselves when those effects impinge inescapably on their lives. It is in her depiction of such epiphanic moments that Gordimer locates the impact of apartheid upon individuals in the novels, and not in any larger or more impersonal representation. For example, Rosa Burger is galvanised out of her apathy and pushed into her flight to Europe by two experiences whose significance owes nothing to what she has learnt at her parents' knees: the death of a tramp on a park bench below the office where she works, and the agony of a donkey at the hands of a carter in the no man's land between township and city into which she accidentally strays one evening (*Burger's Daughter*, 208-209). Equally significant is her confrontation with her father's now adult black protégé, Baasie, on the telephone in the London night. It is his emotional accusations which tip the balance for her towards a return to South Africa, rather than any rational appeal by him to the abstractions of Justice and Responsibility.

That it is often a subjectively swayed sense of morality – an embedded humanism – rather than an objective political commitment which becomes the stimulus to action is a further dimension of this complex interaction between private and public worlds. In *A Sport of Nature*, for instance, Pauline decides to help the Masuku family in their flight into exile, despite her earlier refusal to harbour the refugees even temporarily; her change of heart is presented as the expression of no more than a right impulse,

> the impulse of her nature, which was simply to give. Principles, political allegiances with their attendant reservations were the rational and intellectual restraints laid upon this instinct; she revered them, and so [her] mood alternated with a kind of nervous shame. (76)

In the same novel, the Afrikaner woman Christa, who takes Hillela under her wing, has in the past also acted from the heart – an 'organ capable of keener feeling than the brain' – rather than from the head:

> It was this organ, taking over from all the revolutionary theory she had studied since recruitment at seventeen in a jam factory, that had been responsible for her arrest along with black women protesting against the pass laws. (127)

Gordimer made it clear in 1965 that she believes in the existence of a moral instinct: 'It is instinct which dictates duty,' she said, 'and intelligence which offers pretexts for avoiding it'.[62] Perhaps the most compelling image in the novels of the power of unconscious forces to precipitate actions which are contrary to self-

interest and conscious ideological stances, is that of the hold
which the idea of the buried corpse on his land gains over the
disintegrating mind of the industrialist Mehring, whose faltering
attempts at self-justification collapse into hysteria when the
floods finally wash the body up onto the surface of both land and
consciousness towards the end of *The Conservationist.*

Even Hillela herself in *A Sport of Nature*, in that most politically committed of Gordimer's novels, succeeds in making her
way successfully through the minefield of exile politics in a variety of newly independent African states not because she espouses
the 'correct' positions but simply because of an absence in her of
preconception and prejudice. The necessary quality she possesses
is an adaptability which is the expression of an inherent open-
ness. She represents a psychic and experimental space waiting to
be appropriately filled, and it is a measure of the bleakness of
Gordimer's view of her fellow South Africans that she should
consider such qualities to be 'a sport of nature'. Hillela's history
brings to a culmination the history of all those of Gordimer's
characters whose 'unguarded hearts'[63] allow life itself to mould
and direct their energies, and whose politicisation rests upon the
bedrock of the empirical rather than on the shifting sands of
theory alone. Novels such as *A Guest of Honour* and *A Sport of
Nature* demonstrate that, for Gordimer, history is not the product of vast impersonal forces, but must be understood as shaped
by the decisions of individuals who are swayed as much by the
subjective dimensions of their lives as by their conscious theoretical commitments. That the nineteenth-century 'bourgeois' liberal
humanism which lies behind such a position coexists somewhat
uneasily with Gordimer's attempt, in *A Sport of Nature* in particular, to suggest the extent to which the individual may be subsumed in and redeemed by a self-sacrificing commitment to
collective ends, has as yet scarcely been noted.

Ultimately, Gordimer's reading of the South African dilemma
is an essentially romantic one. Although she referred to herself as
'a romantic struggling with reality' in an early interview,[64] it is
doubtful whether she is aware of how strongly marked this
aspect of her temperament is in her work. It expresses itself in the
consuming idealism which shapes the novels' assent to the Black
Consciousness claim that the real struggle for freedom can only

be waged by black South Africans for other black South Africans – that the future is theirs and theirs alone. It is also there in Gordimer's conviction that there can be no place for the current breed of white South Africans in Azania: that only a new, as yet largely undeveloped type of white man or woman will be able to take up a place honourably and fully in post-revolutionary Africa – a type which would be dismissed as a mere 'sport of nature' in the world Gordimer finds herself in at present. And it is a rampant romanticism which lies at the root of Gordimer's often dismissive treatment of even the best efforts of well-meaning 'liberals' to make a difference, for in her view not only the political and social structures of the country must be altered; its citizens too must undergo a 'sea-change', a transformative process which will ready them for the utopian future whose emergence *A Sport of Nature* celebrates. The need for such a new individual is articulated from the earliest novels onward. Already in *A World of Strangers* Toby hails Steven Sitole as

> a new kind of man, not a white man, but not quite a black man either; a kind of flash – flash-in-the-pan – produced by the surface of two societies in friction. (134)

Steven's exuberant and apolitical vitality significantly carries with it no trace of colour prejudice, of a victim mentality, or of envy of the dominant white culture; he is the forerunner – particularly in his sensuality and his colour-blindness – of Ann Davis in *Occasion for Loving*, 'that new being . . . for whom the black man in the white city waited' [*sic*] (92). In Gordimer's ninth novel, the figure of Hillela represents the culmination of, rather than a deviation from, this theme in her work. She, the 'sport of nature', is another 'flash-in-the-pan', and simultaneously the embodiment of her cousin Sasha's fantasy of what the new Africa will need: 'It will take another kind of being to stay on, here. A new white person. Not us' (*A Sport of Nature*, 187).

The fact that it is possible to trace this theme essentially unchanged through nine novels testifies to the extraordinary degree of continuity and consistency in Gordimer's work. Her grasp of the situation her characters are entrapped in and of their options within such a framework remains fundamentally unchanged over four decades; her informing themes and concerns are established

in the first three novels and remain relatively constant throughout the *oeuvre*. Although her grasp of political and historical
issues changes and develops, her focus upon the individual's
resistance to the political and moral responsibilities forced upon
him by the accidents of birth and historical process, her representation of the conflict between the sensual and the theoretical, her
rejection of the tyranny of ideology, and her validation of empirical knowledge, all fundamentally inform every novel she has
written. In fact, if we avoid a chronological interpretation of the
novels and attempt a thematic ordering instead, we will find that
they fall naturally into four groups on the basis of their major
themes. The two semi-autobiographical novels, *The Lying Days*
and *Occasion for Loving*, offer an enquiry into what is needed in
order to come of age in South Africa. *A World of Strangers*, *The
Late Bourgeois World, Burger's Daughter* and *My Son's Story*
chart the various ways in which the individual may be seduced or
emotionally coerced into full identification with the revolutionary struggle in South Africa, the pitfalls of such a commitment,
and the temptation to and impossibility of escape from its imperatives. *The Conservationist* and *July's People* analyse with an
exceptionally cold eye the anguish of the only partially redeemed
as history catches up with them. *A Guest of Honour* and *A Sport
of Nature*, written at different points in the evolution of post-
colonial Africa, attempt an exploration of the possible shapes
such a future might take. All four themes are, of course, implicit
in one form or another in all of the novels, but it is interesting to
note that only *A Sport of Nature* offers a vision which has the
potential to inspire hope, rather than entrench archetypal white
fears about a black-dominated future.

In addition, such a grouping of the novels reminds us once
again of the extent to which the fiction offers a most particular
and individual response to the dilemma of being a middle-class,
English-speaking, liberal, white South African over the four decades of which Gordimer has written – a personal record fully
consonant with her own emphasis upon the centrality of the private and of the subjective in the public life of a society, one arising
out of the non-representative complexity of a single and unique
life-experience. The reader who searches for a history of the period between 1923 and 1987 in the novels will, as has been sug-

gested, find it only most sketchily and incompletely filled in. The novels are instead perhaps best read in the light of Morphet's suggestion that Gordimer's fiction is, in the end, about her own 'powerful, wounded, entangled self', about a personal 'drama whose pressure skews much of the writing'.[65] It is the tensions between the public face of the novelist and the impetus of the work itself, between the explicit and the implicit, between text and subtext in Gordimer's work, which need to be more fully explored.

Chapter 3

Stereotypes:
Text and Subtext

The writer's work can run counter to his prejudices while the writer, and even large parts of the work itself, remain rooted in these prejudices.

F. Engels[1]

Realism by itself does not reflect us; it shields us from reality.

F.R. Karl[2]

The history of white, English-language South African fiction has been one of increasing engagement with the multiple ways in which apartheid has distorted human relationships at every level in the decades since 1948. That eventually there should have developed a backlash against such an overt politicisation of an entire literature is hardly surprising: not only Albie Sachs and his respondents but as eminent a writer as Lionel Abrahams have recently called for 'artistic freedom, including the freedom to seem politically irrelevant', which, Abrahams says, is 'a *sine qua non* of a free society'.[3] As has been suggested in the preceding chapters, Gordimer's own development has been one from an insistence on the writer's necessary autonomy to an initially re-luctant but later explicit acceptance of the felt pressure on the writer to engage with the manifold dislocations to which life in South Africa is subject: there is a clear movement from the early *Entwicklungsroman* with its smattering of social awareness, be-ginning with *The Lying Days*, to the politically self-conscious later works.[4]

Such a development places her well within the mainstream of South African writing in the last four decades, in which she has both participated in the construction of and deployed in her own work some of the dominant stereotypes of South African life in this period.[5] The ideological perspectives implicitly encoded in such stereotypes tend to correspond with a particular political agenda, and their inscription was encouraged as apartheid became more overtly a target of attack both internally and externally and South African writers found themselves increasingly urged into using their art as 'a weapon of the struggle'. Marquard was among the first South African critics who openly resisted what she termed the 'prescriptive stance' which had emerged by the mid-seventies, and she listed its negative effects on South African writing in a passage worth quoting at length. There is firstly, she argues,

> the symbol of apartheid as a strait-jacket, destroying all freedom, indeed all mobility. The writer is told, or he tells himself, that he must operate from within that strait-jacket, because there is nothing else . . . The second image or symbol is the "image of Africa" which it is the writer's duty to transmit. This usually has something to do with the pre-Colonial past, with ancestors and with the holistic tradition of rural communities. Nostalgia for the past is usually merged with anger against the colonial regime which destroyed it . . . The contemporary white writer now reverses the confident European assumptions of the past by imposing on himself, or his protagonist, rather than on the African, the role of (good or bad) alien. Modern South African literature is full of lost and alienated beings, identity-seekers in a fragmented and "foreign" landscape – burdened by guilt and worry, unable to bridge the gap between cultures, doomed to some form of psychological, if not actual, exile. This "image of Africa" turns out to be tiresomely repetitive . . .[6]

Marquard goes on to suggest that within this context narrative realism is in effect 'prescribed' as *the* mode in which to confront 'the social malaise' which results from the imposition of an apartheid hegemony, and laments South African writers' entrapment in their own symbols as a consequence of their felt need to confront its effects.

Gordimer does not escape these pressures. However, her work not only clearly inscribes the dominant images (or 'symbols', as Marquard prefers to call them) of the overt rhetoric of the anti-apartheid stance in these decades: it also betrays subtextual tensions between her sympathies with the oppressed masses and her origins in that class of affluent white South Africans who are among those who perhaps have most to fear from a successful black revolution. That these tensions are themselves a product of the dilemmas colonial writers around the world have found themselves caught up in is suggested by JanMohamed's distinction between overt cognitive structures and covert emotive and ideological insertions in the typical colonial text:

> The former can be defined simply as the conscious textual "intention" to represent or depict a certain kind of world or a particular theme, while the latter can be defined as the unconscious selectivity and closure according to which the "depicted" world is organised – that is, the emotive structure can be seen as the product of a *will* or *desire* to secure the relative coherence or position of the individual and the group to which he belongs.[7]

Although JanMohamed claims in a subsequent article that Gordimer 'manages to free [herself] from the Manichean allegory' by writing 'symbolic fiction' which confines itself to 'a rigorous examination' of the ' "imaginary" mechanism of colonialist mentality',[8] the contention in this study is that Gordimer's work has not escaped the effects of the tension between conscious intention and unconscious selectivity and emphasis. Although it is incontestably true that her great strength lies in her dissection of the 'colonialist mentality' (we need only remind ourselves of the masterly control of nuance and the unerring ear for tone in her set-pieces on colonial social gatherings in such novels as *A World of Strangers* and *A Guest of Honour*),[9] a close examination of the fiction reveals a powerful subtext of colonialist stereotypes which frequently runs counter to the overt stance.

Sander L. Gilman has highlighted the role stereotypes play in illuminating the assumptions which underlie a culture. These stereotypes are, he asserts:

> a crude set of mental representations of the world . . . palimpsests on which the initial bipolar representations are still vaguely legible . . . Within the closed world they create, stereotypes can be studied as an idealised definition of the different . . . For stereotypes, like commonplaces, carry entire realms of associa-

tions with them, associations that form a subtext within the
world of fiction. In the case of works claiming to create a world
out of whole cloth, such a subtext provides a basic insight into
the presuppositions of the culture in which the work arises and
for which it is created.[10]

This definition suggests that stereotypes will be a particularly
marked characteristic of the literature of a society dominated by
the fear of difference, such as South Africa under apartheid, it
also implies that it would be impossible for a writer to escape
altogether the effects of her society's tendency to interpret the
world in terms of a series of simple binary oppositions. If this is
so, then Gordimer, the quintessential coloniser-who-refuses, cannot be expected to escape the formative influence of her origins[11].

In fact, she herself is clearly aware of the possible difficulties
with which her immersion in the society from which she seeks to
distance herself might confront her. In a thoughtful comment
(not necessarily directed, however, at her own work) she has said
that

> cultural identity [is] "nothing more nor less than the mean be-
> tween selfhood and otherwise" . . . The dilemma of a literature in
> a multiracial society, where the law effectively prevents any real
> identification of the writer with his society as a whole, so that
> ultimately he can identify only with his colour, distorts this mean
> irreparably.[12]

But Gordimer's lucid articulation of the ways in which apartheid
problematises the relationship between self and others should not
obscure the fact that she herself is victim as well as analyst of this
process. For example, the 'fetishisation of the Other'[13] which
JanMohamed identifies as characteristic of the colonialist text is,
as we might expect, emphatically foregrounded (as we shall see)
in Gordimer's fiction as well as in South African literature as
such. The effect of apartheid ideology on the imperialist programme has been to institutionalise further that drive to label
and compartmentalise which, as JanMohamed has persuasively
argued, is fundamental to the colonial vision.

Within the framework of such an analysis, perhaps the most
intriguing way in which Gordimer's novels embody the conflict
between origins and ideology delineated above is in the radical

tensions between overt message and subconscious discourse, between text and subtext, which at times subvert the ideological stance and tend towards a reinforcement of precisely those prejudices the fiction appears to oppose. It is not Gordimer's deployment of the clichés of revolutionary rhetoric which will be under examination here: she justifies the use she makes of those in the fiction by provocatively suggesting that clichés play a necessary role in a culture in so far as they represent 'an attempt to habituate ordinary communications to overwhelming meanings in human existence . . . [becoming] enormous lies incarcerating enormous truths' (*Burger's Daughter*, 328). Nor should we discount Gordimer's own awareness of the incursion of stereotypes into South African literature. At various times she speaks dismissively of the apartheid *Tendenzroman*,[14] of the 'literature of victims' which apartheid has spawned,[15] of the modish 'miscegenation novel' (*A World of Strangers*, 46), and of the growth of an industry in Immorality Act literature.[16] Nevertheless, tensions are set up in her novels by conflicting influences of which she is hardly in conscious control. Most intriguing, perhaps, is the coexistence in the fiction of both a didactic, anti-apartheid thrust, and a secondary stream of response, embedded subtextually, which encodes and implicitly valorises, in a most powerful and immediate way, the myths and anxieties of a white consciousness whose paranoias shape Gordimer's material at a fundamental and perhaps unconscious level. Much of the fiction can be read as paradoxically confirming the deepest nightmares of the beleaguered white imagination, and as supporting at a subtextual level precisely those conservative fears and prejudices which oppose change, and which the surface rhetoric of the texts implicitly challenges.

In a relatively early novel, *The Late Bourgeois World* (1966), we may trace some of these tensions and contradictions particularly clearly. The novel takes its origins from an incident of 'sabotage' which took place in the mid-sixties. A young schoolteacher, John Harris, who was apparently under the influence of the African Resistance Movement (ARM), planted a bomb in the concourse of the Johannesburg station on 24 July 1964 which killed a woman and injured a number of other people. At his trial, Harris was described by a psychologist called *by the defence* as 'a

manic depressive with a paranoid complex'; it was claimed that
he had 'been in a state of manic ecstasy at the time of the explosion, and could therefore not be held to be criminally responsible'. The judge, while rejecting the claim that there were
'mitigating circumstances', agreed that Harris's 'mental condition was something different from normal'.[17] Although Harris
himself, unlike Gordimer's protagonist Max van der Sandt, became the first white man to be hanged (on 1 April 1965) for a
politically inspired act,[18] other ARM members did indeed, as Max
does, turn state witness after periods of imprisonment, often in
solitary confinement, under the 90-day detention laws.

That there are analogies between the history of John Harris
and that of Max van der Sandt is not accidental. Gordimer has
said that her intention in *The Late Bourgeois World* was 'to look
into the specific character of the social climate that produced the
wave of young white saboteurs in 1963-64'.[19] What is of particular interest here is that the insights into the character of that
social climate and its effects on Max van der Sandt, as recorded
in the novel, tend to reflect white public opinion of the time,
which was that violent acts of resistance to the apartheid state by
a young man so demonstrably 'one of us' could only be understood as the action of one who was not 'normal'. Such radicalism
was so clearly associated with mental pathology[20] in the public
mind that the response to Harris was partially coloured by the
sympathy reserved for those who are mentally ill, and published
interviews with Harris's wife sympathetically stressed her
naïvety, her inexperience, and her loyalty to him.[21]

It is highly significant that Max van der Sandt is not allowed
to speak for himself in the novel and is thus absent as a
countervoice. Instead, he is seen through the eyes of his ex-wife,
Elizabeth, in a first-person narration which never deviates from
her perspective. The portrayal of Max reflects both the condemnation and the peculiar sympathy this incident aroused, encoding
conflicting emotions that undermine those passages in which
Elizabeth overtly endorses Max's actions, and that introduce a
curious effect of confusion and inconsistency which ultimately
negates the values Elizabeth uncertainly attempts to articulate.

The novel opens with an epigraph from Gorky: 'The madness
of the brave is the wisdom of life.' Gordimer later claimed that

Max's history constitutes 'a tragedy',[22] and has recently defined a tragedy as being what happens 'when a human being is destroyed engaging himself with events greater than personal relationships. A tragic death results from the struggle between good and evil' (*A Sport of Nature*, 215). But is Max's death presented as indeed *tragic* in terms of such a definition? It very soon becomes clear that Elizabeth's fundamental response is irremediably ambivalent. On the one hand, she appears to defend Max's actions (which include the betrayal of his political associates at his trial, and the driving of his car into the sea in a suicide which appears to represent an attempt to expiate his guilt) as she muses that

> he risked everything for them and lost everything. He gave his life in every way there is, and going down to the bed of the sea is the last. (*The Late Bourgeois World*, 55)

But, on the other hand, her ultimate assessment of Max, as an individual caught in a web of internal tensions and contradictions which reflect a profound degree of personal inadequacy, is summarised in her explanation to their son, Bobo, that Max

> wasn't equal to the demands he took upon himself . . . as if you insisted on playing the first team when you were only good enough – strong enough for third. (18)

The analogy suggests not the individual's failure to live up to a mythical heroic status (thereby suffering a tragic defeat since what has been aimed at is by definition unattainable), but simply that Max was lacking: not 'good enough' to play the game with the best and the bravest (who remain undefined, but may well include Luke Fokase). Max is, in fact, a man who cannot command Elizabeth's respect, as is suggested in her admission that she wanted him '*to do the right things so that [she] could love him*. Was that love?' (49). She interprets his actions as a childish attempt to attract attention to himself, and thus presents the plan to plant a bomb as foolish in conception, the attempt as amateurish in its execution, and the whole affair as of the same order as Max's burning – when he was a child – of his father's clothes in order to force his father to pay attention to him. Elizabeth's initial reaction to his suicide is a sense of outrage that he should again be claiming her attention by yet another extreme and childish ploy. She also presents Max in negative terms as a 'fanatic', and as 'unable to be aware of anyone else's needs but his own' (42, 43). In the end, Max is seen as both too flawed and too unstable either to elicit fear or be worthy of Elizabeth's anger. Her analysis is correspondingly cool and dispassionate, reflecting her symbolically apt occupation as a laboratory technician, engaged in the scientific analysis of blood and urine samples entirely dissociated from the living human entity.

Elizabeth's perspective is neither modified nor contradicted at any point by an alternative vision. It is Max rather than Elizabeth who is the focus of attention throughout the major part of the novel, and Gordimer feels no need to qualify her first-person narrative voice by her characteristic modulation, as in other works, between this and the omniscient mode. No tension between alternative points of view (other than that located within Elizabeth's own ambivalences) exists which would allow a possible metadiscourse to emerge which would encourage an assessment of Max and his actions other than the reading Elizabeth offers. *Her* analysis of Max's background, character and motives, given in so rational and sympathetic a tone, acquires the status of a complex series of 'truths' which, in the end, simply serve to strengthen and confirm the embedded prejudices about the sanity of whites who attach themselves to radical political groupings which were widely held at the time. To a degree then, Gordimer inadvertently undermines our sense of the value of political activism and of the integrity of those involved in it, even as she appears to affirm both.

The tensions between white prejudices and radical commitments already commented upon in Gordimer's attitudes surface not only in *The Late Bourgeois World* but also in later novels such as *Burger's Daughter* and *July's People*. In its depiction of Rosa Burger's inability to deny her inheritance of political activism, *Burger's Daughter* tapped into a popular excuse for avoiding such activism at a time when apartheid was still perceived to be monolithically impervious to any pressures for change. It was an excuse already embedded in one of the first ostensibly anti-apartheid commercial films to be made and screened inside South Africa, *Katrina* (1969).[23] This film presented sex across the colour bar with some insight and compassion, nevertheless concluded against a lasting union between its two protagonists on the basis that it would be indefensibly irresponsible to produce 'coloured' children who would, inevitably, be condemned to a miserable existence in an irremediably vicious racist world. Gordimer's own early pessimism about the fate of such children is inscribed in her representation of Anna Louw's attitude on this issue in *A World of Strangers*. Anna discusses the failure of her own 'mixed marriage' to an Indian South African and, in a passage which might well have influenced *Katrina's* script-writer, she explains to Toby that

> it's a good thing we didn't have any children . . . I used to say, it's too bad if it's hard for the children; you just have to make them understand that they're only misfits in a worn-out society that doesn't count, that, in reality, they're the new people in the world that's coming, the decent one where colour doesn't matter . . . [But] it's not true yet. It's a hell of a life to impose on a half-and-half child in the meantime; waiting for a Kingdom of Heaven that probably won't come to earth in its lifetime . . . You can't measure a historical process against the life of a kid. (176-77)

The underlying premise that racism is a regrettably constant element of unredeemed human society both informs Anna Louw's perspective and gives substance to the ultimately anti-miscegenationist message which surfaces in this novel, and which also undercuts the superficial liberalism of *Katrina*. Nevertheless, within the context of Gordimer's avowed conviction that the 'new' Africa will require a new type of person, it is significant that the novel also gives voice to Anna Louw's idealistic view that although 'in reality' children of mixed race are 'only misfits in a worn-out society that doesn't count', they represent 'the new people in the world that's coming, the decent one where colour doesn't matter'. (176)

Only in such utopian projections can Gordimer suggest a resolution to the intractable problem of race in her society, and the tentative nature of such a hope is perhaps reflected in the fact that she allows Hillela only one child of the 'rainbow family' she so desires in *A Sport of Nature*. In strong contrast, for example, to Rosa Burger's history of co-option into 'the struggle' in *Burger's Daughter*, Nomzamo is the first and only one of Gordimer's children who is allowed a personal liberation from the historical imperative (in contrast to her famous namesake, Winnie Nomzamo Mandela). Only in an Africa at last liberated may a child of revolutionaries opt for the entirely private pleasures of the apolitical, superficial glamour of the world of the international fashion model.[24] Indeed, within such an emotional context, *Burger's Daughter* may be conservatively read as an object lesson in and warning against the destructive effect that political activism has upon the lives of the 'innocent' children of committed parents, despite the novel's suggestion that this might be a necessary price to pay for change. The image of Rosa Burger in prison at the end of the novel, having fulfilled at last her destiny as Burger's daughter, emphasises not only her acceptance of her fate (and claims for her a concomitant psychological 'liberation'), but also, in incorporating an element of pathos in the emphasis on her once again looking 'about fourteen' (360),[25] suggests that she has been the victim of a merciless exploitation.

Such conservative readings represent a travesty of Gordimer's expressed intentions and overt political commitments in these novels, but the fact that they were and are possible suggests the extent to which an alternative and unconscious discourse is embedded in the work, one which may be seen to spring directly from Gordimer's immersion in the society she dissects with so merciless an eye. *July's People* is an especially revealing example, ironically encoding as it does a number of peculiarly South African myths.[26] White fears of the consequences of giving in to black demands (which, in their crudest and most populist form took the simplistic shape of assuming that blacks would do to others as they had been done by, and that a black hegemony would relegate vanquished whites to the rural mud huts vacated by the newly victorious black masses) inform the way in which Gordimer conceptualises the fate of her white protagonists in this revolutionary context. The novel can be read as an ironic inversion of several contemporary literary paradigms: for example, the 'Jim comes to Jo'burg' model, the Conradian notion that a penetration into the African reality will reveal to the intrepid explorer a 'heart of darkness', and the American concern with the search for and a return to 'roots'. The latter semi-pastoral theme, however, serves to remind us here, as it does in *The Conserva-*

tionist, of Gordimer's belief that the white man can by definition have no roots in a country he has only temporarily colonised and exploited. In addition, encoded in an only slightly modified form in Gordimer's treatment of the character of July are some of the more persistent myths of the time in the subculture of Johannesburg's northern suburbs, myths so pervasive that they have recently been labelled 'urban legends'.[27] Gordimer herself has revealingly defined myth as 'a psychologically defensive and protective device . . . an extra-logical explanation of events according to the way a people wishes to interpret them'.[28] Thus, it is probably no accident that we find embedded in the subtext of *July's People* the morbid humour of the frequently repeated 'joke' that, when the revolution comes, either one's own servants or the gardener next door will come to cut one's throat,[29] which is combined with the older Boer myth of the trusty black servant hiding white women and children away in the caves and kraals of the countryside until the war has passed by. The two myths fuse in the depiction of July as not only saviour but also exploiter, oppressor and gaoler of the Smales family. The novel thus, by implication, ironically succeeds in communicating not only Black Consciousness scorn of, but also conservative right-wing contempt for the liberal 'illusion' that genuine relationships of affection and respect might be possible between masters and servants (an illusion still encoded in earlier depictions of employer--employee friendships in such novels as *The Late Bourgeois World* and *Burger's Daughter*).

July is, in fact, determined to give no quarter to his erstwhile masters and mercilessly manipulates them as servants are typically said to do by their madams at afternoon tea parties. Firstly, he refuses to abandon the role of a servant whose loyalty exists only in so far as it is bought and paid for; secondly, in ensuring that Maureen's attempt to establish friendships with the women of the village fails, he denies her the relief of acceptance and integration (96-97); and, thirdly, in his appropriation of the symbols of power ('bakkie' and gun), he symbolically castrates and makes impotent the master-race he exploits. Maureen's flight at the end of the novel towards a helicopter which may represent 'civilisation' at any price can hardly be read as a simple expression of personal liberation: the act inextricably fuses both self-affirmation and betrayal. The novel as a whole tended to confirm its white readers' worst fears of the consequences of revolution, paradoxically strengthening resistance to its representation (by radical groupings) as a liberating scenario, at a time when such a revolution seemed nearly inevitable.

Gordimer's susceptibility to the currents of fear and prejudice in the world she inhabits not only reveals itself in her subtextual incorporation of popular myths, but also has a corollary in that tendency already briefly discussed above to inscribe uncritically in her fiction the prevailing ideological positions of the left-wing groups she had access to at any one time. For example, in the title of *The Late Bourgeois World*, (a phrase taken from the work of the Marxist critic, Ernst Fischer),[30] the term 'bourgeois' has all the force of contempt associated with it by Williams in his definition of the word in *Keywords*:

> It is often difficult to separate [the term 'bourgeois'] from the residual aristocratic and philosophic contempt [which coloured it in the past], and from a later form especially common among unestablished artists, writers and thinkers who might not and often do not share Marx's central definition but who sustain the older sense of hostility towards the (mediocre) established and respectable.[31]

In this novel, Gordimer's corrosive contempt for white South African liberalism extends to embrace the whole of white society in a narrative remarkable for the degree of alienation it inscribes as a norm for both its characters and its author. Her excoriation of the bourgeoisie may be traced to and understood to be rooted in her identification with those anti-racist forces which, in a South Africa in which apartheid consigns all of its oppressed black non-citizens to the working class, have of necessity allied themselves with working-class interests. It is this, rather than a commitment to Marxist or socialist political theory, which gives impetus to the emotional thrust of the fiction in its valorisation of the (black) oppressed against the (white) bourgeoisie.[32] We might note here that, despite Gordimer's awareness that colour prejudice may encompass a form of class prejudice, class itself is not an issue in the fiction.[33] Thus, for example, the extraordinary influence of Black Consciousness ideology in the early 1970s (which destroyed the South African PEN* in which Gordimer had been active), together with white fears at the time that Frelimo's activities in Mozambique would fan revolutionary fervour in South Africa, colour the symbolism and largely determine the anti-white, anti-capitalist and anti-bourgeois resolution of *The Conservationist*. The need to articulate and endorse an ideologically determined prophecy about the fate of South African whites eventually swamps aesthetic judgement in the melodramatic final section of this novel, in which a storm blows in from the Mozambique Channel, uncovering the buried corpse of the unknown black man on Mehring's land and precipitating Mehring's collapse – a collapse in many ways inconsistent with the character so skilfully and sensitively developed in the novel to this point. Mehring abandons the farm and, in effect, conveniently flees 'overseas' at the end of the novel, leaving the land to its 'true' owners, the community of black farm labourers who live on it and off it. In so far as Mehring has been made to be representative of white South Africa as a whole in the novel, such a resolution could only be read as validating popular white perceptions of the Black Consciousness position, which were that the victory of such an ideology would result in the white man being 'driven into the sea': insofar as he was an alien intruder, there could be no place for him in the new Azania. The contrast between the persuasively insightful, complex anatomisation of white liberalism and the lurid melodrama of the novel's politically simplistic conclusion could hardly be more marked. In addition, white fears of the consequences of any capitulation to Black Consciousness positions can only have been strengthened by such a resolution of the novel's tensions.

In a more recent novel, *A Sport of Nature*, we have another example of Gordimer's tendency to pattern her fiction after prevalent trends in radical politics. At a time when interest in the ANC, the politics of external resistance to apartheid, and the activities of political refugees and exiles was growing rapidly, this novel offered a kaleidoscopic and romanticised version of such activities which is, in many ways, essentially improbable. Parker

---

* An international writers organisation consisting of Poets, Playwrights, Editors, Essayists and Novelists.

(1987) has said of the political discourse in this novel that 'the level of the discussion is invariably unsophisticated and tends to culminate in slogans and clichés'[34] – a comment which could well be applied to the enthusiastic political pronouncements of much of her earlier fiction as well. If, indeed, the Censorship Board's belief that Gordimer's work would be read only by a small 'intellectual' segment of the population was correct,[35] it seems likely that her tendency to combine a documentation of the prevailing popular concerns of the day with both a fairly clichéd version of complex political positions and an attack upon the fundamental political integrity of those who constituted her potential readership would go some way towards explaining the lack of enthusiasm with which her work has been received within the country by, in particular, an academic readership which she might have expected to share her perspectives in certain areas.

These novels, then, offer us 'history from the inside' from a rather different perspective than the one Clingman foregrounds: a history of the submerged guilts, fears and repressions of a white consciousness Gordimer's vision has been shaped by, and whose delusions and myths she has internalised and expressed in the subtexts of the novels. Clearly, her work has not escaped the problems that, according to JanMohamed, typically beset colonialist literature. His claim that colonial writers in general are unable to 'negate or at least severely bracket the values, assumptions, and ideology of their culture', and that their work paradoxically 'affirms its own ethnocentric assumptions . . . and codifies and preserves the structures of its own mentality',[36] revealingly illuminates the tensions in Gordimer's work. In many of the novels she articulates precisely those fears of black rule and its consequences which are characteristic of the class from which she seeks to dissociate herself. Although there can be no argument about the subtlety, refinement and precision of her analysis of the inner contradictions of the particular white liberal position in South Africa which she knows so intimately, she clearly cannot be expected to free herself fully of the psychological and conceptual limitations of her class.

We may extend the analysis further. Gordimer is, of course, not only the product of her class position in South Africa; she has also attempted to step outside of it in making herself an analyst of and spokesperson for radical activism in the country. Not surprisingly, her work reproduces both aspects of the anti-apartheid movement's ideology and many of its prejudices, dreams, confusions and stereotypes. A particularly noteworthy consequence of this is the prevalence of what may be termed reverse racism in her work: a tendency to idealise the black world at the expense of the white world. Gilman has suggested that such tendencies may themselves be paradoxically an expression of a vision circumscribed by stereotypes. He argues that 'the idea of the pathological is a central marker of difference', and locates the origins of a sense of racial difference in the perception of sexual differences: the 'other' is by definition seen as diseased within a paradigm which defines the self as healthy and the 'other' as not. Gilman goes on to claim that

> physiognomy or skin colour that is perceived as different is immediately associated with "pathology" and "sexuality". [But] these associations are double-edged. They may appear as negative images, but they may also appear as positive idealizations. The "pathological" may appear as the pure, the unsullied; the sexually different as the apotheosis of beauty, the asexual or the androgynous; the racially different as highly attractive. In all of these cases the same process occurs. The loss of control is projected not onto the cause or mirror of this loss but onto the Other, who, unlike the self, can do no wrong, can never be out of control.[37]

In novel after novel Gordimer presents us with images of a white reality almost exclusively characterised by self-deception, alienation, ambiguous morality, and sterile and atrophied relationships, and sets against these a romanticised black world of vibrant vitality and joyous purpose, to which those whites who seek some degree of psychological and spiritual salvation must attach themselves if they are to be connected in any meaningful way with the positive future which is unfolding. In *A World of Strangers*, for example, Toby's first encounter with 'Africa' in Mombasa is in his lazy swim in the warm sea, during which he feels

> an actual physical melting, as if some component of my blood that had remained insoluble for twenty-six years of English climate had suddenly, wonderfully, dissolved into free-

flowing . . . the last jagged crystals of my English blood melted
away. (14-15)

Not 'Africa' but the colonials among whom Toby finds himself
constitute a problem: 'Were these the sort of people Africa gets?'
he asks, 'Christ, poor continent!' (27). The novel's subsequent
schematisation of South African society into a binary opposition
between the 'abundant life' (129) of the black township world as
epitomised in the character of Steven Sitole, and the isolated and
alienated world of the wealthy northern suburbs of Johannesburg as alternatively epitomised in the character of Toby's girlfriend Cecil (whose name significantly connects her with the
brutal imperialism of Cecil John Rhodes), is fully consonant with
the opening passages.

   Such simple stereotypes dictate in particular Gordimer's stress
on sex across the colour line as a form of redemption for the
white colonial. They shape, for example, the depiction of Elizabeth van der Sandt's attraction to the radical black activist Luke
Fokase in *The Late Bourgeois World*. He is her Orpheus, calling
her to the 'crowded company' of the 'real' world; she is his
Eurydice, trapped in her class-Hades and symbolically associated
with Death via the symbolism of the identical bouquets of snow-
drops sent to her and her senile grandmother by the white lover
she rejects, Graham Mill. Luke's ability to stir her sexual responses reawakens in her the potential for political commitment
and action which had atrophied within her symbolically sterile
relationship with Graham. If she is to free herself of the *anomie* of
'the late bourgeois world', she must betray her class to advance
Luke's plans; her reward, by implication, will be a symbolic 'affair' with Luke, who is, significantly enough, described as

> this young black bull in the white china shop, with its nice little
> dinner, and bookshelves, and bric-a-brac, coffee-cup talk . . . He
> is immediately *there* – one of those people . . . whose body
> warmth leaves fingerprints on his glass. (89, 75, 83)

Political salvation is to be achieved, it is made clear, via a sexual
connection. Here the popular racist stereotype of the superior
sexual potency of the black man[38] is implicit both in the imagery
and in the symbolic representation of the black world as a source

of sensual and spiritual liberation, as well as in the concomitant stress on the sterility of Elizabeth's relationship with Graham. It is worth noting that, throughout Gordimer's work, a willingness to engage in sexual relationships across the colour bar functions as a reliable signifier of spiritual liberation from apartheid ideology and of at least potential political commitment to the advancement of revolutionary change. Gordimer has herself suggested that sexual attitudes in her novels are to be understood as analogues of political attitudes, and it is therefore no accident that, for example, in *The Conservationist*, Mehring's sexual relationships are shown to be directed by that need to exploit, dominate, possess and manipulate which, for Gordimer, represents the central impulse of the capitalist temperament. For him no liberating or redemptive sexual contact across the colour bar is envisaged. His confused and submerged longing for some kind of integration with the land can ironically express itself only in his fantasy of a fleeting friendship with the black overseer of his farm, an impotent yearning which, minimal though it is, is nevertheless refused fulfilment. The novel, in fact, ironically makes his fear of exposure under the Immorality Act symbolic of his general moral corruption.

So simplistic an equation between a political and a sexual revolution appears to have been partially rejected by the time Gordimer came to write *Burger's Daughter*, in which Rosa articulates an awareness of the 'false consciousness' involved in 'using blackness as a way of perceiving a sensual redemption' (135). Yet Rosa's attraction to Marisa Kgosana as a symbol of such a redemption is not invalidated. In an even later novel, *July's People*, it is Maureen's realisation of the impossibility of establishing a sexual bond with the potentially attractive figure of July which is the catalyst for her flight at the end of the novel. Here, once again, as in *The Late Bourgeois World*, Gordimer presents us with an axiomatically sterile relationship between the two white protagonists. Maureen and Bam's marriage is conceived of as one based on a delicate balance of power-relationships determined by each one's willingness to play out predetermined roles within a clearly defined suburban context. The emptiness of these roles is demonstrated when they are shown to disintegrate upon the Smaleses being forced into a physical exile which reveals to them their irremediable inner alienation from each other and from any form of community. However, the emphasis on alienation is too dependent on an insufficiently developed analysis of their situation to be suggestive on any other than a rigidly schematic level. Gordimer's attempt to link that alienation with their political and social position, and to use it as a symbol of both white South African alienation from 'Africa' and of the essential sterility of white culture, is somewhat strained within the finely developed context of a sensitive analysis of the tensions which beset the novel's central consciousness, Maureen Smales.

Equally interesting, in terms of the present study, is the specific character of Gordimer's depiction of white suburban culture, a depiction demonstrably shaped and directed by her own ideological commitment to a vision of history which posits the imminent demise of that class. Her novels have significantly helped to construct and entrench in the minds of a foreign readership an image of the spiritual and material conditions of a white South African lifestyle which, at one level, reassuringly supports the idealist's demand that there be moral justice in the world. Those who are the perpetrators of or profit in some way from the twin evils of capitalism and apartheid are depicted as being trapped in that deadly spiritual and moral malaise which we have already noted as the context of the protagonists' meditations in novels such as *The Late Bourgeois World*, *The Conservationist*, and *July's People*. Material wealth and leisure are the keynotes of this world, not only in the early emphasis on the Fitzgeraldian social life of The High House in *A World of Strangers*, but also in the depiction of dinner parties attended only by those who work hard 'to keep the best for themselves' in *The Late Bourgeois World*, and in the much later representation in *July's People* of the Smaleses' 'typical' suburban lifestyle. The seven-roomed house, the swimming pool, the cars, the farm, are, it is suggested (both here and in *The Conservationist*), normal components of what are called 'the superior living standards of white civilisation in South Africa' (*The Late Bourgeois World*, 27).

Gordimer indeed at times loses touch with credibility as a result of her unquestioned assumption that affluence is a white norm. For example, in *A Sport of Nature* Hillela gives Rey an elephant-hide attaché case with gilt fittings as a birthday present

(114) at a time when it is clear that she would not have had the means to make so expensive a gift (unless, of course, we assume, as we are perhaps meant to do, that Hillela is using Rey's money). It should be noted that such visions of pervasive affluence as marking white lifestyles (even in exile in Dar-es-Salaam) have themselves sunk to the level of stereotype in the literature as a whole. Watson, for one, has recently criticised the extent to which South African poets confine themselves to reproducing a stereotyped version of their social and cultural contexts. What he has to say of poetry is demonstrably true of the fiction of the last few decades as well, namely that the poets reproduce

> unconsciously, helplessly, the flatness, the impoverishment of their culture . . . [South African culture] has remained resolutely stranded within the confines of its own impoverishment. Similarly trapped, its [writers] have stuck largely to reproducing the moribund features of their imprisonment and the muddying tans of their own kind . . . As much as anything else, this cultural situation (or malaise) accounts for the interminable depictions in their poetry of the well-heeled decadence of the English with their swimming pools, tea-times and sun-downers on evening verandahs.[39]

The moral decay of an impotent liberalism is epitomised by Antonia's wistful and only partially ironic desire, in *The Conservationist*, to 'change the world but keep bits of it the way I like it for myself . . . Why not just leave it as it is?' (70-71; see also 77). It is a measure of the subtlety and complexity of Gordimer's characterisation of Mehring that she chooses to allow his voice to articulate a contemptuous response to Antonia's fantasy: 'To keep anything the way you like it for yourself you have to have the stomach to ignore – dead and hidden – whatever intrudes' (79). The typical liberal, it is implied here, simply lacks the guts to come to terms with the clash between reality and fantasy, but Mehring's hard-headed, capitalist pragmatism constitutes another kind of failure and becomes an index of his multiple inadequacies as a human being among other human beings. Antonia (whose face, Mehring muses, is 'full of intelligent stupidity' (71)) is eventually driven out of the country, and Mehring finally flees the farm and presumably sells it (264). With a corrosive irony Gordimer presents his material wealth not only as simply the result of exploitation, the ill-gotten gains of social and economic injustice, but also comfortingly suggests how – as should be the way in general with the wages of sin – this much vaunted high standard of living morally impoverishes those who enjoy it. The pervasive assumption that this is the way in which white South Africans in general live, one implicit in both Gordimer's fiction and in many critical responses to it, is, of course, demonstrably false: such an image of white South African culture must be recognised to function as a stereotype in Gordimer's work, serving her thematic purposes in the novels. It distorts a far more complex reality, while reflecting, pandering and helping to entrench foreign prejudices about white South Africa in general.[40]

In addition, the insertion of the phrase 'their own kind' in Watson's contemptuous dismissal of much South African white English-language poetry, in the passage quoted above, should alert us to the urge to compartmentalisation which is a feature of apartheid society and which has itself achieved the status of stereotype. Such an urge betrays, in Currie's eloquent phrasing:

> the restrictive dyad of margin/center, the deadly circuitry of 'us' and 'them' which informs both Eurocentric literary discourse and its nationalist and separatist alternatives.[41]

Gordimer's tendency to insert just such an 'us versus them' dialectic into her novels is an interesting pointer to some of the submerged assumptions which shape the fiction. At one level, the purpose of such oppositions is clearly ironic, entirely consonant with Wright's suggestion that stereotypes may be deployed, in a Swiftian formula, as a deliberate strategy in 'a total satiric polemic'.[42] The phrase serves a dual purpose: it implicitly satirises the club-oriented, British-colonial insider–versus–outsider cast of mind residually present in the world Gordimer inhabits, and also acts as an indicator of her own alternative commitment, within such a framework, to those conventionally thought of as 'them' – the outsider class rejected by the 'us'. The 'us' (or the individual described as 'one of our kind', or, alternatively, in the third-person narrative voice as 'one of his/her kind') is characteristically identified as a member of a politically right-thinking, anti-apart-

heid and often activist inner coterie, and set against the vast un-
thinking masses of 'them'. Such a simple dialectic, however, also
suggests the smug certainties of a moralistic perspective which
divides the world into those who are either with 'us' or against
'us'; a world of moral blacks and whites in which Gordimer gives
no quarter in her attacks upon the objects of her contempt and
scorn. Watson criticises such 'ideological thinking' as 'an insurmountable Manicheanism' which is 'inherently totalitarian' and
'inclines human beings to the belief that politics rather than religion is the true means of human transcendence and fulfilment'.[43]

The 'us versus them' dialectic expresses itself most clearly in
the underlying assumptions which control the representation of
both black and white protagonists in the novels. The depiction of
each group is visibly shaped and informed by a series of generalisations about characteristics and attitudes which ultimately
originate in the deeply embedded stereotypes and prejudices
characteristic of particular political allegiances. Firstly, since
Gordimer's sympathies are aligned with black aspirations, and
her scorn is directed at the impotent or self-deluding white
liberal, we find that the latter is frequently presented negatively,
and often through the lens of what Gordimer asks us to assume is
a 'black' point of view. This perspective offers images of 'what
whites are like' in the form of a series of generalisations which at
times strike the reader with all the reductive force of prejudice
and stereotype. In *July's People*, for example, the child Victor is
described as being angry 'with a white man's anger' (86), a comment which is deemed to be self-explanatory. In *The Late Bourgeois World*, Elizabeth's unease expresses itself in the unintentional pathos of her attempt to see herself through the eyes of the
black activist, Luke Fokase, as she wonders self-deprecatingly
whether he will see her as 'yet another white woman who talks
too much'. She will later explain that, of course, Luke's lack of a
genuine (sexual) interest in her is understandable because white
women have nothing to offer black men 'except the footing
[they] keep in the good old white reserves of banks and privileges'
(80, 94).

Such distorted and defensive generalisations suggest a psyche
under siege, and modulate into the bitter generalising assumptions about white attitudes and responses articulated in, for ex-

ample, *July's People*, where we are told by the narrative voice
that deviousness is 'natural' to white suburban life and, more
astonishingly, that leisure is a 'suburban invention' (89, 34).[44] We
are also told that whites are impractical, unadaptable and unwilling to work, and that white attitudes to children are distant and
rejecting. White alienation and dislocation are repeatedly suggested by a stress on distorted attitudes to the body (9, 67, 80, 90,
103): sexual puritanism, hostility, prurience and an obsessive distaste for bodily functions mark, in particular, Gordimer's female
characters and their responses to their white lovers. Indeed, the
prevalence of this element in her work has given rise to Parker's
protest that she 'often writes in a manner that might be construed
as appealing to those who read airport type international block-
busters of the more elevated kind'.[45]

At another level, the narratives reproduce, both consciously
and unconsciously, common white assumptions and prejudices
about black behaviour and black qualities. In an early example,
we find the narrator of *Occasion for Loving* telling us without
conscious irony that the 'piccanins' looked with 'dull astonish-
ment' (133) on the sight of Gideon and Ann picnicking together;
behind the flat descriptive tone lies concealed a whole series of
assumptions about rural black children which reflect a number of
white stereotypes about their intelligence and lifestyles. A parallel
betrayal of prejudice is embedded in a similarly unmarked comment in *A Sport of Nature* that the radio was playing 'monoto-
nous African music' (212). In *July's People*, petty theft on the part
of the servant class is presented as a norm and not criticised:
Maureen's lack of surprise or anger at the presence of long-lost
household objects in 'July's huts' is a typical reaction among
white liberals who are plagued by guilt about the gulf between
the white rich and the black poor and thus prohibited from ex-
pressing any disapproval of the urge towards redistribution. At
the same time, black rural life is represented here without any
warmth of interest or intimacy of knowledge, despite the strong
response to 'nature' which is a feature of many of the other novels, and ideology rather than accuracy dictates Maureen's comment that 'they had nothing', in flat contradiction of the
undeniable presence of huts, goats, pigs, chickens and fields.
Maureen's son, Victor, takes up an unquestioned, indeed, auto-

matic leadership among the children of the village, despite the language and cultural gaps which divide him from them and of which the novel betrays no more than the superficial tourist knowledge characteristic of white South Africans faced with black contexts (89, 34, 86, 29). And in *The Late Bourgeois World* the narrative suggests admiration for the alleged efficiency and orderliness of white minds and their hidden resources, in observations which clearly imply the general absence of these qualities among blacks (77, 84, 87).

At yet another level, a third set of generalisations offers a glimpse of those positive stereotypes of black life and customs current among the white liberal élite as a result of its sporadic contacts with some of those on the other side of the racial divide. So, for example, the white 'brats' of *July's People* are shown to 'learn manners' from their black playmates: they begin to clap their hands together as a sign of gratitude when given something. Black physical characteristics normally alien to contemporary white standards of beauty are frequently self-consciously valorised: for example, the narrative voice approvingly suggests all black women are broad and stocky in the generalisation that Lydia was 'of the age blacks retain between youth and the time when their sturdy and comfortable breasts and backsides become leaden weight, their characteristic good thick legs slow to a stop – old age' (30). Another such view of 'difference' is reflected in the description of a black child in *The Conservationist*, 'the elder girl', as 'motherly towards smaller ones as only black or Afrikaans children are' (55). Black children in *Burger's Daughter* are represented as communal property, cocooned within the loving care of the group, in a representation which asks the reader to assume that there are no neglected children in enlightened black circles. Further generalisations surface in *The Late Bourgeois World*, where Elizabeth claims that 'Africans are instinctively tactful in these matters' (relating to the repayment of debts), and that African funerals are occasions on which 'all feuds and estrangements [are] forgotten'. 'It's all so much simpler if you're black,' she finally earnestly explains; 'even your guilt's dealt with for you' (90, 79, 80). Such comments offer us images of a black world altogether simpler and cleaner than the white world, one in which the ambiguities, contradictions and complexities of alle-

giance characteristic of the white world are for the most part refreshingly eased.

The voices which articulate these generalisations are, of
course, very often those of flawed and crippled consciousnesses,
yet it is noteworthy that, despite the frequent complexity of
Gordimer's narrative technique, and particularly of her deployment of point of view, no metadiscourse emerges to contradict
the distorted perspectives quoted above. The pervasive tone of
the narrative voice is one of dispassionate reportage or documentation of 'reality' and its submerged biases arguably unintentionally reflect the subjective distastes and enthusiasms of the author
herself. The tension already discussed between overt message and
submerged response is again apparent here: although Gordimer
was well aware of the extent to which 'the mutually exclusive
"them" and "they" of our daily lives . . . [serve as a signifier of]
the South African caste system',[46] she often does not deploy this
opposition ironically, but frequently offers it without any form of
qualification throughout the entire body of the fiction. The pervasiveness of the 'us versus them' syndrome in the novels, with its
concomitant burden of generalisation and stereotype, should indeed be seen as a primary signifier in Gordimer's work, one
which alerts us to the simple pattern of binary opposition which
underlies the surface complexity of the novels and gives them
much of their moral force and focus. The dissection of confusion
and contradiction in her white characters' internal and external
relationships is implicitly set against a moral world in which
there is no doubt on which side Right is to be found, who the
evildoers are, and what is ultimately required of the individual in
the service of the collective drive to liberate the 'beloved country'.

The limitations of vision suggested by the degree of simplification and generalisation in the political and cultural attitudes expressed in the novels are evident also in the tendency to
romanticise, idealise and mythologise both the revolutionary
process and the lives and attitudes of those working to realise it,
which is a corollary of the didactic element in Gordimer's moral
stance. The problematic ending of *Burger's Daughter*, for instance, highlights this element in the fiction. Rosa has finally
found her way to the prison cell marked out for her as her inheritance, a cell she inhabits, significantly enough, not as a conse-

quence of her actions but simply of her connections. After her temporary 'defection' to a richer set of possibilities overseas, she needs to be rehabilitated and her detention is to be read both as a form of expiation which will lead to redemption, and as a confirmation of her return to the fold as 'one of us'. The sanitised and idealised images offered of her life in prison avoid any reflection of the grimmer realities of imprisonment as a political detainee in South Africa as described by those who have actually gone through the experience, and Gordimer's representation lacks the persuasive power and dramatic force of contemporary prison narratives.

There are other moments in the novels which simply jar as entirely unlikely in a society held in the grip of apartheid ideology, such as the suggestion in *July's People* that a maid and her school-girl charge on the gold mines of the East Rand in the 1950s could have addressed each other as 'darling' in 'affection and ignorance' (33), or the sidelong glance in *The Late Bourgeois World* at an equalising, race-blind, feminist complicity between maid and madam as they together procure joint abortions which are mutually kept secret from their men. Such romantic images of the possibility of a human contact unqualified by race or language, cultural or class gaps, and unsullied by the corrupting influence of the pervasive apartheid ideology, must strike the reader as representing, in a touchingly naïve fashion, a momentary, simple romanticism shaped by Gordimer's need to transcend the numbing realities of fissure and compartmentalisation in contemporary South African society. We may note in passing that the problems inherent in such an attempt to knit together what has been ineluctably divided are further well illustrated, at another level, in the difficulties Gordimer has in constructing convincing black speech patterns in her novels. Although this will be investigated in more detail in Chapter 5, we may note here that she swings between two extremes: the perfect English spoken by her black characters in, for example, *The Late Bourgeois World* and *Burger's Daughter*, which suggests a pervasive whiteness-under-the-skin that elides cultural differences and links the characters together in terms of a common humanity, and the broken grammar of those 'servants' who refuse to be assimilated, in *July's People* and *The Conservationist*, which suggests the essential opaqueness of the black world to the enquiring white eye in a society irredeemably divided. Neither can be a satisfactory solution to the problem of representation, as Gordimer herself has recognised.[47]

The question may be asked whether Gordimer's vision can be exonerated from the charges of simplification, romanticisation and stereotyping by accepting, for example, Clingman's claim that her method of characterisation should be understood as an instance of Lukacsian 'typification'. Lukacs has argued that the ideal protagonist in the socialist realist novel should be 'typical' in a quite specific sense, neither average, eccentric nor 'crudely illustrative'; he should be one who reacts 'with his entire personality to the life of his age', for in him 'the determining factors of a particular historical phase are [to be] found . . . in concentrated form'.[48] Clingman amplifies this in his suggestion that Gordimer's characters should be seen

> to represent, as extreme condensations of more widely dispersed traits and possibilities, a feeling for the socially typical – those ostensibly essential features that represent a whole mood and moment . . . [It is a technique] based upon a principle of significance which selects the extreme embodiment and ignores the particular exception. [49]

Such a claim is, however, based on an essentially reductive model, implying that general agreement exists on what the nature and spirit of an age might be, and what is typical or eccentric in a response to it, and ignoring both the difficulties inherent in acquiring such a perspective while being immersed in the moment itself, and the necessarily subjective, partisan, selective and essentially fictive nature of such a perspective at any time.[50] For example, the claim that Mehring, in *The Conservationist*, 'tends to include all white society in his condition'[51] is difficult to support. Mehring is, firstly, an exception to his class – 'no ordinary pig-iron dealer' (69) – and the claim that his particular blend of defensive cynicism, sexual perversion, racist prejudice, personal alienation and bizarre sentimentality in some way typifies white South African attitudes and dilemmas is at one level not only unacceptable as a gross and inaccurate generalisation, but also does an injustice to Gordimer's subtly analytical characterisation. Simplistic readings of the novel, which represent Mehring as the typical white South African, pander to stereotypical prejudices about white South African attitudes that can only be held by that non-South African 'outsider' audience to which Gordimer's work so frequently implicitly addresses itself. Yet Gordimer herself encourages such readings by inserting the suggestion that Mehring's personal, social and economic position should be read as neatly representative of that alliance between capitalism, liberalism and apartheid which it is her concern at an ideological level to expose and attack in the work. At times the novel therefore reads as a narrowly schematic exposition of a particular, ideologically determined view of South African history in which is encoded a generalised and simplistic view of the nature of 'all white society'. In a movement which takes us from the 'general' to the 'typical' to the stereotypical and, finally, to caricature, Mehring's position unfortunately becomes precisely one 'crudely illustrative' of current left-wing criticisms of socio-economic policy of the time. His breakdown in response to the re-emergence of the black corpse on his land is determined by such stereotypes, and is both melodramatic and inconsistent in terms of Gordimer's subtle development of his character elsewhere in the novel: it is neither 'typical' nor especially credible.[52] Maureen and Bam are similarly reduced to caricatures, strangers to themselves and others, by the end of *July's People*, in which Maureen's much-debated final decision to flee becomes, in Cooke's phrase, merely 'a vehicle to advance the argument'.[53]

Gordimer's necessary entrapment in both class and historical moment indeed reveals itself most clearly in that generalising impulse in which is expressed both her sensitivity to the framing modalities of her colonial inheritance and her internalisation of what Said has called

> the flexible *positional* superiority which puts the Westerner in a whole series of possible relationships with [the Other] . . . without ever losing him the relative upper hand. [54]

In Gordimer's work, the generalising impulse not only betrays that sense of moral superiority already noted above, but also by definition falsifies; it reduces the variety of life to a series of stereotypes which frequently disclose an unacceptable level of prejudice. Thus we are told that Jews get fat as they get older

(*The Lying Days*, 149); that all Jewish parents want their sons to be doctors (*The Lying Days*, 152); that whites age differently from and less attractively than blacks (*A Guest of Honour*, 332); that young girls are often characterised by an 'animated lying look' (*A Guest of Honour*, 286); that defecting Russian ballet dancers have 'wild face[s]' (*A Sport of Nature*, 225) and the list stretches on. Underpinning such generalisations is Gordimer's conviction that the writer's eye can see further, more clearly and more fully than that of the ordinary individual, and that this gives the artist-observer in her society the right to make morally coloured pronouncements about what constitutes the 'typical' and the significant.

Within the context of this discussion of 'typification', it is useful to bear in mind JanMohamed's elision of the distinction between the typical and the general: he suggests that a penchant for generalisation reflects a certain contempt for the ability of an audience to check the 'truth-value' of the representation.[55] At the same time he reminds us that 'apartheid society [is] predicated on stereotypes'.[56] We have seen that Gordimer's necessary entrapment in both class and historical moment in South Africa makes her unavoidably vulnerable to the unconscious inscription of its stereotypes and clichés despite her sharp awareness of such dangers. Such distortions in her fiction should not perhaps be so much a cause for criticism as an illuminating reminder, not only of the extent to which the notion of 'realism' as unproblematically mimetic cannot be sustained, but also of the lack of 'innocence' with which each individual will inevitably interpret his reality.

Chapter 4

Gordimer's Women

We see [her] life and writing as a product of a specific social history. We are not only looking at what she experienced but at how she, and others, perceived that experience; at the concepts with which her contemporaries understood their world, and again, at the consciousness that was possible for her time.

First/Scott[1]

Something that has continued to interest me all my life: the oblique picture of the narrator himself, emerging from the story he tells and the way he tells it; an unconscious self-revelation.

Nadine Gordimer[2]

In Gordimer's ten novels there is a marked emphasis (particularly in the early work) on female perspectives. The narrative voice is female in two (Helen in *The Lying Days* and Elizabeth in *The Late Bourgeois World*), the centre of consciousness is female in another four (Jessie in *Occasion for Loving*, Rosa in *Burger's Daughter*, Maureen in *July's People* and Hillela in *A Sport of Nature*), and the authorial consciousness which manipulates these voices with increasing sophistication is itself, of course, also female. Nevertheless, feminist critics who have found themselves strongly attracted to her work have found themselves at times dismayed by Gordimer's often bluntly reductionist and even at times hostile statements on 'feminism', which have placed her status as a 'feminist writer' in question. Those critics who have found it hard to read her various pronouncements as merely ingenuous have increasingly come to criticise her work as simply 'insensitive' to those issues with which a woman writer might be expected to be directly concerned in the feminist and post-feminist eras;[3] and the apparent gap between her responsiveness to issues of race on the one hand and issues of gender on the other has led Lockett to argue that we need a study of her work which will

> account for her willingness to recognise racial oppression, the oppression of others; but not to perceive that, in terms of gender politics, it is she herself who is the other . . . The challenge for feminists who wish to take up her work is to reveal the male-centred perspective from which she writes and to attempt to account for her strong identification with patriarchy.[4]

But such criticisms arise at least partly out of both a somewhat narrow definition of feminism and a number of misconceptions about the thinking behind Gordimer's undoubtedly non-feminist stance. Her own consistent and unequivocal refusal to allow herself to be labelled as a 'feminist' writer is, in fact, as we shall see, an expression not of insensitivity to women's issues but of a decision to set herself other priorities as dictated by her understanding of the demands of the anti-apartheid struggle in South Africa.

These priorities have led her to dissociate herself quite unambiguously and repeatedly from 'feminist' perspectives. She has said of herself that she is to be seen simply as 'a writer who happens to be a woman',[5] and as recently as November 1988, at a conference of the Congress of South African Women (COSAW), she argued that

> one gets the feeling often, talking to feminist writers, that the women feel that it's their destiny to write simply from the body of a woman, from the mind of a woman.
>
> But I think this is denying what a writer is and what a writer can do. Because a writer can be many things in the imagination, in the creation of a character . . .
>
> What I am saying is that there is a certain gift or ability in writers, a certain gift that comes from observation, cultivated, that comes from hypersensitivity to other people's feelings, from an ability to read people's faces, to hear beyond and behind their words, what they really are saying.[6]

This reformulation of her already well-established view that writers have special powers is not gender-determined, and the 'gift' of which she speaks should quite clearly not be seen as limited by gender expectations. She argues for the freedom of writers to develop any perspective each chooses, subject only to the requirement that they remain true to their characteristic, determining sensitivity to the unique quality of individual experience. Her insistence here on the necessary autonomy of writers originates in that resistance to prescriptive impositions which is so central a theme in her work; it is an issue of such importance to her that she reiterates her point in explaining that she is simply making

> a case for the powers of writers to write not only . . . within the confines of their own sex. I think that women write very well about men.[7]

Although Gordimer often pairs gender-based and race-based issues in her discussions of the particular nature of the writer's perspective (arguing that not only men and women can write convincingly of each other's worlds – black and white can do so too), she does not develop the parallel when she finds herself having to qualify her position. Brought to a reluctant acknowledgement in mid-career, as we shall see, that there are indeed areas of race-determined experience which remain by definition inaccessible to even the most sympathetic outsider, she does not acknowledge concomitant limits on what a female writer may grasp of male experience. Her emphasis instead remains predominantly on the 'amazing things' writers can do: 'the imagination of writers, the ability of writers to project,' she has said, 'is a very mysterious thing. One sex can write about another'.[8] Underpinning this assertion is her conviction that the writer is essentially an androgynous being, a belief which she repeatedly articulates and which is firmly based on pre-feminist thinking on the nature of the aesthetic imagination.[9] For example, in 1975 she wrote that she questions

> the existence of the specific solitude of the woman-as-intellectual when that woman is a writer, because when it comes to their essential faculty as writers, all writers are androgynous beings.[10]

She repeats the point again in an interview in 1984, in which she states that

> writers have very strange powers of identifying themselves with other people and lives different from their own. I think they are strangely androgynous beings as well.[11]

Behind such statements lie what frequently appears to be a de-
cidedly hostile attitude to what she perceives to be the narrowly
polemical concerns of other clearly 'feminist' South African
writers. She is curtly dismissive of Olive Schreiner's feminist concerns in a 1980 review:

> I suppose one must allow that she has a right to concern herself
> with a generic, universal predicament: that of the female sex . . .
> Yet the fact is that in South Africa, then as now, feminism is re-
> garded by people whose thinking on race, class, and colour
> Schreiner anticipated, as a question of no relevance to the actual
> problem of the country – which is to free the black majority from
> white minority rule . . . In the South African context . . . the
> woman issue withers in comparison to the voteless, powerless
> state of South African blacks, irrespective of sex.[12]

However, as feminist issues began to push their way to the
forefront of the liberation movement, Gordimer's characteristic
sensitivity to shifts in political opinion led her to qualify precisely
this passage. Almost a decade later, in 1989, she published a revised version of the original review in which she added:

> . . . but then again, [Schreiner] may have anticipated (as she did
> much else) the realisation, now, by South Africans of all colours
> in the liberation movements, that feminism South African style
> is an essential component in the struggle to free our country from
> all forms of oppression, political and economic, racist and
> sexist.[13]

Nevertheless, this is not as substantial a revision as at first appears. Feminism is presented here as still only one component of
the struggle, and implicitly subordinated to it; the phrase 'feminism South African style' remains undefined; and it is clear that
this passage represents no fundamental shift away from her earlier insistence, clearly articulated in another passage written in
1981, that she is 'not a feminist, except in so far as I carry, still,
the tattered banner of full human rights for all human beings'.[14]
    What underpins such rejections of the demand that she en-
gage herself explicitly with feminist politics is Gordimer's conviction that the drive for 'Women's Liberation' (which appears to be
what she understands 'feminism' to consist of) is simply a form of
white, middle-class self-indulgence on the part of spoilt women

who wish to avoid the imperative to respond to the more pressing issues of their day. In a 1988 interview specifically focused on the issue of feminism in her work, she represents her own class of wealthy, white, 'non-working' Johannesburg wives and mothers as a white female norm (as she does throughout the fiction). Although she clearly recognises the negative dimensions of their position, she avoids developing the implications, in terms of feminist theory, of her perception that

> maybe white women have been conditioned to accept psychological oppression, but I have the impression, having been brought up here as a white female, that it seems to be what so many women really want, even young women . . . There's a whole level of women here who acquiesce in their powerlessness to make decisions because they enjoy the protection, the dependency. They don't realise that it's terrible to be made dependent. But there are many advantages to it.[15]

Despite such minor forays into the fringes of feminist politics, Gordimer continues to dismiss feminism within the context of white South African experience as 'marginal': she characteristically measures its value against the yardstick of *black* needs, and remains convinced that 'feminism' among white women is no more than a form of tokenism, unwilling as it is to confront the specifically apartheid engendered deprivations and difficulties of black women's lives. As such, white South African feminism is dismissed as largely irrelevant, both to the apocalyptic battle against racism and to the life experience of the vast majority of women, whose struggle forms part of the overall struggle against apartheid, and with whose hopes she has aligned herself against the interests of her own class (defined as both white *and* female), in South Africa.

We may identify several reasons for Gordimer's stance on feminist issues. Firstly, she herself cannot be entirely exempt from the effects of that white liberal 'guilt' whose corrosive power over the white South African psyche she has documented so thoroughly. Such 'guilt' designates as 'privileges' what would be taken for granted as basic human rights in other western societies, and dismisses 'feminism', as we have seen, as a mere self-indulgence within the context of the wholesale deprivation of rights in the black community. In 1984, for instance, Gordimer significantly categorised the right to move around as one pleases as a 'privilege',[16] and in doing so signalled her awareness that such rights are not available to all. Similarly, the (private) advantages to be gained by feminist initiatives are to be foregone until a wider (public) justice has been achieved for all: a position entirely consonant with her insistence in general that the personal must ultimately give way to the political in any conflict between the two.

Secondly, white 'privilege' has enabled Gordimer to enjoy a lifestyle in which, as she herself has claimed, she has never needed to feel herself to be oppressed as a woman. On the one hand, her commitment to her art and her success as a writer have made her emotionally and financially independent in important ways, and may well partially account for her lack of identification with typical Anglo-American feminist issues. Indeed, in an interview with Jonathan Paton in 1985 she explained that she has always worked for herself and not for others, and therefore finds it hard to know what other women's working worlds are like.[17] On the other hand, the availability of servants has meant that she has also escaped the household drudgery which fuelled the feminism of her generation. At this level her lack of interest in feminist thrusts is simply typical of white South African women of her class. Interestingly enough, the exploitation of female servants is not emphasised in the novels, where their existence in every white household seems to be simply taken for granted; in *The Conservationist*, for example, the presence of a servant in Antonia's left-wing pad who serves the lovers a very late dinner, well 'after hours', is given no satirical resonance (73).

At the same time, we should note that Gordimer's initial contact with 'the oppressed' was doubtless with typically ill-paid, black, female domestic servants in her parents' household. There is some irony in the resultant perception that the two apparently contrary streams in Gordimer's psyche identified above, her liberal sense of 'guilt' and that failure to identify personally with typically female forms of oppression which partially accounts for her marginalisation of feminist concerns in her work, may be understood to be both at least partly rooted in the exploitation of black women by white madams that is the norm within the South African system of domestic service.

Thirdly, however, we should also note the extent to which Gordimer's insistence on subordinating women's issues to the larger project of political liberation in South Africa is in line with contemporary post-colonial reactions to white Anglo-American feminism. Gordimer has accepted the claim that white and black women are more deeply divided by colour than they are united by gender, and in this is markedly in agreement with such feminists as Andersen, who wrote in 1983 that

> within the feminist movement, white feminists have often asked why black women are reluctant to identify with the women's movement. At the same time, minority women perceive the women's movement as a white, middle-class cause that misunder-stands or ignores their experience . . . Black women are reluctant to affiliate with a movement that divides them against black men or that generalises its politics and analysis from the experience of the dominant group.[18]

Similarly, Gordimer argues in 1984 that

> it's all based on colour, you see . . . The white man and the white woman have much more in common than the white woman and the black woman, despite their differences in sex. Similarly, the black man and the black woman have much more in common than the black man and the white man . . . The basis of colour cuts right through the sisterhood or brotherhood of sex . . . Loyalty to your sex [for black women] is secondary to loyalty to your race. That's why Women's Liberation is, I think, a farce in Southern Africa. It's a bit ridiculous when you see white girls at the University cam-paigning for Women's Liberation because they've been kicked out of some fraternity-type club or because they can't get into bars the way men do. Who cares? A black woman has got things to worry about much more serious than these piffling issues.[19]

In this reductive view of feminism the emphasis is once again upon the triviality of white female concerns within the context of black oppression and dispossession. Gordimer expands upon the issues at stake once again in a comment in 1988, in which she notes that

> black women have a great struggle to assert themselves [against their men]. But it's difficult for them to articulate this too loudly because of a sense of loyalty to the larger struggle. So that's why I

have tended to dismiss feminism as a progressive force in this country.[20]

Gordimer here implicitly acknowledges that a political agenda determines her choice of emphasis: feminism is to be subordinated to the struggle not only because of her general sympathies with the black cause but also because of her specific identification with the main-line position on feminism of her black female counterparts in the movement.

Two problems, however, arise out of her inscription of black women's dismissal of feminism in her own work. On the one hand, such a rejection of an overtly feminist perspective does damage to her own intuitive, creative impulse, which is clearly to focus upon and develop aspects of her own experience of what it is to be a woman in South Africa. For example, her interest in the nature of the relationships women are caught up in with men at every level in African society is evident in numerous cameo pieces throughout the novels. However, on the other hand, her awareness of the extent to which sexism is an oppressive force in the lives of black women is barely hinted at in her largely uncritical documentation of the relationships between black and Indian men and women in a number of the novels: Joosab, Shinza, and their wives in *A Guest of Honour*; successful male politicians and businessmen and their wives in *A Sport of Nature*; Gideon, his girlfriend Ida, and his estranged wife in *Occasion for Loving*; and Steven Sitole's womanising in *A World of Strangers*. Gordimer's failure to enter into the feminist issues at stake here arises out of her belief that her colour necessarily divides her from her black female counterparts: as a white woman she is condemned to remain fundamentally ignorant of the more private dimensions of black women's experience by the barriers set up not only by apartheid but also by differences of language and culture.[21] In its treatment of the texture of black women's lives, therefore, the fiction can ultimately express only an outsider's deferential sympathy with a world of experience closed to the white observer, and cannot escape a concomitant degree of generalisation and stereotype in its depiction of that world. In *Burger's Daughter*, for example, we find both black and white women cast in roles which are of necessity stereotyped as Rosa attempts to articulate her sense of the gulf which divides the two at a tea party:

They [the black guests] didn't know why they were there, but as crosspurpose and unimaginable digressions grew louder with each half-audible, rambling or dignified or unconsciously funny discourse, clearer with each voluble inarticulacy, each clumsy, pathetic, or pompous formulation of need in a life none of *us* white women (careful not to smile at broken English) live or would know how to live, no matter how much Flora protests the common possession of vaginas, wombs, or breasts, the bearing of children and awful, compulsive love of them . . . *these* were everything Flora's meeting was not succeeding to be about. (204)

Although the inclusion at another point in this passage of the unlikely detail that Rosa can distinguish between 'the coal-smoke and vaginal odours of [these] old, poor black women' suggests a reluctant recognition at a sensory level of a shared female inheritance, the emphasis is here overwhelmingly on the ultimate impossibility of grasping the inner dimensions of the lives of those 'Others' whose political oppression at the same time trivialises white feminist urges to make contact.[22] The inherent irony of these difficulties is apparent within the context of recent feminist and post-colonial theory which has located the origins of our sense of the 'Otherness' of those of a different race in patriarchy.[23] In effect, Gordimer's deference in the novels to the political stance of the 'Other' inadvertently furthers those typically patriarchal and sexist attitudes, which themselves seek to trivialise feminist thrusts for entirely different reasons.

Thus as her work develops we find the early interest in female growth and the construction of identity which is at the core of such novels as *The Lying Days* and *Occasion for Loving* increasingly obscured by a growing focus on the overriding necessity to first achieve a political liberation for all. The point is neatly highlighted in a comment Gordimer made in an interview in 1981, in which she claimed that she had recently become 'more radical . . . both as a citizen and as a woman'.[24] Some feminist critics took this to mean that Gordimer had at last become more aware of the hitherto anomalous nature of her stance on feminist issues,[25] but they have looked in vain for evidence of a growing feminist orientation in her work. In fact, this statement must be understood within the particular ideological framework Gordimer has developed over the years. Her emphasis here is on the nature of the relationship which should ideally exist between the individual and society: she is restating her already clearly articulated belief that both men and women are caught up in and inescapably shaped by the historical situation into which they are born. Thus, she argues, women should not be portrayed in literature as existing in a political vacuum, in illusory retreat from the public domain and turned inwards upon the personal and subjective. Instead, fiction should realistically portray the impact of the public upon the private world, which demands of both men *and* women that they should respond to the moral demands made upon them as citizens of the world. Neither can escape the shaping influence of the political nature of the times they live in and through: they 'are what they are because their lives are regulated and their mores formed by their political situation . . . Politics *is* character in South Africa' (my italics).[26]

When this is recognised to be the underlying truth of each individual's position, a personal redemption begins to be possible in the novels. Within such a context, the private self-indulgence of an attenuated, self-conscious and self-reflexive individualism eventually becomes, for each of Gordimer's protagonists, whether male or female, an inappropriate luxury as the moral responsibilities of a full citizenry of the human race begin to take hold upon the imagination. This is as true for the writer as for the citizen. As we have seen, despite her claim in 1985 that *as a writer* she does not wish to find herself 'being answerable to some political or social problem in which [she] may be involved as a citizen',[27] her stance in an essay written a year earlier elides this distinction and is truer to her actual position: in 1984 she writes in praise of Camus that

> in theory at least, as a writer he accepted the basis of the most extreme and pressing demand of our time. The ivory tower was finally stormed; and it was not with a white flag that the writer came out, but with a manifesto unfurled and arms crooked to link with the elbows of the people. And it was not just as their chronicler that the compact was made . . . to be 'no more than a writer' was to put an end to the justification for the very existence of the persona of 'writer' . . . He has weighed within himself his existential value as a writer against that of other functions as a man among men, and found independently in favour of the man

... He has, in fact, accepted its condition that the greater responsibility is to society and not to art.[28]

Implicit here again is Gordimer's belief that not only the woman
but the writer and the citizen as well must subordinate their private interests to the immediate imperatives of the broader political struggle against apartheid.

We should also note, in considering the reasons for Gordimer's
rejection of a 'feminist' label, that it is clear from her statements
over fifteen years that her definition of feminism is a rather narrow one, ignoring some of the dimensions and complexity of contemporary feminist theory. On the one hand, in inscribing a sense
of the gulf which separates the life experiences of white and black
women, she ignores an alternative definition of feminism which
stresses that it is to be seen primarily as a *political movement*:
Coward, for example, argues that feminism 'must always be [un-
derstood to be] the alignment of women in a *political* movement
with particular aims and objectives . . . identified by its *political*
interests, not its common experiences'.[29] Nor does she respond to
recent Anglo-American definitions of a feminist as one 'primarily
concerned with the oppression of women in an androcentric society', whose chosen perspective will represent 'a political act in
which the politics of gender oppression are confronted'.[30]
Gordimer seems to understand and reject the term 'feminism' only
to the extent to which it refers to one now largely outmoded feminist thrust, 'liberal feminism',[31] whose broad agenda for the
achievement of gender-equality within existing social structures
had little appeal for a writer committed to radical social and economic transformation as a prerequisite for true political liberation. Gordimer in fact nowhere debates the merits and demerits of
radical and socialist feminist perspectives, both of which argue for
the need for a fundamental social restructuring as the only effective way to free women from patriarchal oppression, and with
both of which we might expect her to be in some degree of sympathy. Nor do her references to feminist positions acknowledge the
recent post-structuralist conception of gender as 'socially produced and historically changing', a perspective which

> requires attention to historical specificity in the production, for
> women, of subject positions and modes of femininity and their

place in the overall network of social power relations. In this the meaning of biological sexual difference is never finally fixed. It is a site of contest over meaning and the exercise of patriarchal power.[32]

It is possible that the omission of such perspectives is the result of a conscious choice, for it is unlikely that Gordimer is entirely ignorant of them. Advanced feminist and post-structuralist theory has in fact penetrated South African writing elsewhere, particularly in the work of an author Gordimer admires, J.M. Coetzee. Gordimer's tentative treatment of race and gender ought to be seen within the larger context established for these themes in South African literature as a whole, and in particular by Coetzee's sophisticated manipulation of these issues in his novel, *Foe* (1986).[33] Coetzee's female protagonist, Susan Barton, must finally submit to a poignant recognition of the extent to which we 'write' ourselves and our own reality, even as we are 'written' by others. Within this paradigm we are all (regardless of gender and colour) the authors and creators of both ourselves and our worlds, neither of which are ever entirely penetrable by others, while in turn their selves and worlds remain essentially obscure to us. In the end, of course, Susan Barton, discovers that it is language itself which is the ultimate enemy, the ultimate barrier to Truth, for it is in the artifices of language that both the fictions of Self and of Reality are constituted. Within this context, the notion of the possibility of attaining to a grasp of absolute Meaning must finally be recognised as the ultimate, transcendent illusion. 'That art is radical,' says Coetzee, in illuminating disagreement with Gordimer, 'which, facing the abyss between language and the world, turns towards silence and the end of art',[34] thus neatly undermining the absolute validity of *all* the various ideological 'camps' into which white South Africans are encouraged to marshall themselves.[35]

On the other hand, although Gordimer confronts some subtle issues of female identity-construction in such novels as *Burger's Daughter* and *July's People*, she does not deploy such post-structuralist strategies in her work. She is too immersed in the immediate, pragmatic demands which the concrete, continuing struggle for the political liberation of black South Africans makes upon her art to be seduced by the metaphysical relativism and subversion of meaning at the core of post-structuralist discourse –

a different kind of revolution which would place in question the absolute nature of the values to which she is committed and which sustain her sense of outrage at every level. Instead, in asserting an essentially Romantic belief in literature as a privileged mode of access to the Truth, and by retaining her typical emphasis in her characterisation on a nineteenth-century individualism, one which underpins in a diluted form even the experimentalism of *A Sport of Nature*, she attempts to retain a sense of her own continuing autonomy in the face of feminist and other pressures.

Yet, as we have seen, Gordimer's defence of that autonomy is beset with contradictions and heavily circumscribed by her conviction of privilege and her internalisation of a typically liberal sense of 'guilt' as a white South African. Both urge her not towards autonomy but towards finding a philosophically and psychologically valid way to 'belong' to the 'real' Africa of emerging black aspirations. Ironically, it is precisely the privileges of her background which, in encouraging her class-based sense of personal and intellectual independence, enable her to step outside the confines of that class and make an emotional and political commitment to the oppressed – a commitment which seeks to provide her with an answer to her somewhat wistful question posed in 1959, 'Where do whites fit in?'.[36] It is a question which resonates through the entire body of the fiction. Already in Gordimer's first novel, *The Lying Days*, the protagonist, Helen, feels herself to be marginalised: she perceives herself as 'belonging only to the crust, beneath which the real life lay', whereas her activist boyfriend, Paul, is felt to be 'rooted in that life, in the rural slow-gestured past and, more important, the confused and mazelike city life of the present' (240). She envies him for both his male freedom and his access to the world of blacks through the work he does, and both appear to her to have a greater authenticity than her own life. But the privilege of entry into these other worlds is possible in the novels only through a personal commitment to the struggle of black South Africans, one which Helen cannot yet make. However, her successor, Jessie, in *Occasion for Loving*, is more successful: at the end of the novel she makes a tentative commitment to potential political activism, which at last allows her to feel that she is 'beginning to slip into the mainstream, she [is] beginning to feel the substance [is] no longer something she must dam up for herself. Passion [will] not leave the world grey when it [goes] out for her' (274). The implications of this passage are made clear in her husand's recognition that, if power stations need to be blown up, 'it [will] be Jessie who [will] help someone to do it, perhaps, in time' (279).

Significantly, Jessie is grateful that in middle age she no longer needs to make a clear choice between 'passion' (which she sees as the prerogative of youth) and a committed activism (the taking up of a public responsibility in adulthood). Here again we find that opposition between public and private which has already been discussed above. Within the framework of the simple binary oppositions which underlie the surface complexity of the text, youth is presented as a time of irresponsibility, of subjectivity and passion, and of dedication to the self; it is the private world which must be outgrown in favour of the adult world of public responsibility, political commitment, and selfless dedication to the larger world of community and the 'Other'. Jessie's movement from a marginalised private life to a morally responsive public activism is here presented as part of a natural evolutionary process in the individual life, when that life is lived as sensitively as possible, and equated with a full maturity. In each of the novels Gordimer's protagonists are made to travel the difficult path from one to at least intimations of the possibility of the other, and the implication is that only through the dedication of the self to service 'the struggle' in some positive form will the white South African find a way to 'fit in' to the new world waiting to be born.

'to be young and in the sun'

Fuelling Gordimer's rejection of institutionalised feminism are not only the mature perspectives of her adult life but also the hidden influences of her upbringing in an intensely conservative and culturally isolated community at a particular point in South Africa's political and social development. That she herself has been acutely aware of the extent to which the writer's perspectives are limited by the historical position into which she is born, is suggested by the fact that she was sufficiently impressed by First and Scott's reminder that Olive Schreiner's work must be understood as 'a product of a specific social history'[37] to repeat their formulation unconsciously in her own critical consideration of Schreiner as 'a creature doubly trapped by a specific social history and by the consciousness that was possible for her time'.[38] Some attention must be given in return to the question of what sense of herself as a woman was made possible for her by *her* time.

Gordimer has avoided giving the public much autobiographical information, remaining largely true to the belief expressed in an early statement in 1963 that 'autobiography can't be written until one is old, can't hurt anyone's feelings, [and] can't be sued for libel, or worse, contradicted'.[39] Yet she has spoken enough about her childhood and her development as a writer for it to be possible to piece together some sense of the nature and dimensions of the specific type of 'femininity' she was schooled into, and to gain some understanding of the battles won and lost in that field. The colonial society she grew up in was unashamedly sexist in its gender attitudes, and such modalities necessarily had a defining and determining impact on the young girl's development. If it is true that 'our subjectivity and identity are formed in the definitions of desire which encircle us',[40] some grasp of the nature of the definitions to which she was subjected will help us to understand her ambivalent response to feminist imperatives in her adult life.

Her adolescence appears to have been typically marked by the opposing pulls of the pressure to conform and the instinctive need to take refuge in covert rebellion. In an autobiographical piece written in 1963 she outlined the conventional expectations of a young girl of her time, describing a world in which

> many girls left school at fifteen or even before. Then, after a six week's course at the local commercial college, a girl was ready for a job as a clerk in a shop or in the offices of one of the goldmines which had brought the town into being. And the typewriter itself tapped a mark-time for a brief season of glory, self-assertion, and importance that came with the engagement party, the pre-nuptial linen 'shower', and culminated not so much in the wedding itself as in the birth, not a day sooner than nine months and three weeks later, of the baby.[41]

Within the context of such limited choices it is understandable that the young girl believed that she had to at least pretend to community values in order to survive socially. After she left school, she continued to live at home, sporadically writing in secret but not knowing what public direction to take and indulging herself in 'an outward life' of 'sybaritic meagreness'. This existence involved acquiring the conventional skills of a pretty young girl for whom no career and no future independence was envisaged other than within marriage: playing golf, learning how to drink, taking nursing and first-aid classes, and participating in amateur theatricals. She was, as she tells us, 'a dilettantish girl, content with playing grown-up games at the end of my mother's apron strings'.[42] However, the tone of overtly ironic self-contempt in several of the passages of this brief autobiographical sketch alerts us to Gordimer's early inner rejection of such modes of being, a rejection rooted in two powerful influences: the example of her mother, and her own early, atypical fascination with the world of books and writing. On the one hand we have the image of her mother as a 'fearless nomad': Gordimer depicts her as having been one with 'a bland disregard for the sheep-like conventions of the town', who sent her two daughters to the local Dominican convent in defiance both of their father's Jewish origins and of the anti-Catholic sentiment of the town.[43] That her mother's strength and independence of mind deeply impressed the child is made clear in Gordimer's description of the family dynamics in her home. She said in an interview in 1988 that her background was

> very female-dominated. I had no brothers, one sister, and in our household it was very much a female or feminine milieu. My mother was the stronger character in more or less everything that we did and learnt. It came from her, my father was rather in the background. And I mingled a great deal among women, through my mother. I went to a convent school, I didn't go to a co-educational school.[44]

On the other hand this mother was also a domineering and powerfully restrictive force in Gordimer's early life, keeping her out of school, for example, as company for herself, from the age of twelve, on the pretext that the young girl was suffering from a heart complaint. The child who often played truant from school learned early to protect her inner autonomy within such a household by practising an external conformity which served to mask the internalised 'real' life of her passionate and private relationship with literature. She did not overtly challenge the unspoken taboo on intellectual or 'bluestocking' interests in a young girl of her time, and by playing out the roles expected of her in public she was 'enabled to survive and grow in secret while projecting a totally different camouflage image of [her]self.'[45] The authors she studied were preponderantly male at this time; the lists of her reading in these years which she has given at various points show that, among her favourite writers, twenty-two were men and only five were women. In common with her generation she consequently internalised chiefly male perspectives on life,[46] which is likely to have both liberated her imagination and entrenched an identification with the world of male affairs. Inadvertently in line with a long tradition of female writers, she published her first short story anonymously (largely to protect her privacy within the intimacy of anti-intellectual small-town life),[47] and she was later to repeatedly ascribe her successful entry into the larger literary world to the encouragement of a male poet, Uys Krige, who took an interest in her work.

While the budding intellectual found ways to escape the ennui of life on the East Rand, the young woman expressed an inchoate rebellion against the expectations of the community, that she either marry or keep herself busy in some trivial employment, by not taking a job (for nothing she could have done interested her, she tells us) and by continuing to live with her parents. At the same time she also embarked upon exploring the multi-faceted dimensions of her sexuality. It has been deeply significant for her work that it appears to have been out of her pleasure and success in this area of experience that Gordimer initially constructed a viable sense of personal worth and identity. In 1975 she admitted this in representing her sexuality as a powerfully integrative force in her early years:

> As for the specific solitude of the woman-as-intellectual, I must say truthfully that my femininity has never constituted any special kind of solitude, for me. Indeed, in that small town, walled up among the minedumps . . . my only genuine and innocent connection with the social life of the town . . . was through my femaleness. As an adolescent, at least, I felt and followed sexual attraction in common with others; that was a form of

communion I could share. Rapunzel's hair is the right metaphor
for this femininity: by means of this I was able to let myself out
and live in the body, with others, as well as – alone – in the mind.
To be young and in the sun; my experience was similar to
Camus . . . [48]

The reference to Rapunzel suggests that her developing sexuality
presented itself initially to her not only as a means of integration
with her peer group, but also as an avenue of escape from the
restrictive pressures of family and community expectations. She
presents sex both as the one area in which she could 'try out [her]
reach, the measure of aliveness in [her]self', and as a site of rebellion: 'My one preoccupation outside the world of ideas was men,
and I should have been prepared to claim my right to the one as
as valid as my right to the other.'[49] Throughout the ten novels
Gordimer's female protagonists similarly seek both to integrate
themselves through a sexual connection and to find in the expression of their sexuality an escape from stultifying social pressures.

Gordimer's conviction that she had a 'right' to enjoy the pleasures of the body was still, in 1963 when she wrote the passage
quoted above, untouched by any specifically feminist ideology.
She was over forty years old before Betty Friedan's seminal study,
The Feminine Mystique, appeared in 1964 and precipitated a
post-war resurgence of feminist consciousness in the English-
speaking world. Instead, Gordimer's belief in the primal power of
sexuality to redirect and transform lives must be traced back to
the frequently acknowledged and powerful influence of D.H.
Lawrence's work on her developing sensibility.[50] In the novels she
offers us an affirmation of Lawrentian perspectives: from the obsessively detailed and passionately sensitive study of adolescent sexual awakening offered in *The Lying Days*, to the sensual
vision of *A Sport of Nature*, in which Hillela, revolutionary hero-
ine and symbolic mother of the new Africa, is primarily characterised by her 'healthy instinct' to trust in 'her attraction *for* men'
(my emphasis),[51] the emphasis is entirely on sexual liberation as a
precursor and even prerequisite for other forms of liberation.
Thus Gordimer's early rebellion against the contexts she was
born into took at least two forms: the woman rebelled by breaking sexual taboos; the intellectual rebelled by making a serious
commitment to the world of ideas.

Given the contexts outlined above, which initially shaped Gordimer's sensibility and within which the work found its genesis, it is clear that she cannot be accused of a simple lack of interest in what has come to be called women's issues: the female *Bildungsroman* is, after all, her core genre. However, the mainly conventional forms her socialisation took, combined with the later politicisation of her attitudes sketched in above, has resulted in conflicting emphases in her work with which feminist critics have found it difficult to come to terms. A common mistake is to attempt an assessment of the work in the light of perspectives which simply have no relevance to Gordimer's fictional agenda. For example, when Lazar, in a sensitive recent study, finds her 'approach to gender questions . . . highly variable, and her fluctuating sympathy with and antagonism to feminism [to] follow no neat chronological patterns', and goes on to suggest that this is why it is 'difficult to read her stories either as feminist or as anti-feminist representations',[52] both criticism and comfort derive from the misleading assumption that Gordimer must possess a certain feminist awareness which may or may not be adequately represented in the fiction. But such an awareness is an entirely contemporary, mainstream Western phenomenon, and was simply not part of Gordimer's early *Weltanschauung*.

From this perspective Gordimer is in fact correct in insisting that she is not a feminist, either overtly or covertly. Her fundamentally liberal-humanist conception of the nature of the necessary relationship between the individual and society takes little cognisance, as we have seen, of contemporary feminist concerns, given the urgency of the ethical issues forced upon the individual by apartheid. Nor does she deflect any energies towards a later dissection of her early inscription of Lawrentian attitudes in her treatment of sexuality. In fact, the influence of D.H. Lawrence has had wider consequences in her work than suggested thus far. For example, her internalisation of the need for a Lawrentian *sensual* liberation from the restrictions of bourgeois respectability both explains her sympathy with the sexual revolution of the sixties (clearly apparent in the fiction and often misinterpreted as a feminist thrust), and also affords us a glimpse of the deeper subjective and emotional roots to her uneasiness with and later unambiguous rejection of 'the late bourgeois world' which are at least as influential in shaping her work and ideological perspectives as her conscious rejection of her own bourgeois childhood contexts and her growing politicisation within an apartheid context. The appeal of the Lawrentian vision – emotionally and ethically radical at the time – was a powerful one: and although Gordimer later had to make her way alone as a young writer and as a divorced parent in the intensely conservative fifties, an experience which might have been expected to radicalise her in feminist terms, her *conscious* grasp of the multi-faceted dimensions of women's experience still nevertheless heavily reflects the Lawrentian sexual codes of a patriarchally oriented and male-identified vision.

Signifiers of such a vision in the works are Gordimer's consistent choice of the male pronoun as the universalising one and her willingness to privilege male perspectives in constructing female sexual identities. Private rebellion is primarily expressed through a straightforward rejection of bourgeois *sexual codes*, rather than through an interrogation of patriarchy. In so far as these bourgeois codes were premised on an unquestioned racist rejection of 'miscegenation', Gordimer's characteristic representation of sex across the colour bar as both an ultimate form of defiance and as an expression of a yearning for liberation from incarceration in the world represented by such codes, entailed only a short conceptual shift for her. Not surprisingly, the search for a feminist thrust in her work has to date uncovered only a plethora of sexist stereotypes which keep company uneasily with those other, sharp and dismissive analyses of the inadequacies of characters whose personal and political deficiencies she so ruthlessly dissects.

'trust Hillela; she chose well'

The extent to which sexuality is a primary signifier – both a powerfully recurrent motif and a centrally determining metaphor – in Gordimer's narratives of personal and political transformation deserves closer analysis to illuminate the complexity of her vision as 'both a citizen and a woman'. To begin with, the willingness to transgress certain sexual taboos, in particular those which are centred on religious and racial distinctions, becomes an indicator throughout the ten novels of the white protagonist's potential for political redemption. Rebellion against the racist values of the bourgeois apartheid state is, first tentatively and then with ever-increasing energy, sited most obviously in the choice of sexual partner. This is as true of Helen in *The Lying Days*, and her uneasy and unconsummated relationship with the Jew, Joel Aaron, within the context of an exposé of the unspoken but pervasive anti-Semitism of the mining world of the novel, as it is of Hillela's choice, in *A Sport of Nature*, of a 'coloured boy' as friend while at school in Rhodesia: a fragile move quickly neutralised by adult intervention, but one which foreshadows her later preferences and epitomises that sense of personal autonomy which will eventually bring her to the Azanian Independence Celebrations at Reuel's side. Ann Davis's politically and personally irresponsible affair with Gideon Shibalo tests the ethical convictions and political positions of those around her; while Elizabeth van der Sandt and Maureen Smales each attempt a tentative escape from the prison of their whiteness by acknowledging a measure of attraction to Luke Fokase and July respectively. Although such relationships are frequently potential rather than actual, and often characterised by a pervasive political naïvety, they suggest a willingness to contemplate that crossing of boundaries which is a prerequisite for any meaningful growth in the fiction.

Secondly, the urge to free the self from perceived bourgeois prejudices, standards of conduct and values, is expressed through the embracing of what came to be called in the 1960s the 'sexual revolution'. The absolute value of sexual fidelity and later, monogamy, is interrogated with increasing frequency in the novels' creatively flexible acknowledgement of the transformative effects of growth on personal relationships. In *A Guest of Honour* Bray emancipates himself from his potentially compromising position as an ex-colonial officer in a newly independent African country by making the symbolically loaded decision to commit himself to the uncertainties of revolutionary action on behalf of the separatist leader, Shinza. It is a decision made possible only by his liberation, both emotionally and sexually, from the English country-house lifestyle associated with his wife and retirement, a liberation made possible through his developing commitment to the unstructured freedom of his affair with the essentially rootless wanderer, Rebecca. It is a move significantly uncluttered by guilt feelings on Bray's part towards his absent spouse, whose reaction to this betrayal appears to be of no interest either to the husband or to the authorial voice in a novel which is strongly male-oriented in its perspectives. The emphasis is instead on Rebecca's unqualified 'adaptability', which foreshadows that of Hillela as she incarnates at one level the male dream of endless and undemanding sexual availability. Such relationships in recent South African fiction have a metaphoric resonance: in their rejection of Eurocentric sexual morality they symbolise personal liberation through a reunification of the self with Africa as the Great Mother, a trope which is also widely distributed, for example, in the novels of André Brink. Gordimer's narrative affirms Rebecca's undemanding flexibility, which extends to a willingness to share herself sexually with almost all comers in a bid to survive in an uncertain and often hostile context; and her emotional freedom from possessiveness and jealousy is set in strong contrast to the negative emphasis on the aggressive, domineering and insensitively macho attitudes of her itinerant husband, Gordon. The novel's rejection of sexual jealousy as an inappropriate bourgeois response clearly reflects the influence of the sixties decade, but we should note earlier interrogations of the complexity of this emotion in, for example, *Occasion for Loving*, in which a straightforward response to his wife's infidelity is complicated for Ann's politically liberal husband by her choice of a black lover: the desire not to appear a racist stifles the expression of Boaz's sense of betrayal and leaves him feeling metaphorically and actually impotent.

Not only do serial relationships replace simple monogamy from the earliest novels on, but Gordimer goes on to attempt to enter imaginatively into the intricacies of what she perceives to be an African world of polygamous relationships in her representation of Hillela's marriage to the General, Reuel, in *A Sport of Nature*. The novel suggests that Reuel's other two wives present only a minor problem to the socially adept and endlessly resourceful Hillela, and she is shown to graduate with no difficulty from the nuclear family she had set up with Whaila into this more complex set of relationships. Gordimer's conceptualisation of such a relationship is, however, highly conventional under the veneer of Africanisation and remains true to that liberal perspective which, as Bayles reminds us, 'has never, despite its contractual echoes, stopped conceiving of the family as an organic institution'.[53] Thus Hillela *in effect* is shown to enjoy a conventional western marriage with Reuel despite his polygamous unions. She takes up a position, despite her youth and without reference to African traditions of precedence, as first among his wives, appears to live with him rather than in her own home, is his trusted adviser in all his affairs, and manages his large family for him with the aplomb one might expect of the wife of an important man who must deal with his large extended family. Their mutual acceptance of each other's discreetly conducted affairs (305-310) derives perhaps more immediately from Gordimer's romanticisation of European, and in particular French, sexual culture than from any grasp of the real tensions which may beset polygamous relationships in a non-ideal and often westernised African context. It is the utopian and romantic inclination of Gordimer's imagination in this novel which shapes her representation of Hillela as

> not taken in by this African family; she has disposed it around her. Hers is the non-matrilineal centre that no-one resents because no-one has known it could exist. (310)

In Hillela and Reuel's marriage the destructive, coercive or nonfunctioning families of the fictional *oeuvre*, from whose stranglehold Gordimer's characters struggle to escape with varying degrees of success, are finally laid to rest. They metamorphose into a fully supportive, yet marvellously elastic and tolerant structure which symbolically replaces Hillela's dream of a nuclear 'rainbow family' with the larger vision of a 'family of man'.

In this novel Gordimer's emphasis is not so much upon Hillela's personal emancipation as a woman as upon her status in the novel as the ideal type of the 'new African'. She is clearly intended to function as an evolutionary model for those white South Africans who wish to find a way to belong in the emergent black-ruled contexts which Gordimer envisages as Africa's future, when the land will have been returned in reality, rather than merely metaphorically as in *The Conservationist*, to its original and rightful owners. This would explain the otherwise

uneasy conjunction between Hillela's sense of personal autonomy and independence, her creative adaptability and sexual
freedom, on the one hand, and her willing subordination of herself to the men off whom she lives on the other. The narrative in
fact affirms at every level her use of her sexual attractiveness to
ensure her survival, privileging what is in essence a version of
archetypal female prostitution which is fundamentally opposed
by contemporary feminist attitudes. Hillela's opportunism (160),
her willingness to let others (both her men and the communities
she finds herself in) take care of her and take over her financial
and emotional responsibilities to her child (191, 197; 259), and
her unfailing ability to discover, adopt and project 'the appropriate attitude' (190) to ensure her acceptance at every juncture,
suggests a chameleon personality. Such elasticity makes it difficult to accept her commitments at face value when she metamorphoses into a dedicated campaigner for African causes at the
United Nations. Indeed, the personal values which the novel
finally projects have little to do with feminism and everything to
do with that Lawrentian impetus which we have already identified as Gordimer's emotional base. Sexuality as a primary and
decisive force in shaping lives and choices is the true centre of the
novel. Hillela, explains the narrative voice, 'drew upon the surety
of her sexuality as the bread of her being' (283): 'the more she
gave . . . the more she had to give' (259). Pauline knows that
'Hillela's field was, surely, men' (279), and Sasha perceptively
says of her that she 'received everything through [her] skin,
understood everything that way' (318).

This emphasis alerts us more fully to a clear pattern in the
fiction which has already been briefly touched upon: both men
and women are shown to be politicised by their emotional relationships and personal experiences rather than through the intellectual development of a theoretical condemnation of the evils of
apartheid. Hence the importance of epiphany as a structural and
thematic device in the novels. There are clear parallels between
Bray's decision to forsake Mweta for Shinza, in which political
affiliation follows upon physical and emotional attraction,[54] and
Hillela's induction into revolutionary politics through her marriage to Whaila. Gordimer tells us that Hillela 'has *entered South
Africa* through Whaila, where before she was a vagrant'.[55] Thus a

conventionally feminine rather than feminist conception of the fundamental importance of subjectivity and sexuality in human affairs, of the political as rooted in the personal, is at the heart of Gordimer's conceptual universe, making her novels quintessentially what has been dismissively termed 'women's fiction' despite their burden of ideological responsibility to large public issues.

The fundamentally conservative nature (in contemporary terms) of Gordimer's conception of women's options in society is perhaps most fully revealed in a brief sentence in the concluding sequence of *A Sport of Nature*, in which the narrator asserts, 'Trust Hillela; she chose well' (331). The assumptions behind this unintentionally ironic statement are illuminating, for it reminds us that Hillela has chosen well not only in political and ethical terms, but also in the realm of typically bourgeois values. In effect, she is praised for having achieved the middle-class goals of money, status and power as she stands on the platform at the end of the novel as the influential young wife of the Chairman of the Organisation for African Unity, wealthy, elegant, pampered, and admirably fulfilling the age-old female role of the 'power behind the throne'. There is a suggestion here, at a subtextual level, that it is power which is the ultimate prize, for within a context in which powerlessness is the bitter corollary of oppression, liberation becomes synonymous with the access to power. But not only political power is Hillela's prize: her sexual liberation has also and simultaneously given her a form of power over men which is presented with unqualified approval in the novel.[56] 'One can offer without giving. It's a form of power' (198), we are told, as Hillela discovers that her sexual attractiveness allows her to manipulate the men around her. Later, sexual and political power are combined in her willingness to use the former to achieve the ends of the latter: 'lust', we are told, 'is the best aid-raiser' (245). Here the political arena becomes in effect an extension of the bedroom. However, we should not assume that Gordimer here generally sanctions the spread of sexual amorality: given the underlying commitment in the novels to a clearly defined moral agenda, deviations from bourgeois rules of behaviour are sanctioned only when they advance the cause of personal and political liberation from various forms of oppression. In sharp contrast to Hillela, Mehring is unequivocally condemned in *The*

Conservationist for sexual transgressions which, in not advancing any cause, are rejected as simply exploitative. Nor should we be tempted to read the emphasis on female power as possibly after all implying a submerged feminist thrust in the work: Tilly Olsen warns us against such a reading in her observation that we should not confuse 'sexual liberation (genitally defined) with the feminine liberation of women'.[57] Instead, as we have seen, in making sexual liberation symbolic of the possibility of a more general political and wider human liberation, Gordimer lends weight and significance to the complex personal dramas which the fiction largely concentrates upon, but does not in any way commit it to explicitly 'feminist' goals.

Parallel to such emphases, and in a move still fully in accord with her representation of the transgression of sexual boundaries as a potentially redemptive act, Gordimer also develops metaphors of psychic and spiritual alienation as a necessary consequence of sterility of relationships locked within bourgeois paradigms. Political and personal impotence is symbolised by her characters' entrapment in meaningless relationships; for example, in *The Late Bourgeois World* and *July's People*, both Elizabeth's and Maureen's fear of putting themselves at risk morally or emotionally expresses itself in their willingness to stagnate in relationships which are severely challenged by their attraction to figures such as Luke Fokase and July, who represent a forbidden aggressive and politically liberated male power.

In fact, throughout the novels, sexual alliances betray the true political allegiances of Gordimer's characters. We have already seen how Mehring's drive in *The Conservationist* to possess, dominate and exploit his women in a sequence of relationships which contain an increasingly overt incestuous component betrays a similar substratum in his relationship to both his land and his society. His submerged fear of 'exposure' may be interpreted as a fear that he will finally be revealed as one who breaks not only the racist laws of his country but also his own disregarded internalised ethical codes, and his violation of both public and private moral law threatens him with that psychological dissolution which is symbolised by his simultaneous fear of and obsessive identification with the corpse. The true extent of his corrupt collusion with forces he professes to despise is symbolised by the way he is addressed by the Afrikaner observer-policeman, who benevolently warns him of 'muggers' in the eucalyptus plantation below the mine-dumps: the man treats him as a fellow, as 'one of us', and his assumption exposes Mehring's pose as an enlightened, politically liberal businessman and gentleman-farmer-cum-conservationist as the distorted fantasy it is. Here we might also note that a similar symbolic resonance is given to Ann Davis's encounter in *Occasion for Loving* with the Afrikaans farmer on whose land she and Gideon are picnicking. His warning also arises out of his assumption that she is 'one of us', and its insertion at this point may be seen to foreshadow her eventual abandonment and betrayal of Gideon (233-34).

Not only do sexual propensities betray political affiliations in the novels: collusion and compromise in one's political allegiances undermine the possibility of harmony in the personal sphere. Mehring is one of several figures in the novels who are rejected by their women because they attempt to maintain positions in opposing two camps. Helen's criticism of Paul's attempt in *The Lying Days* to support radical black initiatives while working for the Department of Native Affairs – 'to do the impossible' (295) – is an early example of Gordimer's rejection of liberalism as a viable political stance in South Africa. Since she is convinced that the system cannot be changed from within, she represents those who attempt to do so as finding themselves beset by so many internal contradictions that they are driven into a frustrated impotence. It is only those who succeed in making an unequivocal commitment to that radicalism which will sweep the world they know away from under their feet who are granted a degree of fulfilment and harmony in their personal relationships. Thus Bray is only able to affirm his commitment to Rebecca when he sets off on his final mission for Shinza: and it is her grief at his death which becomes the measure of his ultimate worth.

Contrasted to such a resolution are the many relationships in the novels whose inauthenticity is marked by the partners' willingness to play out conventional roles vis-à-vis each other as a substitute for their lack of any genuine sense of connection. Such a personal lack of integrity is a symbolic corollary of their superficial grasp of the ideals to which they pay lip-service in the political arena. The players in these charades of intimacy remain in essence strangers to one another within both the personal and the public spheres, a fact which gradually becomes clear, for example, to both Bam and Maureen in *July's People*, as they fail to adapt to unfamiliar contexts. Their flight to the bush village has stripped them of the familiar frameworks that made extensive role-playing 'back home' possible. Maureen discovers that both Bam and July are after all essentially strangers to her, while Bam muses that

> for the children [Maureen] chose to appear as 'their mother', 'his wife', this morning. But she was no one to whom he could say that the chief was going to tell them to go. He had no idea how she would deal with this certainty . . . How to accept, explain – to anyone: after all these days when his purpose (his male dignity put to the test by 'Maureen', 'his wife', Victor, Gina, Royce who were living on mealie-meal) had been how to get away – now it was how to stay. (105)

With the loss of the keys, the bakkie, and the gun – the novel's symbols of power – Bam becomes in Maureen's eyes a 'man who had nothing now' (145); she then inappropriately tries to offer July – the one who has acquired these symbols and represents the new power relationships developing within the novel's revolutionary climate – the unwanted intimacy of her feverish honesty.

> She told him the truth, which is always disloyal . . . The incredible tenderness of the evening surrounded them as if mistaking them for lovers. She lurched over and posed herself, a grotesque, against the vehicle's hood, her shrunk-jeans poked at the knees, sweat-coarsened forehead touched by the moonlight, neglected hair standing out wispy and rough. The death's harpy image she made of herself meant nothing to him, who had never been to a motor show complete with provocative girls. (153)

Maureen's carelessness of her sexual attractiveness in the eyes of this man symbolises the collapse of her willingness to continue to play out the roles of wife, mother and sexual partner which bourgeois suburban society had assigned to her.

Given the link between sexual and political liberation in the novels which has been outlined above, it is not surprising to find that, despite marked continuities in Gordimer's sense of what it is to be female in her work, her women liberate themselves with increasingly less confusion and anguish as their author finds herself more and more committed to clearly demarcated political positions. For example, whereas Maureen can only recognise the extent to which she has been imprisoned in bourgeois roles but is given no clear sense of alternatives, Hillela's personal liberation is marked by her ability to freely adopt whatever role will be most fruitful within a given situation without any sense of coercion or oppression whatsoever.

Nevertheless, certain assumptions which inform Gordimer's construction of the feminine in the texts reveal the extent to which she herself has remained subject to her own bourgeois (and, in feminist terms, essentially sexist) education in what it is to be female; although she is exceptionally clearsighted about the deformative effects the internalisation of imposed role-playing demands has upon the lives of her women, she nevertheless frequently encodes entirely 'unliberated' assumptions about the nature of the options open to them in the novels. To begin with we should note the general physical and emotional *passivity* of her female protagonists in their relationships with men and the outside world. Their tendency to react rather than to act is consonant with the 'learned helplessness' which is an important component of female socialisation, and is reflected both in their dependence on men in the field of public affairs (they are fundamentally 'campfollowers'), and in their inclination to resort not to confrontation but to simple physical flight when at their wit's end. Helen, Ann Davis, Antonia, Rosa and Maureen all at various points take up the option of flight from the untenable situations in which they find themselves. In addition, Gordimer's representation in the novels of what might be allowed to women in the public sphere of active involvement in political change seems equally fixed in what have increasingly come to be thought of as outmoded and sexist paradigms; and we should remember that she herself served her political apprenticeship during a period in which women's roles in left-wing circles were, as Lessing tells us, defined by a characteristically unpoliticised and cheerful sexism which kept them in an inambiguously subordinate position. In the novels, the dimensions that women's lives are allowed to take on – indeed, at times their very identity –

frequently entirely depends upon the nature of their relationships with the male characters. Helen's relationships with Joel and Paul, Jessie's sympathy for Gideon, Elizabeth's meeting with Luke, and Maureen's frustration with July, all serve to open the women's eyes to the dimensions of public realities outside the domestic sphere which they are only vaguely aware of until their relationships with the men in their lives provide them with a conduit into that larger world. Rosa finds herself in prison at the end of *Burger's Daughter* not because of what she has *done* but because of who she *is* – her father's daughter. Hillela needs to be vouched for first by her lovers and then by her husband, Whaila, before she can gain acceptance in exile circles, and it is primarily her identity as Whaila's widow rather than her personal qualities which provides her with the credentials which allow her to be employed by the international liberation movement after his death. In *The Conservationist* women's dependence on men is ironically inscribed in the use Antonia makes of Mehring's willingness to give her access to his expensive lawyers when she finds herself on trial for the radical friendships with which she has enlivened her somewhat dull suburban life. Like Rosa, she too has in effect 'done' nothing although she is victimised for her sympathies.

Although there seems to be some tension in the novels between the conservative view that women chiefly acquire value to the extent to which they are sexually and otherwise affirmed by men, and the apparently more 'liberated' view that they acquire value through their commitment to abstract and idealistic ends, a closer look at these two perspectives reveals that, in so far as both paths to self-fulfilment require an unquestioning subordination of the self to outside influences and standards of judgement, they also both entrench pre-feminist constructions of the female role, such as the expectation that women function as the civilising, nurturing, all-giving and all-sacrificing power which would redeem the crude excesses of the male world. Gordimer's resistance to violence as a political option throughout most of her career may fruitfully be seen as an expression of this paradigm.

In this connection we should also note that a powerful subtext in the novels rejects those women who do commit themselves to the 'unfeminine' option of direct, self-motivated political activism: they are granted respect and a degree of admiration, but are shown to be unable to attract a full sexual response from their men. Gordimer appears to assume that such a commitment to activism, in bringing to the fore the 'male' elements of independence and aggression, robs the women in question of a substantial degree of their sexual attractiveness. Toby, in *A World of Strangers*, longs for the amoral Cecil (whose literary precursor seems to be Fitzgerald's morally corrupt but fascinating Jordan in *The Great Gatsby*) even as he kisses the divorced, middle-aged civil rights lawyer, Anna Louw. Intellectual attraction and respect do not translate easily into a fulfilling sexual relationship. In *Occasion for Loving*, Gideon Shibalo's first affair with a left-wing white woman, Callie Stow, with her 'tweed skirt and sensible shoes', perplexes him because, although he is 'not unattracted', it is 'the first time he had desired a woman mentally . . . [yet] in the end, the very thing that had made the open relationship possible killed it off, for him. He did not feel like her lover' (123). Clare Terblanche, Rosa's earnestly committed activist cousin in *Burger's Daughter*, is significantly contrasted to Rosa at a physical level: Rosa's body had 'the assurance of embraces . . . men would recognise it at a glance', while Clare's 'flesh was dumb . . . a body that had no signals; it would grow larger and at once more self-effacing. Few men would find their way, seek her through it' (122). When Rosa finally commits herself and finds herself in prison, it is suggested that she has reverted to an asexual state: 'She looked like a little girl again . . . about fourteen,' comments a visitor (360). Yelin has interestingly argued that Rosa's position at the end of the novel may be read as a regressive move *towards* the father and patriarchy, and *away* from self-determination.[58] In fact, although patriarchy is overtly rejected by Gordimer as a political model, it clearly continues to be valorised in the private arena, and the novels tend to swing uneasily between a narration which 'privileges the personal, individual, private dimension of experience', and the contrary insistence in the overt thrust of the work on the idea that 'the struggle against apartheid [must take] precedence over sexual liberation or personal fulfilment'.[59] The latter emphasis on the necessary subordination of private needs to public responsibilities is most clearly present in *Burger's Daughter*, in which, at the insistence of Rosa's parents, she plays out the charade of being a political prisoner's fiance while still an adolescent in order to get messages to him in jail, regardless of the personal and emotional stress such role-playing causes her. On the one hand Gordimer repeatedly implies that sexuality and political commitment cannot successfully coexist in a life: they have their individual seasons, and only when sexuality has burned itself out can the passion which fuelled it be transferred to political *engagément*. Thus her effective female activists are all middle-aged women, either divorced or with conventionally dull marriages in which emotional estrangement rechannels female energies into idealistic and selfless service to others. But on the other hand, given Gordimer's focus upon the life-enhancing power of a fully realised sexuality, such emphases can only reinforce our sense of a subtextual resistance to the imperative to embrace political activism, and serve to support our sense of Gordimer's protagonists as the 'reluctant revolutionaries' which we have already identified in the fiction.

Elements of a consciousness still 'unliberated' in feminist terms also appear in Gordimer's unsettling representation of what seems at times to be an obsessive degree of female physical prudery and self-consciousness as a norm. In her exhausting sexual arena, in which each player seeks to make 'an amused and attracted audience of the other' (*Occasion for Loving*, 134), women must remember to hold in their stomachs as they move about (*A Guest of Honour*, 28), and it is assumed without criticism that Rebecca will be embarrassed by trousers which reveal her to be 'a bit heavy in the thigh' (*A Guest of Honour*, 489); Ann turns towards Gideon in a way which will 'liven the angle of her neck' (*Occasion for Loving*, 136); sweat is a pervasive problem; and Helen does not want to be kissed until she has cleaned her teeth (*The Lying Days*, 315); while Gordimer chooses to symbolise Hillela's indifference towards certain bourgeois values on the novel's opening page by causing her to refuse to shave her legs. Such details usually carry no ironic resonance: they are apparently inserted into the text simply to enhance that sense of authenticity, of a 'felt life', which the realist novel traditionally seeks to impart.

Make-up, however, does acquire a cumulative significance. It is taken for granted in the early fiction that it will be worn, and it soon comes to be represented as an essential disguise without which the individual is uncomfortably naked and exposed. Jessie significantly dispenses with it in her retreat at the sea-side in *Occasion for Loving* and is surprised to find that its absence makes her feel liberated; commenting on the gulf between the artificial and the natural, she says:

> What extraordinary things there might be in a face naked, open, weathered by an absolute freedom to take on the cast of feelings, as rain and sun and wind move through the sky. (194)

Ann, whose motives are entirely confused and who will ultimately betray both husband and lover, uses make-up at all times, but Rebecca, in *A Guest of Honour,* transparent in her emotions and thoroughly honest in her sexual response, never uses it (238). Such contrasts also serve to alert us to the distinction that Gordimer draws between what it is to be 'female' and what it is to be 'feminine'. She implies that the latter is learned, while the former is purely instinctual and sexually predatory. For example, amoral Emmanuelle walks with a 'sloppy stalk, very female in its disdain of femininity' (*A Guest of Honour*, 351), while adaptable Hillela exhibits a 'feminine friendliness' as she asks for directions to her mother's house (*A Sport of Nature*, 298).

Gordimer's occasional inscription of the clichéd and often sexist terminology of popular 'pulp' fiction, and her tendency at times to view female behaviour and attributes from crude, male-identified perspectives, further contradict the attempt to attribute a submerged feminist perspective to the novels. For example, there are points in the fiction when a singular coyness dictates her euphemistic presentation of the penis as 'the flesh' or as a 'poor blind thing' (*A Sport of Nature*, 9), while the linguistic liberation of the 1960s expresses itself in Gordimer's use of 'cunt' as an expletive in *A Guest of Honour* – Bray admits to being 'cunt-struck' as he describes his attraction to Rebecca, in an authorial move which is perhaps designed to shock a readership assumed to be conventionally bourgeois (371). Within such a context the search for the telling metaphor at times takes on a bizarre tinge – for example, Joosab's eyes are described as steady among 'wrinkled skin the colour and texture of a scrotum' (219), while

Gordimer's identification with what she assumes to be male perspectives issues awkwardly in the musings of Toby, who wonders at one point, 'Who knows what women feel in their queer gratuitous moment?' (*A World of Strangers*, 155). Throughout the novels there is also a conventional and clichéd emphasis on breasts, eyes and hair as primary signifiers of sexual attractiveness. In this connection we should note Fido's persuasive analysis of the extent to which Gordimer's internalisation of male standards in *A Guest of Honour* is revealed by the narrative focus upon Bray's simple sexual satisfaction in the early stages of his affair with Rebecca, one which excludes any consideration of her needs within the context of an assumption that she is simply happy to make him happy. Such 'sexist' perspectives are also revealed in the choice of such terms as 'old maid' and 'old woman' to communicate a negative assessment of Dando, Boxer and Wentz. On the other hand, Shinza's baby in his arms is envied by Bray in that he sees it not as a vulnerable infant but as a symbol of Shinza's continuing sexual potency: the appearance of the baby is, in fact, a catalyst in Bray's decision to transfer his political allegiance from Mweta to Shinza.[60] Such emphases remind us again of the repeated intrusion into the fiction of a characteristically Lawrentian voice, for example in such blatant generalisations as the one implicit in Helen's sense of Joel's thighs as possessing 'the unconscious lordliness of any young male's legs' (*The Lying Days*, 201).

Male sexuality is, however, also frequently seen as disturbingly and elementally threatening. An intrusive sense of the male as disconcertingly 'Other' underlies Jessie's first intimations of adult sexuality as she sees her stepfather's hairy legs pass by her bed in the hotel bedroom she shares with him and her mother (*Occasion for Loving*, 43). It is also present in Maureen's alienated perception of Bam as possessing 'the menacing aspect of maleness a man has before the superego had gained control of his body, come out of sleep. His penis was swollen under his rumpled trousers' (*July's People*, 39). Further, Gordimer's male 'Other' acquires a doubly significant and threatening aspect as the black male 'Other', the fear of whom is activated in Rosa's imagination as she accidentally meets the old chief at dawn outside her parents' bathroom; as Helen's nerve snaps towards the end of her clandestine visit to the mine's Concession Stores when she sees the 'native boy' urinating; and in Jessie's fantasy of a black rapist lurking behind the door of the bathroom in her mother's house. Such images encode the obsession with race which will express itself in the directing of sexual desire toward the feared 'Other', and in its corollary, the romanticisation of powerful black males, which reaches a climax in Hillela's fascination with her 'obsidian god'.[61]

'salvation exists, or doesn't it?'

Despite the tendency in Gordimer's work to represent women's lives as essentially subordinated to the more active and aggressive activities of men, the fiction continues to express a shaping interest in the precise and subtle nuances of women's experience in apartheid society, and to examine the options and roles available to them. Although it is the men who act, the emphasis is generally upon the impact of these actions upon their women. Men are repeatedly pushed off-stage as the focus turns to the confusion about roles and identity which beset the female voices. In *The Late Bourgeois World*, for example, Elizabeth's meditations about the origins and impact of Max's actions are privileged at the expense of developing Max's own perspectives on the events of which he was in fact both catalyst and victim.

This interest in women's experience is grounded in Gordimer's own vested emotional connections to the condition of being female in her world, and adds levels of depth, sensitivity and sympathy to the novels. But these are at times negated by the demands of the political vision which overlays them and determines plot development and character assessment. This vision with its didactic polemical elements, which articulates Gordimer's understanding of the pressures the public realm of communal action places upon the individual, is given an essentially ambivalent response in the fiction. Although her characters are brought again and again to succumb to its demands, the bulk of the work focuses upon their resistance to the invasive and distorting pressures the demands of the public realm bring to bear upon their private lives. The hard certainties of the political vision frequently run counter to the emotional logic which operates at subtextual levels in the fiction, and the unwelcome task of disciplining the wayward psyche into a firmly reliable commitment to public issues constitutes the central problem which Gordimer's characters must confront again and again.

In investigating why Gordimer has chosen to make this theme the controlling force in her fiction, we need to return to the history of her own emotional growth and subjective life as both a citizen and a woman in apartheid society. Gordimer's own emphasis on the prevalence of privilege in white South African society tends to obscure the fact that, from a different perspective, her life and attitudes may be understood to have been fundamentally shaped at a subliminal level by the twin experiences of powerlessness and marginalisation, both personal and political, in an authoritarian and patriarchally ordered world.[62] As a woman in a male-dominated society, as part-Jewish within the anti-Semitic contexts of the East Rand,[63] as a liberal and an English-speaker within a nationalist and Afrikaner hegemony, and as a white South African in a political context increasingly dominated by a Black Consciousness ideology,[64] she has been herself demonstrably the victim of stereotype and prejudice. Given her own conviction that the roots of public action lie in private experience, her sympathy with the oppressed is therefore perhaps best understood as originating in her own experience of marginalisation at multiple levels. The powerful emotional intensity which welds together the three prongs of her work – her withering denunciation of the moral hypocrisy of the class to which she belongs, her valorisation of the political aspirations of the oppressed black majority, and her consistent concern with female options in an entirely corrupt society – may be seen to be grounded in her identification with the state of victimhood which is arguably the ultimately generative experience which prompts all committed activism in both life and fiction.

Gordimer's identification with the predicament of women who are trapped in their own marginalisation thus 'naturally' allies her with those other marginalised and dispossessed peoples, black South Africans, whose quest for a voice and for power she perceives to be even more fully frustrated than that of white women in the historical contexts of which she writes.[65] Hence the concern with the need for escape and the desire for power in the novels, both in their own way offering a solution to the dilemma of marginalisation. Hence, too, the juxtaposition of the world of the body to the world of ideas in the fiction, for the indulgence of sexuality as surely allows an escape from external pressures into the private world of sensual experience as the intellectually responsible life provides an answer to the experience of oppression by encouraging a liberating political activism. It is within the context of so fundamentally romantic a conception of the options open to the individual that we should understand the complex roots of the authorial praise lavished on Hillela at the end of *A Sport of Nature*: fulfilled both sexually and politically, she has achieved a position of personal and public power which must satisfy every fantasy of escape and revenge.

However, our perception of such subliminal connections between the personal and the political spheres of action may illuminate the origins of, but cannot eliminate our sense of contradictions in the fiction. Whereas the authorial stance is consciously committed to a politically engaged and semi-didactic response, the subconscious needs and fantasies outlined above fuel powerfully contradictory subtexts in the novels. The tensions between the two uniquely shape Gordimer's representations of the interior histories of her female characters as they struggle to find space for their voices and appropriate ways to respond to both political and gender contexts. Such a space is difficult to both find and maintain within the context of the political agenda Gordimer sets herself, for, in bringing her novels to a resolution, Gordimer repeatedly chooses to privilege the political perspective over her tentative histories of subjective consciousness. The polemical intent which determines this choice generates tensions which at times nullify the subtlety and sensitivity of the preceding analysis of ambiguity and ambivalence in the emotional lives of the characters, and frequently causes the novels to collapse into inconclusive and unsatisfactory endings.

Such tensions clearly beset the conclusion to *July's People*, Gordimer's examination of the possible fate of liberal whites in a South Africa in which the Armageddon of violent revolution has finally arrived. The credibility and power of this novel is seriously affected by Gordimer's uncertainty about the precise nature of her project here. On the one hand, the novel may be seen to function at the level of a political allegory. The Smales couple is clearly intended to be representative of the 'decent', fair-minded, liberal response of Johannesburg's northern suburbs to the impossible contradictions inherent in being affluent, liberal and white in the post-Sharpeville era; the weaknesses and internal contradictions of this position are exposed by Gordimer with a characteristically detached, cold and merciless eye. In focussing on the personal relationships within the South African family structure between husband, wife, children *and* servants, she suggests that the artificial separation of human beings from one another brought about by the apartheid régime, and the patterns of guilt and often involuntary collusion which this separation has forced upon even the liberal white grouping the Smaleses represent, have created a society in which the fullness of emotional response between human beings has been stunted and the deeper dimensions of a spiritual life appear to be entirely absent. The shallowness and sterility of the emotional relationships this family is caught up in are, as we have seen, epitomised in Maureen and Bam's inability to relate to each other except in terms of the playing out of the roles their society has assigned to them. Bam is the provider and later the hunter; Maureen is consigned to the domestic sphere and, later, to the hut: stereotypes of what late bourgeois or capitalist man may be seen to have been reduced to under the cumulative impact of the apartheid régime. The authorial narrative voice takes care to distance itself from an identification with the moral sordidness of their dilemma in, for example, the tonal patterning of the opening generalisation about what July's 'kind has always done for their kind' (1). The phrase not only demarcates the gap between master and servant but also establishes an unbridgeable distance between the reader and the characters on both sides of the racial divide. Names, too, are given an ideological resonance: Royce, Gina and Victor, are (perhaps too obviously) named to signify their paramountcy over their mostly nameless black countrymen; while the satiric intentions in the naming of July and the link thus established between Gordimer's text and Robinson Crusoe's naming of Friday are only too clear.

At this level, then, the morally didactic purpose of the novel is unambiguously present. It is clearly implied that the Smaleses' attitudes are to be understood as *typical* of the morally culpable stance of liberal white South Africans as such; the affluence of their lifestyle has an emblematic significance, and their futile and rather absurd attempts to behave 'decently' within the frame-work of a liberal 'correctness' towards July are sharply and mercilessly satirised. No sympathy or irony softens the element of self-flagellation in the implicitly contemptuous description of the Smaleses as

> sickening at the appalling thought that they might find they had lived out their whole lives as they were, born white pariah dogs in a black continent. They joined political parties and "contact" groups in willingness to slough privilege it was supposed to be their white dog nature to guard with Mirages and tanks. (8)

Within the parameters of the stereotypes which the novel encodes, it is their attachment to precisely these nonexportable privileges which prevents them from following the promptings of their drive for self-preservation by emigrating 'in time' and which encourages in them that characteristically ostrichlike stance which finally makes them first fugitives from and then prisoners of history. The total destruction of all they have clung to is presented by the authorial voice with so fertile a wealth of improbable detail about how the revolution erupts and progresses (6-12), and in a tone of such implicit satisfaction, that their losses cannot be read as intended to be anything other than morally and poetically just within the wider scheme of things.

Then, true to another *typos* – that of the morally didactic *Entwicklungsroman* – they embark on that odyssey into the 'heart of darkness' which becomes, for Maureen at least, also the classic journey of self-discovery. It is at this point that the fable softens and extends as Gordimer begins to move beyond the purely polemical dimensions sketched out above to develop the character of her female protagonist more fully. (Bam and the children remain one-dimensional characters, whose flatness fades into insignificance as Maureen's perspective comes to dominate the narrative.) Now Maureen's origins in the class and milieu from which Gordimer herself has emerged begin to colour the narrative significantly, allowing the narrative voice to develop the specific details of her 'appalling' experience 'in the bush' with an element of empathy and a complexity of insight which contrasts sharply with the novel's detached and coldly ironic treatment of the Smaleses' predicament at the level of fable. The story of Maureen's shifting reactions to her captivity in the bush becomes a subtly developed account of both destruction and transformation, as her old certainties are progressively broken down and she is forced out of the dead shell of the past into an uncertain present, as much as a moth – doomed nevertheless to self-destruct against the light – might emerge from the dead chrysalis within its cocoon.

Initially it is the family and the roles it has imposed upon its members which becomes the focus of interrogation and the primary casualty in the novel. As Maureen begins to move towards painful and incomplete glimpses of the true nature of her situation, one defined by the inescapable realities of her race and sex, Bam metamorphoses from a husband into the merely chillingly distant 'blond man' (138), and her children are reduced to a 'litter' (47), and cease to be invested with any clear emotional significance of any kind. Their voices (in the final sequence of the novel) blend unintelligibly with Bam's by the river in the meaningless chatter of strangers, which represents a danger to Maureen only in so far as they speak in the language that might betray them all as fugitives to a listening enemy (159). Maureen's tentative moves to establish a bond with July as a friend and her attempts to establish some relationship with the black women of the village (on the basis of her superficial notions of universal sisterhood), are frustrated not only by language and race barriers but also by July's obdurate refusal to allow her to escape from her class role as 'the white madam'. Although he strips her of her illusions about her adequacy in that role, he will not allow her sentence to be transmuted. At the same time, the fact that the black women do nothing to facilitate Maureen's tentative efforts at friendship is another expression of Gordimer's rejection of the feminist notion of universal sisterhood.

Painful disillusionments are, however, shown to be also accompanied by muted and embryonic forms of transformation. Maureen's initial alienation from her body, one which has stood as a symbol of a more general and pervasive alienation from reality as such, has informed her 'disgusted' scrubbing at vagina and anus as she realises (incredibly for the first time in her life) that her body can smell (9).[66] A tentative movement towards a repossession of that body is suggested in her discovery of the possibility of a fierce possessive joy in it, when she performs her solitary dance in the rain (48): a dance which represents the beginnings of a movement towards a self-awareness and a self-possession which will ultimately express itself in her flight from the village at the novel's end.

But it is precisely at the point of flight that the novel breaks down into a problematic inconclusiveness which causes its political polemic and its tentative feminist perspective to collapse into a confusion which undermines the whole project. How are we to interpret Maureen's flight from the village? We might read it as a 'suicide run' into the arms of an enemy, one which is ironically intended to 'liberate' her from the unbearable actual and emotional isolation which is the consequence of her alienation from family and society in the village. It could be read, on the other hand, as an affirmative action, a gesture which represents an attempt to take control of both herself and her destiny, as she

> [trusts] herself with all the suppressed trust of a lifetime, alert, like a solitary animal at the season when animals neither seek a mate nor take care of young, existing only for their lone survival, the enemy of all that would make claims of responsibility. (160)

In this reading her flight might be intended to break the cycle of fear and impotence by precipitating a confrontation with the feared. Alternatively, it could be understood as a pathetic attempt by a deranged consciousness to recover a lost, familiar past as Maureen is drawn on by 'the smell of boiled potatoes (from a vine indistinguishable to her from others) [which] promises a kitchen, a house just the other side of the next tree' (160). (Here Gordimer encodes a long and familiar tradition in which women are driven into insanity both by their inability to play out the gender-roles assigned to them, and by Africa's refusal to mould itself into forms familiar to them.[67]) Maureen may also be seen as fleeing not only *towards* domesticity, but also *from* so-called Third-World deprivation into First-World comfort: the helicopter (regardless of whether it contains friend or foe) may be understood as a symbol of modern technology and of the resources of an urban civilisation Maureen is desperate to recover. To confuse matters further, the helicopter may at some level represent not only the unknown future but also some kind of redemption, a reading which is strongly suggested by the baptismal imagery which accompanies Maureen's improbable fording of the river, in waist-deep water, through which she wades with her shoes held above her head in defiance of the dangers posed by unseen rocks in the waters underfoot. In the heavy-handed imagery of the passage, she emerges 'born again' (159).

Gordimer's text offers us little assistance in our attempt to make sense of the indeterminate elements in this passage, nor are her later comments on the novel's ending much more helpful. In a 1985 interview she merely says that Maureen is

> taking her life in her own hands. My theory is that you never make sudden decisions. Things begin to decay inside her and something else begins to grow. So we reach at the end of that book for me a moment of growth. But it is also a Pascalian wager, you know . . . Salvation exists or doesn't it?[68]

Pascal argued that, although it is impossible to establish the existence of God without doubt, it is also impossible to be certain there is no God; in this situation of radical uncertainty, man does best to act 'as if' there is a God in order to secure salvation *if* it exists. The reference to Pascal is illuminating, for it suggests that the indeterminacy of the novel's conclusion is intentional within a context which stresses the collapse of all certainties, and reduces Maureen's flight to little more than a physical reflex which, at best, can only express her overwhelming rejection of the black African world she has fallen into and which seems to constitute her only future. That she has achieved some sort of personal liberation as a woman and as an individual is strongly suggested, but her political redemption remains in question. Moreover, any attempt to read the novel's ending as one articulating a feminist solidarity with Maureen's struggle to achieve a fuller sense of self finds itself in conflict with the overwhelming emphasis, in the tonal patterning of the text as a whole, on the Smaleses' inadequacies as fully human beings on almost every level. This emphasis is made necessary by Gordimer's determination to offer her readers a political fable, but her morally didactic purpose here cannot simultaneously sustain a true sympathy for or sense of solidarity with Maureen's struggle. Ultimately, Gordimer reverts to the inscription of a stereotype in her decision to condemn the Smaleses as both the typical products of and the guilty collaborators with a régime which (within the framework of an essentially clichéd conception of historical process) must be seen to be finally brought to a richly deserved and catastrophic end by the triumphantly victorious forces of a successful revolutionary movement.

The naïvety of both the political analysis and the political vision embedded in this novel has already been noted in Chapter 3.[69] Little work has, however, been done so far on the significance of Gordimer's decision to tell the story through Maureen's eyes and to concentrate specifically on her experience. That Maureen's movement towards rebirth *must* be represented as stillborn in terms of the politically didactic ends the novel has been designed to serve (which will, of course, determine that white South Africans such as the Smaleses cannot be granted any form of redemption in a vision of the future almost completely dominated by an implicit Black Consciousness perspective), reduces and skews the novel's imaginative thrust and prevents it from achieving that degree of fullness, depth and humanity of analysis which would rescue it from being little more than an interesting political tract.

Such tensions are not confined to *July's People* alone: similar difficulties beset Gordimer's endings in several of her other novels. As Cooke has noted, the affirmative ending of *The Lying Days* does 'not grow out of the body of the novel',[70] while the conclusion of *Burger's Daughter*, is equally problematic. Rosa's decision to return to South Africa, and the idealised images offered of her final sense of well-being in her prison cell at the end of the novel, do not arise convincingly out of the body of the work; they are clearly a product of the novel's political agenda and coexist uneasily with the complex history of Rosa's emotional development with which the bulk of the work is concerned. Tensions also arise in *The Late Bourgeois World*, where the narrative suggests that Elizabeth's decision to agree to Luke Fokase's request is determined not so much by her tentative attraction to the idea of helping the 'struggle' onwards as by the extent to which she is powerfully sexually drawn to him. It is an attraction both she and Gordimer attempt to discount – to the novel's detriment – in the musings upon the American space-walk and its significance which form an uneasy conclusion to the novel. Here too Gordimer's characteristic insistence upon making sexual preference an indicator of the individual's potential for moral and political salvation or redemption within the context of apartheid undermines, and threatens to negate, the subtlety and intelligence of the analysis in the novel as a whole, reducing aspects of the work to the level of stereotype and caricature.

Not only does Gordimer fail to do herself justice in allowing her novels to collapse repeatedly into such conclusions, but the weakness of such endings betrays again the extent to which her work encodes that conflict between her concerns as a citizen and as a woman which we have been tracing in this chapter and which, to a significant degree, remains unresolved. As we have seen, the two streams of concern at times work against each other in unproductive ways, and their dissonances contribute to a significantly damaging diffusion of focus in the novels. Such insights must encourage us to treat Gordimer's insistence that neither a feminist impulse nor a politically didactic thrust has shaped her work with caution: it is clearly at best ingenuous, and at worst suggests a genuine confusion in her sense of the nature of her fictional project.

Chapter 5

Images of Blacks

Adam, even as he learnt to see what was true, learnt also to lie: truth itself was no longer whole but partial, incomplete, corrupted. And the lies that are perhaps hardest to discern, the most insidious, are those that tap the power of the imagination to root themselves in our consciousness – the lies, that is, that come in the guise of imaginative truth.

Hazel Waters[1]

The prejudiced individual creates his own stereotypes, very often unconsciously, by reading into situations involving Negroes those stock meanings which justify his emotional and economic needs.

Ralph Ellison[2]

Gordimer's conviction that race prejudice and its consequences have crippled the South African psyche at its very core has not only shaped but also powerfully redirected her aesthetic and creative thrust from the earliest point in her career. This conviction is clearly rooted in that liberal tradition of English-speaking intellectual life in South Africa with which her wide reading had made her familiar and of which she quickly became a part. When she wrote in 1961 that 'the greatest single factor in the making of our *mores* in South Africa was and is and always will be the colour question',[3] she was simply adding her voice to those of an established line of eminent South Africans who had spoken out before her, and articulating sentiments which reflected in broad outline the general attitudes of the affluent, liberal English-speaking circles of the northern suburbs of Johannesburg within which she was moving in her late thirties at the time. The extent to which her politics were in fact shared by many of her class and time is documented in Nat Nakasa's comment in the late sixties that 'apart from Cape Town, Johannesburg has what must be the largest number of whites who don't want the colour bar'.[4] Indeed, within her own still largely expatriate colonial circles, it was not her moral and political convictions which initially set her apart but her willingness to write about, to explore, the complexities of life within South Africa at a time when those around her still spoke of England as 'home' and when every public gathering, every cinema showing, was still concluded with a rendering of 'God Save the Queen' while the audience stood to attention.

Within this context, both Gordimer's early identification with her own South Africanness, and her generous sense of the overwhelming attractiveness of that other, black world from which apartheid sought to divide her, were exceptional. The courageous independence of spirit initially needed to write of her own world in the face of the general contempt for local literary efforts, which was widely current at the time, also soon expressed itself in her attempt to represent aspects of the black African experience in her work as well – despite the extent to which she knew herself to be separated from that world by the racist conventions of her upbringing and by the subsequent restrictions of the apartheid régime. Within such a framework, in which she knew the entire life of the culture to be distorted by the principle of enforced division imposed by an alien Afrikaner hegemony, Gordimer's rebellion against racism also of necessity expressed itself politically, despite its philosophical origins in European liberal humanism. That her determination to defend her right to connect with that 'other' Africa and to write of it was, in consequence, understood by her to be a primarily *political* act of dissent, is shown in her early representation of friendships across the colour bar as a 'conspiracy against keeping apart' (my emphasis) (*Occasion for Loving*, 120).

So political an act soon became enmeshed in typically political difficulties. Her characteristically humanist belief in that fundamental brotherhood of man which allows the artist to enter imaginatively into the life of the other, regardless of gender, creed or colour, quickly found itself at odds with the political argument that, within the specific contexts of the resistance struggle, such an appropriation of the experience of the 'Other' was unacceptably arrogant.[5] The fundamental philosophical conflict between these two positions has never been entirely satisfactorily resolved in Gordimer's work. In her search for a compromise, her shifting

pronouncements on the issue have been marked by a reluctance
to abandon in its entirety her claim that whites may write
'authentically' of black experience, despite her increasing sensitivity to the possibility that a writer who is both white and a
woman may find herself to be seen as simply both patronising
and presumptuous in her attempt to do so.

A vigorous defence of her early practice is to be found in an
essay written in 1961, in which she acknowledges the opposing
position in passing but puts forward her own views with enthusiasm and sensitivity. Praising Olive Schreiner for not having any
of 'the intellectual timidity that would make her limit herself to
the things she knows, the little world she knows',[6] she observes
that

> we all await with tremendous interest the novels to come from
> the twelve millions who, with only one exception I can think of,
> have not yet written any novels in English – which it seems almost
> certain is destined to be their literary language. But I do believe
> we should await these books as an appeal to the intellect and
> imagination rather than to curiosity. For that is the true business
> of the writer . . . The satisfaction of curiosity . . . belongs to the
> newspapers. Below the level of the meretricious satisfaction of
> curiosity – how it all looks to someone who really *is* black – there
> is little reason why a straightforward novel of events in which the
> protagonists are black men should not be written just as authen-
> tically by a white writer as by a black one. Just so long as he
> makes it his business to know the social forces that shape his
> protagonists, as the writer who writes of men at sea must know
> the sea.
>
> The novel in depth, the novel that is not authentic but imagi-
> native, that does not seek to create the semblance of life but to
> create life out of its own elements – that, perhaps, can be written
> of the black man only by himself. But even of this we cannot be
> sure.[7]

Here, as in her defence of the female artist's right to imaginatively
enter the world of male experience, her argument is premised
upon her belief in the writer's special ability to see further and
deeper than the ordinary person. It is a position she has never
entirely abandoned. Yet the simple distinction drawn here between the 'authentic' and the 'imaginative' novel, between one

which merely creates 'the semblance of life' in a 'straightforward novel of events' and one which miraculously creates 'life out of its own elements', is one she would probably not wish to apply to a classification of her own work; she undoubtedly sees herself as a writer of '*imaginative*' novels, yet, in choosing first to incorporate and then to centre her work upon 'the colour question', she has had to confront the problem of '*authentic*' representation of black experience.

Despite Gordimer's concern with this issue, however, black voices appear infrequently in the novels. We find only one black character developed in any depth in the novels, Gideon Shibalo in *Occasion for Loving*, and even here the internal monologue and stream-of-consciousness techniques so frequently used to develop characterisation elsewhere are notably absent. Indeed, the degree of identification with a protagonist made possible by such techniques is not encouraged here. Black voices are seldom heard from independently of their interaction with the white characters; interesting enough, and when they do emerge, they are almost without exception male: Gideon and Jacobus in *The Conservationist* and July in *July's People*. Such caution in her representation of the inner worlds of black South Africans suggests Gordimer's rapidly developing awareness of how problematic it might actually be to claim to 'know the social forces that shape' black experience.

Already in 1959 she had said of township life that 'what it means to live like this from the day you are born until the day you die, I cannot tell you. No white person can'.[8] By 1972 in an appendix to her 1961 essay, 'The Novel and the Nation in South Africa', she had heavily qualified her earlier claim that whites can write authentically of blacks. Referring to Lukacs, she wrote that

> a writer, in imaginative creation and the intuition that comes with it, cannot go beyond the *potential* of his own experience . . . [and] living in a society that has been as deeply and calculatedly compartmentalized as South Africa's has been under the colour bar, the writer's potential has unscalable limitations. There are some aspects of a black man's life that have been put impossibly beyond the white man's potential experience, and the same applies to the black man and some aspects of a white man's experience. Both can write of the considerable fringe society in which

black and white are 'known' in a meaningful sense to one another; but there are areas from which, by iron circumstance, each in turn finds himself shut out, even intuitively, to their mutual loss as writers.[9]

In 1975 she repeats the point in almost the same terms:

Any writer's attempt to present in South Africa a totality of human experience within his own country is subverted before he sets down a word. As a white man his fortune may change; the one thing he cannot experience is blackness – with all that implies in South Africa. As a black man, the one thing he cannot experience is whiteness – with all that implies. Each is largely outside the other's experience-potential. There is no social mobility across the colour-line. The identification of class with colour means that breaching class barriers is breaking the law, and the indivisible class-colour barrier is much, much more effective, from the point of view of limiting the writer's intimate knowledge of his society, than any class barrier has ever been . . . The white writer, aseptically quarantined in his test-tube *élite* existence, is cut off by enforced privilege from the greater part of the society in which he lives.[10]

However, despite the manifest difficulty of authentically representing black experience in her novels, Gordimer has continued to attempt to do so, maintaining a delicate balance between the known and the unknown which is grounded in both her fascination with, and respect for, difference. By 1983 her emphasis had shifted again, and she reasserted her right to incorporate black points of view in her work in an interview in which she defiantly stated that, after all,

as a writer I think I have arrived at a stage through my work where if I write about blacks or I create black characters I feel I have the right to do so. I accept the limitations of what I know.[11]

Gordimer's repeated return to this issue, and the sophisticated ambivalence of her response to it, should alert us to its centrality as a marker in the fiction. For it is precisely in her attempts to represent black experience and black/white relationships in the novels that the themes that control Gordimer's representation of the South African reality become most clearly apparent. It is revealing, for example, that she has less to say about differences in culture and language as alienating forces within South African society than we might expect. Achebe has emphasised the divisive power of such differences explaining that:

> I am not saying that the picture of Nigeria and Nigerians painted by a conscientious European must be invalid. I think it would be terribly valid, just as a picture of the visible tenth of an iceberg is valid . . . [But] no man can understand another whose language he does not speak (and "language" here does not simply mean words but a man's entire world view) . . . [12]

But for Gordimer it is apartheid alone which divides white and black in South Africa, and in her work she, in effect, marginalises that 'profound silence between cultures which finally cannot be traversed by understanding' which has recently been identified as 'the signifying difference of the post-colonial text'.[13] She opts instead for a reading of the South African situation which we might at one level call essentially optimistic: for, whereas a 'profound silence' is not susceptible to change, apartheid is, of course, eradicable, and it is conceivable that the damage it has wrought may be both healed and transcended. This conviction is at the core of Gordimer's conceptualisation of the artist's role as essentially political: for if all difference is the illusory consequence of racist ideologies, then our common humanity will inevitably unite us once racism is defeated. Her emphasis in the passages above on apartheid as the single, all-consuming source of evil within her society hints at the obsessive force with which this theme has understandably dominated her writing. Within such a paradigm, political change *alone* (which may be encouraged by those insights art affords us) can eradicate difference and leave us with that triumphant vision of harmony offered in the closing passages of *A Sport of Nature*. Yet in failing to confront the enormous power of culture and language to entrench division in societies, Gordimer confines us to a reading of the larger South African drama which at times comes perilously close, as we shall see, to being unacceptably simplistic, romantic and sentimental.

Gordimer's emphasis on the crippling effect of white 'privilege' (as an obvious corollary of apartheid) expresses, of course, that characteristic sense of guilt by which sensitive white South Africans have found themselves overwhelmed; as a consequence of her growing politicisation it also reflects attitudes prevalent in South African left-wing thinking of the time. For example, Parker anticipates Gordimer's point of view in his comment in 1971 that

> it is . . . this position of privilege which isolates [white writers], rather than any myth that 'whites cannot portray black people'. They may choose to mix – and the choice is theirs – with their black cultural counterparts at a party or discussion in those relatively balmy days between the forties and sixties, but they will deny that this mixing is not in fact between equals.[14]

And that such a perspective upon the effects of 'privilege' is also consonant with a Black Consciousness ideology is suggested in Steve Biko's uncompromising assertion that

> no matter what a white man does, the colour of his skin – his passport to privilege – will always put him miles ahead of the black man. Thus in the ultimate analysis no white person can escape being part of the oppressor camp.[15]

In assenting to such perspectives, Gordimer in effect voluntarily restricts her sense of what might be possible for the artist within the South African context. Initially, her determination to confront the difficulties associated with an imaginative crossing of apartheid barriers in the fiction is marked: when Toby makes a rueful comment to Anna Louw in *A World of Strangers* that 'it's so easy to be ridiculous when you're trying to identify yourself with the other person', Anna replies, 'Of course . . . But it's a risk you have to take sometimes' (75). However, the form that risk takes changes as the *oeuvre* develops. Although black characters have continued to appear in the novels close to centre-stage, as they must be, given the themes Gordimer has chosen to develop, the confidence which marked her construction of the character of Gideon in *Occasion for Loving* falters in succeeding works, and her developing sensitivity to the perceived dilemmas that 'privilege' and political orientation have trapped her in constrains to an increasingly externalised, respectful and distanced representation of black figures. Thus July is understood solely within the confines of the novel's focus upon the Smaleses' predicament, and no image of him independent of Maureen's own growing grasp of the untenability of their relationship is developed as a counterbalance to his status as pawn of the novel's thesis. The works almost exclusively privilege white voices who function as centres of consciousness, while a neutral omniscient narrative voice confines itself to objective description and reportage when the focus shifts to those black lives hidden from white eyes in the townships and the kraals of *The Conservationist* and *July's People*.[16]

'we were all like sleepers, coming awake'

Gordimer's acute awareness of the severe practical restrictions on her knowledge of the actual and spiritual lives of the blacks around her has expressed itself in her decision to confine her representations of black figures to three broadly delineated categories, each of which she clearly feels she has some personal knowledge of, both as a white employer and through the contacts with blacks which have developed as a result of her attraction to the non-racial 'fringe' culture of Johannesburg's political underworld. She focuses firstly upon images of blacks who might have been encountered in that 'grey' world of Sophiatown shebeens and liberal dinner parties that she knows from first-hand experience: black men and women whose education, politics and energies sufficiently match those of their white counterparts to enable imagination and empathy to bridge the gaps and allow that illusion of 'equality' in at least social intercourse (which Parker treats so contemptuously above) to arise. Here the racist stereotypes of apartheid culture are deliberately exploded,[17] but in her emphasis on a common humanity, and in her development of the theme that each man is his brother's keeper, the danger she risks is of offering her readers black characters who seem to be merely 'white-under-the-skin'. Parker has argued that such a

> desire to demonstrate by the elaborate balancing of white characters with black characters that underneath their skins people are the same is otiose . . . What is of overriding importance [instead] is the power relationship: how those in power can continue to maintain their position; how those without power can evolve strategies for the acquisition of power.[18]

However, Gordimer's passionate identification with the justice of the black struggle against an oppression of which she is simultaneously both an accomplice and a beneficiary paradoxically expresses itself in what may be understood to be a 'colonisation-by-the imagination' of an alien black world. Its effect is to defuse the threat of the 'Other' as he is assimilated and becomes 'one-of-us' in a typical process of imperialist appropriation.

Given the paradoxes and tensions inherent in such an identification across the colour/class barrier, and the areas of profound ignorance which necessarily underlie her eager attraction to black Africa, it is not surprising that the second level at which Gordimer's fascination with black Africa is expressed is in that romanticisation and even idealisation of the idea of blackness which we have already noted in Chapter 3, and which increasingly dominates the fiction. Although current insights into the complexity of both black spiritual life and the potential destructiveness of inter-black political rivalries, which have recently further problematised liberal perspectives in ways unforeseeable to Gordimer,[19] were not available to her in the period in which she was writing, the reductionist force of her images of blacks is nevertheless surprising. For example, the deliberate reversal of Western colour symbolism, which is so marked a feature of much of her work, results in an emphasis upon black physical beauty which frequently depends upon a denial of the ability of white to attract. The effect achieved at times strikingly illuminates the authorial ideology at work, as in her description of the burnt, black winter veld of the Transvaal as possessing a blackness 'not of death but of Life' (*Occasion for Loving*, 267). A similar reversal underlies her romanticisation of that figure most likely to be feared by the average white South African reader, the black revolutionary. These trends find their culmination in the prophetic fantasy of *A Sport of Nature* in which images clearly indebted to Gordimer's readings in the philosophy of négritude and Black Consciousness are deployed in a defiant expression of what might strike the reader as a form of reverse racism. In noting the passionate emotionalism underlying such patterns (as opposed to the astute, lucid and even-handed approach of the non-fiction) we acquire some sense of the power the ideology which directs the novels' development has had over her imagination.

Such simplifications not only animate the consciously subversive perspectives of the fiction, but also enable negative stereotypes characteristic of a racist society to survive at a subtextual level in the fiction. Consequently at a third level, the novels' population of servants and the occasional worker (from whom class barriers additional to the colour bar most effectively separate the writer and problematise those emotional identifications which inform the other two categories delineated above) may frequently be found to carry the burden of the subconscious residues of typical white South African racist clichés from which Gordimer has struggled to emerge. Gordimer's personal friendships with black Africans animate the first set of representations; her passionately idealistic commitment to an image of Africa which she finds her white skin excludes her from inspires the second; and the third lays bare in its contradictions, as we shall see, the true extent of the gulf between white writer and black subject which experience, empathy and goodwill cannot altogether bridge.

Gordimer has attempted to cross this gulf not only through the development of close personal contacts with black South Africans and the concomitant political commitments this has entailed, but also through the cultivation of those imaginative identifications which art makes possible. She has read widely in African and other colonial and post-colonial literatures, and it is no accident that the first major essay to be published on black African writing within South Africa was her 1973 monograph, *The Black Interpreters*. The title reflects both her sense that a black interpretation of South African realities will be different from a white one, and her belief that white South Africans not only urgently need to have the black world interpreted for them by black writers, but also might need someone from within their own camp to act as further intermediary.[20] She herself has repeatedly acknowledged her dependence upon black African literature to provide her with a window upon a world which, as a white South African, she has felt that she may never truly enter, and her belief that literature has the power to alter and deepen understanding arises at least partially out of her sense of her own particular debt to that literature. As she stresses in an essay she wrote in 1967, deploring the banning of the work of black South African writers:

> If we want to know, not the 'African', that laboratory specimen, that worker bee of fascinating habits, but the Black men and women amongst whom we live, these writers are the only people from whom we could learn . . . [They] offer a first-hand account of the life that is lived out of sight of the white suburbs, and the thoughts that lie unspoken behind dark faces.[21]

The earnest need to find a way to transcend the barriers created by apartheid speaks vividly through such passages. But Gordimer is of course also typically a product of apartheid in the extent to which she finds herself hampered at both conscious and unconscious levels by the habits of prejudice entrenched by a lifetime's entrapment in a society premised upon division. It has been a legacy impossible to slough off entirely, as revealed in the trend we have already noted towards various forms of generalisation and stereotype which run as a sub-text below the surface of the fiction. For example, Gordimer makes no apology for the degree of prejudice which informs her depiction of Afrikaners in the novels. They constitute a pariah group for anti-apartheid liberals, from whose culture all other South Africans have been separated by numerous factors, not least of which has been the language-segregated schooling system to which all children are subjected in the country; and they are given short shrift throughout the fiction.[22] In the area of race, however, Gordimer's sensitivity to the immense difficulty of freeing oneself of even the more crass impulses of prejudice has been acute. Her powerful awareness of her need to find ways to defeat the alienation and suspicion bred by apartheid has expressed itself at one level in her concern with censorship, not only as it has affected her own work, but also as it has sought to silence black voices and thus close off one of the few remaining avenues to some understanding of black lives available to the excluded white consciousness.[23] At another level, the writing earnestly charts how slowly a sense of the black South African as a fully human being initially emerged for both author and protagonists. In *The Lying Days*, published in 1953, Helen is shown as not only attempting to escape a set of stereotypes, but also struggling with the very impulse of the mind to think in terms of stereotypes. The tendency is always to replace discarded generalisations with new ones as a desperate substitute for the empirical knowledge which apartheid denies her. Initially Helen experiences simply an overwhelming and threatening sense of difference: through the eyes of the child growing up on the mine in the cocoon of conscious race prejudice, the servants and the black miners are seen as curious, alien and faintly sinister, leading lives akin to those of animals,

> wondering, receptive, unthinking, taking in with their eyes as earth takes in water, close-eyed, sullen with the defensive sullenness of the defenceless; noisy and merry with the glee of the innocent . . . [The boy, Joel, dodged] through the mine boys as if they were the fools, making up their minds for them when they did not seem to know whether they wanted to step this way or that. (24, 21)

No corrective retrospective voice intrudes here to offer an ironic perspective on these perceptions, and we are left with a powerful insight into the dimensions of Helen's sense of alienation from the blacks around her. It is an alienation which defeats her later tentative overtures to the black student, Mary Seswayo, which collapse into an unresolved and quintessentially South African unease. Blacks may become a passing source of entertainment but finally constitute no more than an exotic backdrop to the unfolding drama of Helen's 'real' life with Paul and Joel: '[The Africans] had passed before me almost as remote if not as interesting as animals in a zoo . . . [Their] language in my ears had been like the barking of dogs or the cries of birds' (161, 186). Although the past tense is used here, an alternative vision is only hinted at in the emphasis on Helen's uncomprehending frustration at her inability to reach Mary across the gap. The impossibility of breaking out of, or transcending, racist colonial paradigms in black-white interactions gives rise to the sense of defeat with which the novel concludes. In an ironic recapitulation of the history of the early development of white relationships with blacks, Helen's imagery at a final moment of intense frustration at the awkwardness and discomfort of her relationship with Mary reflects her sense of the limits set to black-white interaction in the angry protest of her words to Joel[24] on the one hand and missionaries on the other: 'She was horribly grateful. I felt like a bossy missionary presenting a Bible to a little savage who has no shoes and chronic hookworm' (142).

Such discomfort also expresses itself in that characteristic denigration of the 'Other' which reappears, for example, in Jessie's childhood perception of Africans in *Occasion for Loving* as being 'like a cage full of coloured parrots screeching at the zoo' (35). Gordimer herself wrote in 1963, in an autobiographical sketch, of 'the black people among whom we lived as people live in a forest among trees'.[25] That she herself was capable of an unintentionally ironic deployment of such animal imagery is demonstrated in an early essay written in 1955, in which she describes the newly arrived 'Bantu' in Johannesburg as 'the half-naked primitive, fresh from the kraal, clutching his blanket as he stares gazelle-eyed at the traffic'.[26] The images in such passages are all of the non-human or the sub-human; trees, dogs, birds, parrots in cages and 'worker bees' only gradually modulate into living black men and women for both the writer and her characters.

Freeing the self of prejudice is possible in fact only through a kind of moral and psychic rebirth, Gordimer suggests, and

> even when it was achieved in the mind, in the moral sense and the sense of dignity, there remained the confusing pull of habit and use as well as the actual legal confines.
>
> We were all like sleepers, coming awake from a long lull of acceptance . . . It was as painful and confusing as the attempt to change what has grown up with the flesh always is . . . We could not [simply] triumph and say: There – it was everywhere, in the memory and the eye, the hand and the laugh. (*The Lying Days*, 161-62)

Helen's humanist impulse to befriend Mary Seswayo founders, not on a lack of humility and sympathy but on her sense of the sheer, ineradicable and unbridgeable gap between her world and Mary's. Her sensitivity towards Mary's 'otherness' initially takes the form of an attempt to deny the gap, 'to make her feel less different from me' (185), but Mary's brief explanation of how difficult she finds it to study in the house in the township in which she lodges jolts Helen into reviewing and discarding the various stock images her imagination harbours of township life, and into admitting finally to a profoundly helpless ignorance of the true conditions of Mary's life:

I saw the old motor car tyre with the fern straggling out of it; the children shouting, the flatness, the dust, the noise. I imagined the woman with the sewing machine stuttering and the bits of material everywhere. Probably she chattered while she sewed. No, probably that was wrong, too; native women are always far more gay or far more serious than white women, so one mustn't try to visualise their moods from one's experience of Europeans. They sing and shout in the street over nothing, and they are solemn under the weight of some task we shouldn't even feel. There was no way of knowing, no way of knowing. (*The Lying Days*, 186)

That habit of thinking in clichés and generalisations which is the overt expression of the ignorance born of a sense of insuperable difference is, nevertheless, as we have seen, one that Gordimer herself has remained subject to in certain ways, and the entrenchment of an 'us-versus-them' mental set symbolically underpins Gordimer's fictional discourse throughout her work. However, whereas in the later novels division is understood to be based on ideological and political differences, Helen experiences 'difference' in *The Lying Days* as a simple 'fact of nature'. Her world is premised on the idea of the binary opposition between white and black which apartheid has transformed into a 'given', and her sense of alienation and exclusion is overwhelming:

I had an almost physical sensation of being a stranger in what I had always taken unthinkingly as the familiarity of home. I felt myself among strangers; I had grown up all my life among strangers: the Africans . . . (186)

The centrality of Helen's insight for Gordimer herself is attested to in her choice of title for her next novel, *A World of Strangers*. Thus, we may say that, paradoxically, both Helen and Gordimer in a sense come full circle: the threatening but fascinating 'Others' who are initially defensively relegated to a sub-human context prove themselves after all to be unassimilable into the white world despite the most generous of impulses to include them, and the extent to which they remain ineluctably strangers must be reluctantly accepted. Gordimer's own tentative overtures towards the black world must be seen as taking place within the context of these early perceptions, and both the respect granted to and the idealisation of black figures in the later fiction – figures who remain always just beyond our grasp within their own remote and infinitely unfathomable worlds – are arguably rooted in the frustrations of such experiences.

In *The Lying Days* Gordimer offers us in effect a history of this growth to a kind of bitter knowledge. At the level of generality the novel lays the blame for failures in black-white relationships at the door of prejudice, and goes on to indict both the self-indulgent liberalism which fails to combat it effectively and the racist régime which institutionalises it. Helen must learn to accept the reality of the barriers set up by apartheid and the impossibility of breaking them down through an individual and isolated act of goodwill; her naïve idealism must make way for an understanding of the extent to which she too is imprisoned by the system she is learning to reject. The attempt to bridge the gap between herself and Mary is abandoned as irresolvable, and in Part III of the novel she retreats into the private world of her love affair with Paul Clark, her involvement in the issues raised by apartheid restricted to her irritation with Paul's futile attempts to work within the system to change it. Although she becomes increasingly more sensitive to his compromised position, she herself is only jolted out of the indefinable malaise of her immersion in subjectivity when, in a characteristically epiphanic episode, she finds herself inescapably confronted with the brutality of the system under which she lives when she witnesses the death of a black 'rioter' who is shot down by the police before her eyes. Her sudden grasp of the fact that she has failed to 'connect' meaningfully both with those close to her and with her social situation in general is the catalyst for her decision to leave Africa for Europe in an attempt to escape the apartheid impasse.

But Helen has more to learn in her last few days in Durban while waiting for her ship to leave. In the case of Mary, she had experienced the divide between the two of them as imposed by forces external to herself; now she must learn how thoroughly entrenched in her own psychic life the universal phenomenon of prejudice is. Thus the novel's commentary on the public invasiveness of institutionalised racism is combined with a dissection of the ways in which unconsciously internalised prejudices

such as anti-Semitism may also distort and blight potential.[27] Part
of Helen's task is to discover what it is that has stunted her relationship with the Jew, Joel Aaron. The answer to her question to
Joel at the end of the novel – 'Do you really think it might have
been because you are a Jew and I'm a Gentile?' (*The Lying Days*,
359) – is self-evident. That Gordimer clearly intends her readers
to see the prejudices which fuel both racist and anti-Semitic responses as arising from a single source is evident at a number of
earlier points in the novel. Helen links Joel and Mary as equally
positive influences upon her emancipation from her parents'
mores: earlier in the novel a symbolic weight is lent to the fact
that Joel has grown up at the mine's Concession Stores, which are
patronised only by blacks and are out of bounds for the child
Helen, and his origins there link him with the oppressed and suggest a shared victimhood. The novel goes on to develop construc-
tive parallels between anti-black and anti-Jewish feeling, which
are apparent in the emphasis on the subconscious processes
which cause Helen to link apparently unrelated experiences.
Memories emerge and connect with perplexing intensity at apparently inappropriate moments: Helen's uncomfortable feeling,
after she has heard Paul's anecdote about the harassment under
the Mixed Marriages Act of the coloured woman and her old
white husband (259), that her love-making with Paul is under
threat of being exposed to humiliating public scrutiny is strengthened by the sudden invasion of memories of the afternoon she
spent with Joel at MacDonald's Kloof: an afternoon thick with
sexual tensions which were made crudely explicit by the used
condom she discovered stuck under her shoe on her return to the
car (146). This bringing together of three superficially unrelated
incidents has the effect of equating Helen's latent, privately held
anti-Semitism, which prevents the consummation of her relationship with Joel, with the overtly public, destructively absurd,
racist prejudices which seek to justify the excesses of apartheid.
For Helen, the 'unconscious taboo' of 'the difference in national-
ity' is experienced as 'very old, very deep, very senseless' (359-
360). Its effect is a self-generated alienation, experienced as a
form of self-imprisonment, which is all the more painful because
it can neither be blamed on an easily identifiable external source
nor depends upon such simple markers as the colour of a skin.

Helen's inability to transcend the barrier between Jew and Gentile thus becomes symbolic of Gordimer's sense of the immense difficulty of surmounting race barriers not yet even challenged in this early novel. Indeed, *The Lying Days* reflects that earlier and typically South African conviction (upon which the edifice of apartheid comes to be constructed) that differences of blood separate not only black and white but also, in Coetzee's formulation, 'Englishman and Afrikaner, Hottentot and Xhosa, Gentile and Jew. Blood is thus race'.[28] Thus the identification between the oppression of the African and of the Jew introduced in this first novel surfaces repeatedly in Gordimer's fiction; for example in *Occasion for Loving* Gideon Shibalo is presented, in a telling simile, as momentarily forgetting that 'he was an African, burdened, like a Jew, with his category of the chosen, and was aware of himself as a man' (135). The comparison rests upon the assumption that 'the black man's burden' – the task of eradicating the evil of racist oppression – makes his a chosen race, morally elevated above that of his opponents in its defence of absolute, God-given values. Gordimer thus significantly inverts Fanon's well-known equation of Jew and Black as brothers chiefly in misery[29] in a thrust characteristic of her romantic elevation of 'the struggle' throughout her work.

Such inversions are early indicators of the fiction's demonstration of the impossibility of entirely eradicating colour consciousness once it has taken root. It might metamorphose into reverse racism (as in Black Consciousness ideology) or resurface as *négritude*, but it cannot be entirely destroyed. Having accepted as an inescapable 'given', then, the existence of a 'colour problem' in the world she inhabits, Gordimer finds herself confronted with two interrelated problems: firstly, how to represent the black 'Other' in ways which will counteract negative stereotypes and eventually make conceivable an ultimate transcendence of colour-consciousness in a utopian future; and, secondly, how to live as a white African in what she is convinced from very early on is both morally and pragmatically the black man's Africa. The *leitmotif* of the ten novels is in fact to be found in Toby's early question. 'If I went on living here, how should I live?' (*A World of Strangers*, 258).

'No, I'm go to Gala. Colonel him back'

In confronting the first problem, that of the representation of the black 'Other', the fundamental issue Gordimer has had to resolve in the fiction has been that of language; that is, how to cause her black protagonists to speak. On the one hand, it is through the manipulation of language patterns that she has most revealingly 'placed' her black characters in relationship to white culture. On the other hand, however, the choices she has made have not only advanced the ends she has set herself but also serve to illuminate in perhaps unintended ways the extent to which her own consciousness remains affected by the principle of division which underpins her society.

Fanon (with whose work Gordimer is familiar) has eloquently illuminated the issues at stake in the choice of a language for her black characters in his assertion that

> to speak . . . means above all to assume a culture . . . A man who has a language consequently possesses the world expressed in and implied by that language . . . Every colonized people – in other words, every people in whose soul an inferiority complex has been created by the death and burial of its local cultural original-ity – finds itself face to face with the language of the civilizing nation; that is, with the culture of the mother country. The colonized is elevated above his jungle status in proportion to his adoption of the mother country's cultural standards. He becomes whiter as he renounces his blackness . . . Nothing is more astonishing than to hear a black man express himself properly, for then in truth he is putting on the white world . . . he is a complete replica of the white man.[30]

Gordimer herself has resolved the issue of language in the fiction in two uneasily coexistent ways. As we have seen, in the early novels, written at a time when hegemonic apartheid seemed to have a monolithic and unshakeable hold upon the country, her project is simply, in Ellison's words, to 'challenge the apparent forms of reality',[31] and to claim an implicit equality for black South Africans on the basis of their common membership in a 'family of man' within the framework of Western humanist values. This is primarily done by presenting the black South African as 'one of us' through the medium of language: thus the black

student, Mary, depicted as struggling with abysmal living standards in *The Lying Days,* almost entirely isolated by colour and
origin on the white campus, and too ill-educated to be able to
discriminate between the important and the peripheral in her
note-taking at lectures, is made to speak what Helen illuminatingly describes as

> the faint stilted English of the European-educated African
> woman, out of whom all the buoyancy, music, and spontaneity
> that is in the voices of nursemaids and servants seem to have been
> hushed by responsibility. (130)

A marked ambivalence of response is concealed below the bland
surface of this depiction. On the one hand, the imagery implies
that European influences have an alienating impact upon black
Africans and that the English language does not 'belong' in
Africa, as is made evident in the presentation of the black
woman's language as both itself devoid of and simultaneously
destructive of Africa's 'buoyancy, music, and spontaneity'. At the
same time, embedded in the passage is the information that European expectations of Africans are determined by their limited
contact with the serving classes in the reference to nursemaids
and servants and, indeed, that the 'true' African is the working-
class African. On the other hand, Mary's English is represented as
fluent and idiomatic despite the inclusion of the qualifier 'stilted',
and Gordimer inserts no markers to suggest cultural unfamiliar-
ity, or variations in accent or grammatical construction. Mary is
almost as indistinguishable aurally from her white counterparts
as are all of Gordimer's educated black protagonists.

The effect of such a representation is twofold. On the one
hand, the fluent English given to black Africans throughout the
fiction where there is a conjunction of class, or an ideological
brotherhood, between white and black, suggests the symbolic
collapse of the barriers erected by apartheid, and offers an affirmation of the possibility that the dream of a class- and colour-
blind community of men might one day be realisable. Thus the
linguistic ease of Steven Sitole in *A World of Strangers*, of Gideon
Shibalo in *Occasion for Loving*, of Luke Fokase in *The Late
Bourgeois World*, of Mweta and Shinza in *A Guest of Honour*, of
Marisa Kgosana and her friends in *Burger's Daughter*, and of

Whaila, Reuel and their associates in *A Sport of Nature*, is made
to symbolise the possibility and promise of a non-racial and egalitarian post-apartheid society. But, on the other hand, such a
society is conceived of entirely within the framework of those
decent, Anglo-Saxon social values encoded in the linguistic habits
of that class of well-educated, upper-middle-class, white, English-
speaking South Africans to which Gordimer herself belongs, and
on whose language patterns the black characters model their
own.[32] In essence, therefore, Gordimer, though excoriating the
hypocrisies and ambivalences of her own segment of white society, nevertheless salvages its traditional values (such as 'fair play',
politeness, ironic understatement, and tangential, throw-away
humour to name a few) in the linguistic codes which deny the
differences so emphatically stressed elsewhere in the fiction, and
so produces a group of black Africans assimilable by the white
imagination precisely because they appear to be fundamentally
white-under-the-skin. They are each 'one of *us*', in so far as they
appear to share the cultural values of an English colonial society.

The historical tendency among black Africans to adopt white
Western values has of course been criticised by Fanon, among
others, as a form of cultural neo-colonialism. He attacks the
black man's eagerness to adopt European forms and styles as in-
dicative of the Negro's continuing inferiority complex, which he
identifies as most prevalent among the educated. Gordimer gives
us an intriguing example of such eagerness in *A World of Strangers*, in which she describes Sam's attempt to 'live decently' amid
the squalor of the townships (131-32) in a passage strongly remi-
niscent of Dickens's description of Wemmick's 'castle' in *Great
Expectations*.[33] The echo may not be accidental, since Dickens
and Gordimer are both confronting similar issues of survival in a
hostile society, but Gordimer is not content with a simple representation of Sam's solution to his problem. Toby is made to wonder whether, 'if living decently, following a modest taste for
civilised things, meant living eccentrically, or remarkably, one
might prefer to refuse the right masquerading as a privilege', as
Steven Sitole does (*A World of Strangers*, 133). Most illuminating
to note is that here, as elsewhere in the fiction, 'decency' and 'civilisation' are implicitly defined from an entirely Eurocentric perspective, in strong contrast to Fanon's position: the values remain

unquestioned even as the possibility of their attainment within a particular politico-historical context is problematised.

Implicitly contrasted to such figures as Sam, Gideon, Mweta and Whaila in the fiction, and separated from them by class and language, is that other group of black Africans with which the ordinary white South African is most familiar, and which appears frequently – occasionally even at centre-stage – in the novels: the servant population.[34] That white protagonists will have servants is taken for granted, as we have seen, throughout the work. Not only Maureen, Helen and Jessie, growing up on the East Rand, have servants in their homes, but Cecil Rowe, Rosa Burger, Antonia and Pauline all employ maid servants to wait upon them and to care for whatever children there may be; and, in the independent African country of *A Guest of Honour*, Gordimer ironically reverses this South African norm by making Bray's white lover, Rebecca, for a short time the servant of a black family.

Yet, with very few exceptions, certain atypical characteristics strongly mark these relationships between employer and employee. To begin with, the text emphasises a degree of consistent loyalty, trustworthiness, responsibility and indeed affectionate friendship between master and servant extraordinary in what is traditionally a stressful relationship. It is noteworthy that Gordimer's white protagonists are invariably greeted with deep warmth, enthusiasm and pleasure by their black servants and friends. (Rosa's midnight telephone conversation with Baasie in London seems an exception; but Baasie was, of course, never a servant.) Kalimo, Bray's old servant in *A Guest of Honour*, who has 'come more than a thousand miles, out of retirement in his village, to claim him . . . to cook and clean for him as if his were the definitive claim on Kalimo's life' (113), becomes the prototype of all those servants in the novels whose devotion reinscribes the comforting myth of the affectionate loyalty of the old family retainer which Gordimer, surprisingly, appears to appeal to without qualification in such passages. It is a myth which has traditionally helped to salve the consciences of those who have benefited from the inevitable exploitation of others that is fundamental to a class-based society even when race is not an issue, and its deployment in Gordimer's work here is curiously at odds with her political insight at other levels.[35] She neither offers images of mutual exploitation nor attempts to reproduce the stock complaints which are understood to be usual between maid and madam. Indeed, that her images of this type of relationship are highly idealised is suggested by the contrary picture given by Jacklyn Cock and Ellen Kuzwayo, who have both highlighted the typical problems of black South African women working as domestic servants in illuminating accounts which stress unwanted pregnancies from their employers, the killing of infants thus conceived to prevent prosecution under the Immorality Act, inadequate accommodation, low wages, exploitative hours, and a variety of other well-documented disabilities.[36]

Three points may be made about Gordimer's idiosyncratic representation of employer/employee relationships within an apartheid context. Firstly, we may speculate that, by remaining silent about the problems which typically beset such relationships, Gordimer deliberately distances herself from the clichéd complaints about 'the girl' and 'the boy' which, in terms of another stereotype, are said to form the typical substance of white female chit-chat at South African suburban afternoon tea-parties. Instead, her idealised representation suggests that traditionally problematic relationships can be transformed by a mutual respect which is both colour-blind and premised upon a belief in the fundamental equality of master and servant within the framework of a sense of shared humanity. In support of this argument, Gordimer shows her black servants as interacting with their white employers in ways which elide the traditional divisions premised on a sense of hierarchy which have been historically fundamental to such relationships around the world. For example, Jethro and Bettie in *A Sport of Nature* initiate conversation with Hillela around the swimming pool and in the kitchen in an atypical assertion of implicit equality, while in the heyday of apartheid Rosa Burger settles down to tea and a chat in the kitchen with the black woman who comes in to do her chores before the day's work is begun.

Secondly, it is clear that Gordimer's emphasis upon warm friendships between master and servant is intended to establish the credentials of her white characters as well-meaning liberals by showing them as succeeding in relationships which apartheid ideology seeks to make impossible. In this reading, every successful relationship of this kind is in essence a subversive and potentially revolutionary one, and contributes in its own small way to the furtherance of the struggle. Thirdly, the insistence on presenting black servants as always cheerfully devoted, and black friends and acquaintances as always enthusiastically welcoming, constructs in the novels an image of black society for white readers as one of overwhelming human warmth and mutual support under oppression, in sharp contrast to an alienated and spiritually sterile white world. Such an emphasis is aimed at allaying white fears of *swart gevaar* (the 'black peril'), and implicitly promises those whites who place their faith in 'African humanism' both absolution and ultimate acceptance in the new Africa which will emerge from the ruins of the old.

There are of course a few servants who lead a double life in the novels. Jacobus, in *The Conservationist*, and July of *July's People* represent two instances of Fanon's insistence that

> the black man has two dimensions. One with his fellows, the other with the white man. A Negro behaves differently with a white man and with another Negro. That this self-division is a direct result of colonialist subjugation is beyond question.[37]

Gordimer, however, in contrast to Fanon, sketches in the gap between masks and reality as a strategy for that self-preservation and survival which will enable the individual to retain a sense of power, rather than as a symptom of self-division, and we find neither gap nor self-division suggested in her depiction of other servants in the novels, such as Eveline (of *A World of Strangers*), Kalimo (of *A Guest of Honour*), and Jethro and Bettie (of *A Sport of Nature*). As we gave seen, she also typically avoids dealing in any detail with the realities of what it might be like to be a black servant under the apartheid régime. Instead, she either takes the presence of the servants for granted without problematising their existence in white lives, or focuses upon the effect of the gap between appearances and reality upon her white characters' perceptions, rather than attempting an analysis of the effects of such role-playing on, for example, the identity construction of her black figures. Consequently her servants and workers remain curiously flat and one-dimensional figures. Gordimer does not ironise their status as mere foils to the drama that unfolds in the lives of those they serve, although she is well aware that servants are typically relegated to such a status in the consciousness of those actual white South Africans whose failings Gordimer so caustically dissects at other levels.

A further anomaly in Gordimer's representation of black servants in the novels, given the perfect English her revolutionaries and 'fringe' blacks speak, is that she chooses to make them speak in *pidgin* English. For example, although Bray and Kalimo can converse in the Gala language which Bray learnt to speak fluently while on his previous tour of duty as a colonial officer in the province, Kalimo's first words are in broken English:

> Festus he send me. He send me say, Colonel he coming back, one month, two month, then go to Gala. I'm greet my wife, I'm greet my sons. They say where you go? No, I'm go to Gala. Colonel him back. No, I go. I must go. (*A Guest of Honour*, 112)

Although July and Jacobus speak correctly when they converse with other blacks (in what we are asked to read as an English translation of the African language they speak), they speak in pidgin whenever they talk to whites. Here such linguistic variations are intended as ironic reminders of those masks of which Fanon speaks which are worn by blacks in the presence of whites. It is worth noting here that, other than Bray, not one of Gordimer's protagonists – not even Hillela – learns to speak a black language. White failure to do so has frequently been attacked as a typical expression of white cultural arrogance; but, in an interview with Anthony Sampson in 1987, Gordimer attempted to justify this aspect of her work by claiming that, although she herself would like to be able to speak an African language,

> knowing the language doesn't necessarily mean understanding between yourself and those who speak it; identification with them is the real understanding – the real connection.[38]

The untenable equation here between identification and understanding is given some specious substance in Gordimer's claim in the same interview that, while Bram Fischer spoke no African language, exploitative and racist white farmers often do. However, in implicitly denying the extent to which culture is encoded in language and becomes accessible to the outsider only with the acquisition of that language, Gordimer again betrays the Eurocentric and colonialist bias of her perspectives, one which is also evident in her implicit patronage of blacks in her deployment of pidgin English in the novels. Fanon is again a useful guide to the way in which pidgin functions as a marker of oppression in colonial fiction:

> The black man is supposed to be a good nigger... To make him talk pidgin is to fasten him to the effigy of him, to snare him, to imprison him, the eternal victim of an essence, of an *appearance* for which he is not responsible... What is important is... to teach the Negro not to be a slave of their archetypes.[39]

Gordimer, however, appears unaware of such connotations attached to the use of pidgin, and is instead, at one level, clearly simply interested in finding ways to transcribe with accuracy the speech patterns she has heard about her within her own Johannesburg context. Thus the pidgin English given to Kalimo reappears with exactly the same patterns of linguistic aberration in the speech of every servant and worker from *The Lying Days* to *A Sport of Nature*. On the one hand, we might interpret this both as evidence of Gordimer's commitment to realism and of her respect for those whose speech patterns she listens to and transcribes with such careful accuracy. But it also becomes clear as we follow this phenomenon through the ten novels that the use of pidgin must be read as a class marker, differentiating the largely invisible serving classes from those blacks whose English marks them as 'one of us'. Although the insensitivity to regional and tribal differences in Gordimer's reproduction of pidgin English may be intended to foreground the pervasiveness of class and racial oppression in colonial Africa, her stress on the unique amity of the relationships between master and servant in the novels deprives such an emphasis of political and ideological significance, and makes of it a curiously empty gesture.

'the very first man was a black man'

That Gordimer was aware of a certain interpretation which could be attached to her representation of black characters by unsympathetic readers within a racist context is clear throughout the fiction, particularly in those passages in which she ironically places racist insults in the mouths of her characters, or forestalls criticism by delineating the parameters of the response her images might stimulate. In *A Sport of Nature*, for instance, Hillela is shown to be aware that her friendship with Sela might well be seen by others to be the stuff of farce: 'Selina Montgomery and Hillela Kgomani – personages in some race joke: there was this black woman married to a white man, and this white woman married to a black man . . . ' (203). Gordimer responds to such challenges with an energy and defiance born both of her contempt for racist attitudes and of her long and thoughtful consideration of the problems associated with her treatment of such sensitive issues in her work.

The intensity of commitment she brings to her interpretation originates in the weight she gives to the second problem with which she grapples in the novels: how to escape the colonial heritage and become a true 'white African'. Hillela is the first figure in the fiction to liberate herself fully from the taint of apartheid. Helped by fate, fortune and history into her position of solemn pre-eminence at the Independence ceremony at the close of the novel, she represents Gordimer's solution to the problem implicit in Bray's complaint that 'a white man in Africa doesn't know what to see himself as' (*A Guest of Honour*, 139). The core theme which connects the ten novels is indeed the search which runs through all of them for a way to achieve integration with an Africa that has appeared to allow its white children only the mutually untenable options of either internal or external exile: imprisonment within the jails of the apartheid régime has seemed the only alternative to that imprisonment within a white skin which is a fundamental metaphor in the work as a whole.

A Sport of Nature offers a recapitulation of and a guide to the various escape routes from and solutions to this dilemma which the earlier novels have tentatively explored. Gordimer's liberal whites, who have suffered the rejection of their efforts to liberate both self and other by the exclusivity of Black Consciousness ideology, finally succeed in transcending that ideology in a triumphant Pan-Africanism. Pauline glories in her renewed (albeit anonymous) contact with blacks at the 'All-in African Conference' 'after having been shut away, so white, so long' (59), and Sasha probably articulates Gordimer's own sense of liberation from the strictures of Black Consciousness in his comment: 'There was a lot of shit to take from them – blacks . . . Not being needed at all [was] the biggest shit of the lot' (319). For, by this stage, explains the narrator, in a comment which revealingly suggests Gordimer's Eurocentric assumption that the Black Consciousness Movement grew primarily out of an African sense of inferiority, 'Blacks had sufficient confidence to invite whites to join the liberation struggle with them again' (321).

Despite the emphasis on a non-racial utopian future in this novel, however, colour does not cease to be significant. In a movement of tit-for-tat, whites come to suspect their colour to be a liability in a liberated black Africa in which they find themselves subordinated to blacks in a neat reversal of the previous historical situation. Hillela comes to feel that her pale body is 'unfinished, left off, somewhere' (177), and finds (in a deliberate reversal of a metaphor first given general currency in Ralph Ellison's 1952 novel, *Invisible Man*) that 'in a black country, to be white was to feel invisible' (168). The answer, it is implied, is to 'give up being white', and Hillela, in a tentative retrospective defence of white South African liberalism, muses on the difficulty of this: 'I was in a family . . . they wanted to but they didn't seem to know how?' (186).

Hillela's singularity lies in her ability to intuit a way through this mine field, but an ongoing uncertainty as to the 'how' of such an identification with Black Africa shapes both the choice of perspective and of narrative voice in the novels. Indeed, the narrative tone suggested that it may well be safer, when faced with such a dilemma, to stand back rather than to make efforts which will almost certainly be misunderstood. Thus the invitation to identify with her protagonists' confusion which is implicit in Gordimer's use of a stream of consciousness technique, is undermined in novels such as *The Conservationist* by the ironic detachment of the narrative voice, whose characteristic and self-protective stance is that of the observer, of the reporter and of the historian. Ironic detachment not only serves to mark the narrator's distance from the anguished impotence of characters marginalised both by subjective guilt and by objective historical process, but also protects both author and reader from the challenge of direct action. As we have noted, in fact, it is those throughout the novels who agonise over the dilemmas of the South African deadlock whose voices are foregrounded, whereas those who choose to act recede further and further from centre stage. Thus, as we have seen, Max has no voice at all in *The Late Bourgeois World*; Gideon and Ann's affair is presented through the eyes of Jessie; Bray is killed before he can put his plans to assist Shinza into action; Antonia's voice is heard only in Mehring's memory of her castigation of his pseudo-liberalism; and in *Burger's Daughter* and *A Sport of Nature* Rosa and Hillela progressively disappear into the distance of speculation, third-person reportage and rumour as their commitments draw them into the maelstrom. The emotional energies of the novels are clearly focused upon dilemmas rather than solutions; at one level they may indeed be seen as themselves standing as evidence of the spiritual malaise which they seek to identify and condemn.

Yet it is the overwhelming need to find ways to 'belong' and the repeated frustration of this quest which lie at the core of the novels. Gordimer offers her characters what appear to be only two routes to integration: through a powerful identification with the public struggle which is given concrete expression in, and integrity by, the political activism that such emotional commitments make possible, and which finds its conclusion in either jail or exile; and through a passionate emotional and physical identification with the 'Other' in private love affairs across the colour bar. It is the latter route upon which the novels most frequently focus, as we have seen, and the tensions between the self-preserving need for detachment and the heat of passionate identification become most noticeable in the complexity of Gordimer's treatment of the issues aroused by sexual attractions across the colour bar. This area has traditionally offered rich pickings to the South African writer, but Gordimer has been sharply aware of the dangers associated with 'the miscegenation novel'. In *A World of Strangers* she designated such novels (in Toby's sharply dismissive words) as 'as regular a South African export as gold or fruit' (46), and in 1968 she attacked

> the rubbishy work by whites in the past few years, stories and books calculated to skate just near enough to certain areas mined by censorship to provide the reading public with a vicarious thrill, but not close enough to blow the author into the limbo of the banned. The region chosen is invariably that of the Immorality Act, needless to say; and it is one of the paradoxes brought about by censorship that, by making a feint at the colour bar law without actually connecting, the potboiler producer lays claim to being a 'serious' writer, however execrable his writing may be.[40]

Gordimer's awareness of the extent to which this area is beset by stereotypes goes some way towards explaining why only three of her novels (*Occasion for Loving*, *A Sport of Nature* and *My Son's Story*) attempt a representation of such love affairs, although sexual attraction across the colour bar outside an actual affair is given a significantly central place in the fiction. The evidence of the novels suggests that the dearth of full-blown love affairs in the fiction is at least partly a consequence of Gordimer's sense of how psychically deep-rooted the taboos against miscegenation in a racist society are. For example, in the early novels she implicitly suggests that the archetypal identification of the black man with rape and murder, which traditional Judaeo-Christian colour symbolism has encouraged, implants almost insurmountable unconscious barriers to such affairs. In this paradigm, the oppressor invests in the 'Other' that capacity for invasion and violence of which he himself is guilty and of which he fears to become a victim in his turn. It is this spectre which Gordimer has her protagonist confront in *Occasion for Loving*: Jessie's need to come to terms with the affair between Gideon and Ann pushes her towards a realisation of the extent to which she herself has harboured such unconscious sexual fears of the black male in the depths of her psyche from her earliest girlhood. She gradually comes to understand that for her, as for other young colonial girls, the figure she feared might materialise behind her back in the empty bathroom was the figure of the predatory black male:

> . . . the shape of cold terror that used to impress itself on the back of her neck when she turned her back to the dark passage behind

the bathroom door at night, bending to wash her face. Had she ever, in the twenty or so years since then, found out who it was that threatened to come up behind her? (69)

The very first man was a black man ... the black man I must never be left alone with in the house. (253)

Only when she realises that 'she herself could have been Ann once, somewhere' (249) does she come to the end of her own personal journey towards a grasp of the true nature of her situation as a South African. In this way the centrality of Jessie's observer status in relation to the affair between Ann and Gideon in the resolution of the novel's themes is made clear; their affair is the catalyst for the slow growth of Jessie's ability to understand in her heart and in her bones what she has known hitherto only with her head: the shared humanity of black and white. The fear she suffered from is finally demythologised and neutralised in *A Sport of Nature*, where Hillela actually encounters the figure of Jessie's bathroom nightmares and finds him entirely harmless, even somewhat pathetic. He metamorphoses into an old black man (probably intended to represent Chief Albert Luthuli), who is a house-guest like Hillela in Pauline's home:

The two guests in the house – the permanent one and the temporary one – met face to face again. She was in her skimpy cotton pyjamas, running barefoot at dawn to the bathroom, he was coming from there, the big, slow black man, knotted calves bare, feet pushed into unlaced shoes, wearing an old army surplus greatcoat over his nakedness. Against the indignity, for him, the child and the old man passed each other without a sign. (25)

The incident carries no thematic weight in the later novel, except in so far as we recognise it as a resonant sequel to Jessie's fears, and take note that the emphasis has shifted away from Jessie's self-directed concern for her own inviolability to Hillela's other-directed concern for the old Chief's dignity. Only when Jessie frees herself of such unconscious fears, and emerges from the innocence of limited self-awareness and ignorant good-will into the complexities of a flawed reality, can she achieve a true liberation from her unconscious heritage of race prejudice, and thus leave 'her mother's house' once and for all (for, at the novel's beginning, we are told that 'she had never been out of the garden or challenged the flaming angels at the gate' (*Occasion for Loving*, 9).

Yet, in the decades before *A Sport of Nature* was written, such knowledge brings with it no forgiveness. Gordimer posits no conclusion to or escape from the bleak impoverishment of the human spirit which apartheid imposes upon its victims. The romance between Ann and Gideon in *Occasion for Loving* is given short shrift within a moral context which stresses that the corollary to his private commitment to Ann is the betrayal of his public responsibilities to himself and his community. For him, as for Steven Sitole in *A World of Strangers* before him, that positive identification with his 'blackness' which will absolve and integrate the homeless psyche is represented not as a given but as something to be aspired to; liberation into the new Africa must be earned, *even* by black men, only by a conscious embrace of the responsibilities imposed by a particular political destiny. It is within such a framework that Sam's caustic dismissal of politically cynical Steven as no more than 'a white man in a black man's skin' (161) may be justified, while Gideon is condemned for his defection into the self-indulgence of a romantic apoliticism which 'the struggle' cannot afford and which destroys both his integrity and his sense of identity as a black man. Both Gideon and Ann indulge themselves at the expense of betraying other commitments which should have priority: thus Ann's flirtation with Gideon not only makes a cuckold of her husband, but also gradually exposes the fundamentally destructive irresponsibility of her ultimately exploitative apoliticism. The fact that she is a foreigner, and has therefore never internalised the colour bar, means that she feels neither guilt nor defiance in the face of the legal restrictions on such affairs as hers, and her concomitant freedom from the moral agonising which liberal South Africans are prey to is initially very attractive to Jessie, who is somewhat envious of that political innocence which enables Ann to see only the 'warmth and vitality, the zest and freshness', and 'the defiant fun' of township life, and none of its 'uncertainty, pain, and brashness' (*Occasion for Loving*, 224). Gideon, too, finds her innocence both extraordinary and refreshing, and is unwilling to disillusion her: he values the fact that 'she did not love him *across the colour bar*; for her the colour bar did not exist' (268). Never-

theless it is significant that the novel does not validate such romantic colour-blindness. Ann's ignorance of and insensitivity to
the realities of the world she moves in is a central factor in their
failure to convert the relationship into one which could respond
productively and creatively to the political issues which circum-
scribe them, and her very lack of a true emotional connection
with that reality makes it impossible for Gordimer to make her
the central consciousness of a novel fundamentally concerned
with the growth of the insider's understanding of how thoroughly apartheid has succeeded in making prey to corruption
even the most private of worlds, that inhabited by two lovers.

Hillela is the only one of Gordimer's characters in the novels
to cross the racial divide successfully in her affairs with black
Africans, but that she can do so only outside the country, and
that she reaches her apotheosis only in some mythical future
time, emphasises Gordimer's belief that no such experiment can
be successful within the framework of the apartheid state as she
knows it. The novel attempts to weld a symbolic connection between two of Gordimer's most cherished dreams: on the one
hand, the individual's fullest realisation of her capacity for sensual and emotional fulfilment, and, on the other, a public and
political resolution of the problems that beset Southern Africa
within the framework of the finest Western ideals of democracy
and civilised values. Yet Hillela's sensual innocence and her
politically eclectic upbringing, the combined effect of which
leaves her as much without an internalised colour bar as Ann
Davis (and which makes her in essence as much of a foreigner as
Ann is, but in this case within her own land), cannot guarantee
her or her society a more promising future while she remains
within the boundaries of the apartheid state. Gordimer's construction in this novel of a metaphoric framework which opposes
the idea of internal South African imprisonment to external Pan-
African freedom once again emphasises that she cannot conceive
of an individual freedom within the confines of apartheid which
would be capable of transcending its public moral corruption.
The myth which the novel inscribes articulates a perspective of
yearning in which the object of desire is distanced ever further
from us, until at the novel's end, as we have seen, Hillela appears
only as a distant, depersonalised speck on the stage of the inde-

pendence celebrations, entirely subsumed within her African identity, while the actual white political activists of the novel, Sasha and his mother, Pauline, ironically follow the proceedings only on television from their separate places of exile in Holland and England.

The symbolic significance of Hillela's sexual career for the beleaguered liberal imagination is suggested in a passage in which Glenn, in an article which focuses not on Gordimer but on Plomer's *Turbott Wolfe*, directly offers a summary of the paradigms developed in *A Sport of Nature*, and ironically illuminates surprising common elements between Millin's and Gordimer's vision:

> The crucial element of the future would not be political ties but the sexual-emotional ties between liberated Afrikaner/South African women and educated black men . . . The well-meaning sensitive white liberals lack the force to impose their vision on the future, which they abandon for exile, leaving the marriage between a member of the new black élite and the white woman willing to become indigenous as the only challenge to colonial power and prejudice . . . The highly educated or particularly talented black man . . . becomes appealing as a new social force to a white woman who senses some kind of social decadence or spiritual or emotional etiolation in white men.[41]

Such a scenario is both implicitly foreshadowed in the illicit attractions between black and white in *Occasion for Loving*, *The Late Bourgeois World* and *July's People*, and also reflected in the stress placed upon the symbolic value of Hillela's marriage to Whaila as an impetus to hope in *A Sport of Nature*. In the latter novel, we are told that, whenever political exiles in London came across

> a white South African a black had taken as mate, there was to be seen in the union assurance that they too could be given absolution for their country's colonial past . . . [Hillela was] an embodiment of their political and ethical credo, non-racial unity against the oppression of race. (197)

It is in such emphases that Gordimer escapes the sensationalism associated with the stereotypical miscegenation novel, replacing its cheap appeal to curiosity with her own particular style of romantic idealism. It is an idealism which is unexpectedly reflected in the scant attention Gordimer pays to the well-established tradition in colonial fiction of focusing on the liaisons between white men and black women; instead, the novels concentrate almost exclusively upon the emotional and sexual attractions which arise between white women and black men. Although Fanon has suggested that such relationships should be understood as merely another form of colonisation ('In loving me she proves that I am worthy of white love. I am loved as a white man'[42]), Gordimer both offers the more conventional reading that the possession of a white woman is a source of prestige for black men – no more than another notch on the stick in the age-less game of male competition (*A Guest of Honour*, 417) – and at a more general level presents the relationship between the alien-ated female insider and the oppressed male outsider as symbolic of their mutual need for liberation from the oppressive restric-tions of apartheid in its many manifestations. In fact, the empha-sis here is curiously enough on a revised version of the white appropriation of black resources characteristic of the imperialist stance: the vision is one of black empowerment of atrophied white energies – a symbolic fertilisation of the white world in a final transformative and redemptive endeavour. Such a pattern is latent in the relationship between Helen and Joel as insider Chris-tian and outsider Jew in *The Lying Days*, between Anna Louw and her South African Indian husband in *A World of Strangers*, between Ann and Gideon in *Occasion for Loving*, and in the flir-tation between Elizabeth and Luke Fokase in *The Late Bourgeois World*. It is consummated in Hillela's two marriages in *A Sport of Nature*, where the reversal of pattern is made explicit in Hillela's quest to be accepted as the *white outsider* in *black Africa*. It is also the model governing the abrasive relationships between Rosa and Baasie, and between Maureen and July. In the one instance in the novels where a white man 'stoops' to a sexual interlude with a 'coloured' woman, Mehring's encounter with the hitchhiker in *The Conservationist*, the incident symbolises the reverse of the potentially redemptive connections listed above: it serves simply to confirm his own inner corruption as a closet racist. The girl's youth in this episode is as significant as her col-our, and the powerful parallels drawn between her and Mehring's other three women (his white leftist girlfriend Antonia, the daughter of Mehring's friend the deceased businessman, and the Portuguese girl on the airplane) blur the distinctions between all of them in order to emphasise symbolically the essentially exploitative impact of Mehring on his environment, both in his private and in his public life, which places renewal and redemption beyond his reach.

'the Ruritanian pan-Africa of triumphant splendour and royal beauty'

The intense colour consciousness which directs the development of such paradigms will alert us to that other centrally significant marker in the fiction: Gordimer's increasingly defiant incorporation of an element of *négritude* in the novels, and in particular of the concept that 'black is beautiful'.[43] Indeed, one of the most startling components of her work, for a liberal South African readership which has traditionally believed in the virtues of colour-blindness, is her inscription of images and attitudes which foreground rather than elide racial differences. In emphasising these precisely observed markers of difference, Gordimer paradoxically reverses their effect, constructing instead a celebration of differences in the novels which implicitly answers Jessie's early agonised question in *Occasion for Loving*:

> if you did not find blackness abhorrent and outcast, was the only alternative the fastidious repression of all personal responses in the common denominator of a shared humanity? (249)

Gordimer's refusal to allow her protagonists to repress such personal responses, and the resultant foregrounding of a pervasive colour-consciousness in the novels, produces at times the effect of a reverse racism – as Coetzee has pointed out, such a focus upon what he terms 'ethnic markings' in South African writing has been 'the embodiment in novelistic practice of what we can justifiably call a racial consciousness'.[44] We may note, however, a degree of contradiction in Gordimer's responses here: on the one hand, her practice elevates colour to the status of an absolute difference which, in effect, suggests her inability to emerge entirely from the racist cognitive paradigms of the world in which she grew up. As

Gates has argued, if we see society as fundamentally constituted by the difference between black and white, and thus submit to a colour-based construction of reality, then within such a determining paradigm *all* difference must be reduced to this simple binary opposition.[45] On the other hand however, the impetus in the work towards the ideal of non-racial equality and the emphasis on a universal brotherhood of man under the skin implicitly incorporates that sense of race as historically constructed and politically contested, one which we have already noted as shaping the representation of Steven Sitole and Gideon Shibalo, and which coexists in some tension with the entrenchment of difference inscribed so powerfully in the imagery of the novels.[46]

Colour consciousness asserts itself in the novels in two forms. On the one hand, there are numerous images which (in passing) articulate a wondering, sometimes negative sense of the exotic 'Otherness' of blackness. For example, Bray notices a servant whose grin shows 'some pigmentation abnormality in a pink inner lip spotted like a Dalmatian' (*A Guest of Honour*, 34); the servant, Bettie, is seen by Hillela to be 'crying, the flanges of her black nose lined with rosy wet' (*A Sport of Nature*, 37); Toby describes an African waiter as having 'the sweaty monkey-face that I associate with the few new-born babies I've been unable to avoid seeing' (*A World of Strangers*, 18), and he must finally unwillingly acknowledge that Steven 'was not like us, after all; after all, he was black' (173). In their apparent inscription of a residual race-prejudice made evident by the sharp distaste which at times clearly informs them, such images implicitly counterbalance the charge of reverse racism in their focus upon what appears exotic or ineluctably alien in the 'Other'. When we bear in mind, however, that the same precise and impersonal observing eye is frequently trained with an equivalent distaste upon white characters as well, such images may also be read more simply as evidence of Gordimer's characteristically liberal-humanist sense of the inexhaustible fascination of the variety of human phenomena.

Pleasure in the sheer, exotic 'Otherness' of the African is, on the other hand, indeed, a more persistent note in the fiction than the muted element of alienation present at times in Gordimer's inscription of difference; it emerges very early in the novels, already clearly directing the minutely observed description in *Occasion for Loving* of Ann's tentative delight in Gideon's 'smooth skin, hairless, contoured by rib and muscle; the colour of aubergine, but there was no shine to it' (181). The sense of difference as potentially a positive and empowering force is emphasised again in that romantic idealisation of black figures which informs Rosa's description in *Burger's Daughter* of Marisa Kgosana as she is glimpsed in a crowded street:

> In the swaying forward movement of her crested head as she disappeared and reappeared through the shoppers there was only consciousness of the admiration she exacted, with her extravagant dress, the Ruritanian pan-Africa of triumphant splendour and royal beauty that is subject to no known boundaries of old custom or new warring political ideologies in black countries, and to no laws that make blacks' lives mean and degrading in this one. (139)

Rosa's passionate attraction here to a beauty conceived of as quintessentially 'African' should be linked to Fanon's dry comment that 'the presence of Negroes beside the Whites is in a way an insurance policy on humanness. When the whites feel they have become too mechanised, they turn to men of colour to ask them for a little sustenance'.[47] The 'love-affair with black Africa' which informs Gordimer's idealisation of such figures as Marisa and others in the fiction is an index not only of the strength of her need to identify herself emotionally with an idea of Africa which will symbolically both justify and promote revolutionary commitment, but also of her determination to jettison her 'white' allegiances. Thus in *Burger's Daughter* Marisa's 'spendour' acquires its power over Rosa's imagination precisely because it represents everything the spiritually sterile culture of the white suburbs in which Rosa lives is not.

It is in *A Sport of Nature* that Gordimer's ongoing attempts to come to terms with the ineradicable nature of colour-consciousness find their culmination. Her characteristic solution is to turn the awareness of difference on its head and to make of it an asset rather than a liability, thus replacing the conventional humanist claim that 'they' are really like 'us' under the skin with an insistent counterclaim that 'we' are really like 'them' under the skin. In a passage which begins with a reminder that 'skin and hair [in

Africa] . . . has mattered more than anything else in the world'
(177), and in which Hillela goes on to defy a variety of liberal and
racial taboos in a series of apparently naïve questions which
paradoxically serve to emphasise various stereotypes of sexual
difference between white and black, she finally says:

> When you touched me at the beginning (she takes his black hand
> and spreads it on her hip) this was a glove. Really. The blackness
> was a glove. And everywhere, all over you, the black was a cover.
> Something God gave you to wear. Underneath, you must be
> white, like me . . . because that's what I was told, when I was be-
> ing taught not to be prejudiced: underneath, they are all just like
> us. Nobody said we are just like *you*. (178)

In such a celebration of simultaneous similarity and difference,
significantly made possible by the absence in Hillela of both a
rigorous logic and a self-defeating cynicism, the creative force of
her vitality and adaptability is made to overwhelm the potential
embarrassment of those readers who feel, like the white American nurse in the hospital in which Hillela's daughter, Nomzamo,
is born and whom Hillela asks whether the light-skinned baby
will 'grow black', that Hillela's 'confusing joy [in her baby's
blackness] . . . was surely vulgar, if not in some way racist?'
(189). Hilella's resolution of the problem of prejudice in a whole-
hearted affirmation of the *creative potential* of difference characteristically valorises those life affirming, impulsively subjective
thrusts which both override and ultimately give emotional sub-
stances to the 'abstractions of race and politics' (*A World of
Strangers*, 36). Gordimer clearly intends to vest in Hillela those
values which Senghor has claimed as traditionally African, in
opposition to the intellectual detachment of Western culture:

> All these values are essentially informed by intuitive
> reason . . . The sense of communion, the gift of mythmaking, the
> gift of rhythm, such are the essential elements . . . which you will
> find indelibly stamped on all the works and activities of the Black
> Man.[48]

It is the 'African' values vested in her which make Hillela 'a sport
of nature' as far as her white compatriots are concerned[49], but in
the larger world outside South Africa they make her the first true
'white African' in Gordimer's fiction. In the perfect balance of

Hillela's two marriages, Gordimer finally symbolically resolves the tension between public and private commitments: temperament, inclination and history combine to produce an ideal and absolute harmony between the internal and the external worlds.

Hillela's fully achieved assimilation brings with it not a loss but an expansion of identity, and it is the life-giving creative power of variety which Gordimer celebrates in her insistent focus on 'Otherness' which finds its culmination in the novel's passionate celebration of Whaila's thoroughly romanticised blackness. He is 'the disguised god from the sea' (*A Sport of Nature*, 198) equated, in a moment of hyperbole, with both Moses and Du Bois, and, in the passage in which he swims out to sea to meet Hillela and her lover off the beach in Dar-es-Salaam, we are told that

> to eyes accustomed to the radiance above water his blackness was a blow, pure hardness against the dissolving light, his head a meteorite fallen between them into the sea, or a water-smoothed head of antiquity brought up from the depths, intact; basalt blackness the concentration of time, not pigment. Even the hair – black man's kind of hair – had resisted water and remained classically in place as a seabird's feathers or the lie of a fish's scales. (170)

The melodramatic intensity and unashamed romanticism of this deliberately contrived passage brings together two elements in Gordimer's vision worth noting. Firstly, Whaila's beauty is presented as quintessentially African, but invested with a heroic substance and dignity through imagery which links him to the classical figures of Western antiquity, although the implicit reference to Greek statuary is 'Africanised' in the deployment of 'basalt' and in the later emphasis on the 'obsidian' quality of his beauty, strength and firmness of purpose. Secondly, such imagery coexists in a certain tension with the organic simile with which the passage concludes, which interestingly echoes and yet inverts the rhetoric of prejudice in terms of which, as we have seen, the black man was relegated to a subhuman level in the scale of being. Here, however, the comparison between man and bird or fish is intended to draw attention to a perfected beauty of integrated natural form which foreshadows the ideal order of an imagined

world in which the corruptions and distortions of artificially constructed racist perspectives will simply be irrelevant, and of
which the love which develops between Hillela and Whaila will
be the guarantor.

'if one is not afraid, how can one be not attracted?'

In the eclectic conjunction of a heroic intention with imagery
drawn from nature, however, other submerged stereotypes in
Gordimer's construction of black identity become apparent. The
African as both 'natural man' and classical hero replaces with a
certain emotional logic the subhuman and non-human images of
the unemancipated imagination which we noted earlier in this
chapter. Elements of a romantic pastoralism and a concomitant
moral innocence underpin such images, elements which already
inform Gordimer's vision in her earliest writing. Already in 1952,
in a brief magazine piece, an implicit biblical pastoralism informs
her depiction of an Africa in transition, and reveals her uncritical
affirmation at that point of myth of an original innocence corrupted, a paradise lost, as urbanisation takes its toll among black
South Africans:

> Already the black Eve, balancing the calabash on her graceful
> head, has reached for the apple; already the black Adam is fum-
> bling for the rags of factory made clothes to hide his innocence.
> The gates of the garden are closing. The push of something irre-
> sistible and cruel as the push of birth is carrying the people of
> Africa towards Johannesburg.[50]

African tribal innocence is set against Western-induced urban
degradation as the trope at the heart of this passage, a contrast
given an added political weight by Gordimer's grasp of the extent
to which the urbanisation of blacks in South Africa has been
manipulated to meet the ends of the apartheid régime. Three consequences may be seen to flow from this opposition in
Gordimer's work: affirmation of an African mysticism, a rejection of the degrading realities of the apartheid-imposed urban

black present, and an idealisation of the vitality and resistance of blacks to such oppression, as vested in particular in the romanticised image of the black revolutionary. These three themes now need to be examined more closely.

Firstly, Gordimer's acute awareness of the extent to which colonialism and apartheid have together succeeded in erasing the African past and its traditions informs her urge to assert and romanticise African connections with the land, connections which serve to symbolise those continuities which apartheid sought to destroy in her work. Such a past is conceived of, however, essentially within the framework of a Western pastoral nostalgia which does more to illuminate the white liberal sense of exclusion – indeed, of exile – from Africa than the realities of rural lives. Jessie, watching black women washing clothes in the river in *Occasion for Loving,* responds (with unintentional authorial irony) as a tourist might, feeling keenly only her exclusion from a rural world which, however denuded and debased by apartheid policies, seems to her nevertheless to have retained vestiges of a connection to a meaningful African past which is closed to her:

> In this continuity she had no part, in this hold that lay so lightly, not with the weight of cement and tarmac and steel, but sinew of the earth's sinew, authority of a legendary past, she had no share. [But] Gideon had it; what an extraordinary quality it imparted to people like him, so that others were drawn to them as if by some magic. It was, in fact, a new kind of magic . . . [which belonged to those] who held in themselves for this one generation the dignity of the poor about to inherit their earth and the worldliness of their masters. Who else could stretch out and put finger-tips on both touchstones at once? (269)

The romanticisation of the rural African past which inspires the emotional force of this passage is also apparent in the use Gordimer makes of the enigmatic quotations from Callaway's *The Religious System of the Amazulu* in *The Conservationist* which function as epigraphs to the different sections of the novel. They resonantly contextualise Gordimer's conviction offered here that: black connections with the land are so deeply rooted in an intuitive identification with a mythical ancestral past that they must finally triumph over the white man's temporary tenancy. There is a bitter prophecy in Mehring's self-reflexive irony as he imagines himself telling Antonia that he is 'planting European chestnuts for the blacks to use as firewood after they've taken over' (223). The farm-labourers' traditional remedies are shown to have a self-healing power which enables them, at the end of the novel, to take back possession of the land symbolically in the ritual burial of their 'brother', the nameless black corpse, who (like the Africa he stands for) has at last come back to his own. Gordimer consistently suggests that the eclectic mixture of Christian forms, tribal superstition and empty ritual which is the debased heritage of urbanised blacks should nevertheless be respected as concealing at its core an authentic link to a sense of meaning from which whites are permanently excluded. Early in the *oeuvre* Jessie sees only a tragic degeneration in the mine dances which she is reluctantly persuaded to watch; she is appalled at the extent to which they appear to be merely 'fun':

> It all meant nothing. There was no death in it; no joy. No war and no harvest. The excitement rose like a breath drawn in, between dancers and watchers, and it had no meaning. The watchers had never danced, the dancers had forgotten why they danced. They mummed an ugly splendid savagery, a broken ethos, well lost . . . They sang and danced and trampled the past under their feet. Gone, and one must not wish it back . . . [Her tears] came from horror and hollowness (*Occasion for Loving*, 37)

But by the time Gordimer came to write *The Conservationist*, the dance of Phineas's wife in her trance, however uneasy it makes her half-detribalised community, is shown to have the power to connect her with 'those dreams of hers' which link her to an ancestral past which infuses and enriches the present, spiritually stabilising her people. At the subsequent celebration 'dancing conferred a balance of its own' (165, 172) and becomes a prelude to that reconciliation between past and present which the novel's final pages celebrate. Indeed, although Gordimer has more recently appeared to reject what she has termed 'a mysticism of the land', in a 1983 interview with Diana Cooper-Clark, a continuing attraction to such a notion is apparent in the way in which she formulates her point:

> I distrust people – writers, too! – who lean upon a mysticism of
> the land and the earth, but the fact is that there is something that
> comes through from the earth itself in each continent.[51]

The qualification here should alert us once again to the extent to
which those romantic assumptions that informed her early attempts to recapture aspects of a black African past through senti-
mentalised images of lost tribal traditions and pastoral
harmonies have been a powerful shaping factor in her commitment to the emotional *leitmotif* which runs throughout the work:
that Africa belongs to its black peoples alone.

Secondly, set in opposition to such fleeting intuitions of a
meaningful tribal past, rich in cultural complexity and now almost entirely lost to the urbanised black South African, is
Gordimer's multivalent apprehension of township life, one
uniquely shaped for her by the contrast between contemporary
Soweto and her early experience of Sophiatown before its transformation into the white Afrikaner suburb of Triomf. The bleakness and squalor to which all black South Africans are
condemned in such ghettos are well documented in both black
and white South African fiction, and Gordimer's sense of the
appalling ugliness of life in such a context clearly informs, for
example, her emphasis on Jessie's uneasy perception of what
Ann's decision to commit herself to Gideon might mean: she
'found fear in herself at the idea of being allied to this life' (*Occasion for Loving*, 270). Such fear is, of course, the result of a vivid
apprehension of the concrete effect apartheid has on individual
lives; Jessie's response is essentially an indictment of the régime
rather than of herself. The ironically distanced narrative tone of
the somewhat dismissive account given of Callie Stow's romanticised view of the townships implies that the apartheid ghettos
need to be condemned as the slums they are:

> [Callie] thought of the townships as places exalted by struggle;
> like treasure saved from the rest of the plundering world in a
> remote cave, she believed the Africans kept love alive. (126)

The physical squalor and spiritual degradation of ghetto life is
perhaps the most immediate and concrete symptom for the sympathetic observing eye of the inhumanly oppressive impact of
apartheid policies upon individual lives. In *A World of Strangers*,

Toby sees Steven's defiant vitality not simply as a manifestation of the teeming life of the townships but as representing a defiant victory over what Toby understands black life under apartheid to be reduced to: 'A meaningless life, without hope, without dignity, the life of a spiritual eunuch, fixed by the white man, [yet] a life of which [Steven] had made, with a flick of the wrist, the only possible thing – a gesture' (252). In *The Conservationist* the township which abuts onto Mehring's farm is a sinister presence in the novel, spewing forth strangers and murderers at random: neither Mehring nor the reader is allowed to enter it; while in *Burger's Daughter* the no-man's land on the fringes of Soweto where Rosa encounters the carter beating his donkey is presented as the very type of hell, and plays its part in precipitating her flight. Gordimer's sense of the spiritual and actual ugliness of a life marked by countless deprivations also informs the corrosive tone of the passage in *A Sport of Nature* in which Hillela's dream of 'a rainbow family' (207) is contextualised after Whaila's assassination, within a larger debased African reality, with devastating effect:

> Acronyms the language of love . . . No need ever to run out of acronyms . . . [But] the real family, how they smell . . . The real rainbow family stinks. The dried liquid of dysentery streaks the legs of babies and old men and the women smell of their monthly blood. They smell of lack of water. They smell of lack of food. They smell of bodies blown up by the expanding gases of their corpses' innards, lying in the bush in the sun. Find the acronym for the real family. (250-51)

Gordimer's increasing contact with the realities of Third World politics on the African continent clearly made it necessary for her to qualify the romantic elements in her image of black Africa; but the fundamental theme of her faith in and attraction towards its vitality and potential remains a constant in the fiction and must be understood as a concentrated *act of faith* in the face of white cynicism, doubt and fear about the future of the continent.

It is this faith which informs the third level of response to the black predicament in the fiction: that ironically Conradian conviction, which implicitly underpins Gordimer's protest throughout the fiction, that the individual may redeem himself through action. It is a theme implied in both those alternative images of a regenerative and redemptive vitality in township life, in which she offers us a white echo of the work of the writers of 'the Drum Decade', and in the sheer magnetic force of physical and spiritual attractiveness with which she invests her black revolutionaries. Not only Whaila and Reuel, and before them Mweta and Shinza, possess this quality; already in *Occasion for Loving*, as we have seen, Jessie romantically invests Gideon (admittedly chiefly a revolutionary only in so far as he is both an artist and willing to rebel against the anti-miscegenationist laws of the country) with the power to bridge the gap between the old order and the new world. Similarly, in *The Late Bourgeois World* Luke Fokase's compelling sexuality exerts an Orphic power over Elizabeth, and arouses her to exert herself to find an avenue of escape from the particular Hades she is entrapped in. Here again we should note that the images of a teeming, life-affirming, sensual vitality in the black underworld acquire their persuasive power largely because of the extent to which they are opposed to contrasting images of an etiolated, sterile self-indulgence in an alienated and benumbed white world.[52] At this level in the novels, squalor and degradation become (in a passage to which the narrative voice clearly assents) a mere backdrop to Rosa's sense of

> the comfort of black. The persistence, resurgence and daily continuity that is the mass of them. If one is not afraid, how can one not be attracted? (*Burger's Daughter*, 143)

Nowhere is the tension between that fear of and attraction to the black 'Other' which is fundamental to Gordimer's construction of the liberal white South African psyche more clearly reflected. But its intriguing corollary is an affirmation of precisely those aspects of the black physical presence which most often motivate racist contempt. Pauline, flattered that Donsi Masuku has sought her out to help him and his family flee from South Africa, finds her resistance to him – as a representative of the anti-white, Black Consciousness Movement by which she has felt rejected – melting in her pleasure in at last simply, after all, being needed:

> The innocent bodily warmth, the faint odour of black *beneficed* the house, absolved whiteness. (*A Sport of Nature*, 74)

In her symbolic foregrounding here of 'the faint odour of black', Gordimer directly confronts white prejudices about unwashed black township bodies, in a characteristic reversal which challenges the crudities of white stereotypes by setting up an alternative vision no less informed by the powerful emotional subjectivities of a pervasive colour-consciousness. We should note too that, in this passage, whiteness needs absolution precisely because blackness is oppressed. Such connections alert us again to Gordimer's insistence on the unavoidable *political* base to white/black friendships: it is precisely the charismatic energy associated with black willingness to resist oppression which attracts the timid and spiritually impotent white liberal in Gordimer's model. The corollary of such a vision is of course to make an active willingness among white liberals themselves to commit themselves to the goals of the black liberation movement, the prerequisite for their acceptance by the black revolutionaries in the novels. Out of the 'persistence' and 'resurgence' of blackness (metaphorically rooted in the soil of Africa and, hence – given the trope of the black as 'natural man' – 'innocent' in its groundedness in a physical and sensual life) will come that transformative revolutionary impetus whose final victory *A Sport of Nature* celebrates in its conclusion.

Gordimer has in fact consistently insisted, as we have seen, that not only her white but also her black characters submit to the imperative of a commitment to radical politics. The latter can find their identity as Africans only in such activism, she suggests, for it is only through full political independence that the black man in general can achieve his ultimate spiritual emancipation. In a sequence of debates central in particular to *A World of Strangers* and *Occasion for Loving* she argues that an apolitical stance is a particularly irresponsible one, for blacks as well as for whites, within the historical contexts within which her characters find themselves. She thus suggests, in *A World of Strangers,* that Steven's death is not merely tragic but at one level symbolically just, while the artist Gideon Shibalo, in *Occasion for Loving,* is significantly instructed in his duties by Callie Stow in a passage which may perhaps be read as begging a comparison between what is expected of him and what his author, likewise an artist, might expect of herself. Callie tells him that

the only thing that means anything if you're an African is politics.
. . . What's the good of saying it's terrible that you can't be [a
painter]? There it is. You've got politics, that's all. Why drink
yourself silly, mooning over the other? You're a man of your time.
Different times, there are different things to be done, some things
are possible, some are not. You're an African aren't you? (121-
22)

Callie's argument is given force by Gideon's later reluctant admission to himself that, like other both black and white characters
after him (such as Rosa), he had found a sense of identity through
a stint in prison:

The one place in which he felt in possession of himself was when
he was in some small room with the men with whom he planned,
argued, and several times had been in prison . . . Here he knew
himself to be what Callie Stow had reminded him a black face
didn't necessarily make one – an African . . . Here there was no
shade of ambiguity; he was a man who had given up the life of
choice . . . and accepted the one thing possible – struggle. (176)

'All warmth and truth was there,' he muses a few pages later.
'Away from that, cut off from it, when his life was over he would
be a dead cat flung in the gutter' (181). Not surprisingly, therefore, his abandonment of the struggle, which is a consequence of
his decision to commit himself to Ann, leaves him metaphorically
stranded. As he lies on the sand between Jessie and Ann on
Natal's South Coast, the narrative voice comments that 'on this
lonely beach destiny and history overlooked him; he could ignore
both Shaka's defeated kingdom around him, and the white man's
joke about it that he read each time he went to the lavatory'
(247). The tragically self-destructive impact on his life of his decision to become 'the revolutionary-who-refuses' is embodied in
the closing images of Gideon, deserted by Ann, drinking himself
into oblivion at a party, 'his face . . . grey, and the dark of his lips
. . . split with red, . . . flowering patches of bloody colour, scarlet
and purple, like some strange streaked tulip' (288): the bizarre
flower imagery does not obscure the idea of a metaphoric death.
    We might note here that, whereas white women are shown to
seek redemption through their acknowledgement of their attraction to the black world and to black men, black men are fre-

quently fatally diverted and potentially destroyed by their relationships with white women; their redemption is to be achieved
through a public and political commitment rather than through a
private and emotional liberation. In apparent contrast to
Gideon's tragic end, Hillela's husband, Whaila, is allowed to
glimpse, like Moses, the promised land, but he dies soon after. In
a passage rich in symbolic resonances he is shown as strangely
exalted by his visit with Hillela to the black-built harbour of
Tema in an independent African country:

> The deep-water harbour was achieved, there under their feet.
> They were walking along great stone platforms that held half-
> circled the power of the sea. The waters tilted massively at them
> . . . The cargo ships in harbour from all over the world were
> tethered to something Africans had conceived and realised. The
> harbour dominated the sea as only foreigners' fortresses . . . had
> done for centuries. Whaila stood before the sea as no black man
> could before the harbour was built. The salt-laden humidity in
> late sunlight was a golden dust on him, risen from the victory
> over those years. His closed lips were drawn back in the thin line
> that was the price of such victories, as well as failures. (*A Sport of
> Nature*, 193)

The romantic magnification of such figures in Gordimer's fiction
should be read not only as an expression of that 'love affair with
Africa' which we have already traced in the imagery of the novels, but also as a symptom of the many ways in which the policy
of enforced segregation has distorted relationships between individuals: there is arguably a clear connection between the white
South African sense of guilt, alienation and exclusion and the
enthusiastic willingness to embrace idealising generalisations.

That Gordimer is, however, acutely aware of the moral distortions that even (or particularly) her enlightened, liberal, white
characters are prey to under the impact of a racist, colonialist
régime is amply testified to in one final twist in her representation
of such individuals: she repeatedly depicts such whites as reduced
to an anguished impotence when confronted by or finding themselves victims of black exploitation or brutality. It is a dilemma
made possible only by their painful sensitivity to the fact that
their white skins mark them as members of an oppressor race
which they wish to dissociate themselves from and disown. The

South African left-wing commentator, Denis Beckett, has persuasively identified such a sense of impotence with a distorted residue of racist response. He writes that

> we're such deep-died racists that we suspend our critical faculties when we're faced with black stupidity and black primitiveness. We don't demand the same standards from blacks as we do from whites, and that's about as insidious a racism as there is.[53]

Examples of such self-flagellation abound in the novels and are given an implicit assent in most cases by the refusal of the narrative voice to do more than simply report them. Thus Ann's cuckolded husband, Boaz, finds himself unable to confront Gideon in *Occasion for Loving* for fear that his jealousy will be misunderstood as an objection to Gideon's colour: his fear of being thought a racist is so deep-rooted that it takes precedence over his love for Ann and renders him impotent. Similarly, Hjalmar Wentz in *A Guest of Honour* feels he cannot voice his objections to his daughter Emanuelle's affair with the much older Ras Asahe because of the latter's colour. In *A Guest of Honour* Bray cannot confront Mweta with the fact that his police-force is resorting to torture to extract information from suspects because he does not want to be thought of as a typically paternalistic white colonial 'interfering' in the affairs of this newly independent country. And Rosa in *Burger's Daughter* grasps with considerable moral acuity the intolerable ambivalence at the root of her inability to intervene to stop a donkey from being brutally beaten:

> I had only to career down on that scene with my car and my white authority . . . I could have put a stop to it, with them, at no risk to myself . . . I could have stood between them and suffering – the suffering of the donkey . . . I drove on . . . I didn't do anything. I let him beat the donkey. The man was a black. So a kind of vanity counted for more than feeling; I couldn't bear to see myself – her – Rosa Burger – as one of those whites who care more for animals than people. (209-210)

Rosa finds the moral dilemma so insoluble and the sense of self-alienation so intolerable that, like so many before her, she decides to leave South Africa because, as she says, 'I don't know how to live in Lionel's country' (210). It is an admission of defeat which echoes throughout the fiction. That such crippling scruples recur so frequently is testimony to Gordimer's overwhelming sense of the extraordinary complexity of the moral issues which must be daily confronted by those who have been sensitised to the colour bar to an almost unbearable degree by the accident of having been born into a racist society. That Gordimer can ultimately offer her protagonists no way out of such dilemmas, since neither flight, good works, nor imprisonment can function as final solutions, is one reason why her vision has recently been labelled 'tragic'.[54]

What emerges from such a study as this is not only the history of Gordimer's own gradual politicisation as it is unconsciously revealed in the novels, but also extraordinary continuities of perspective which testify to the presence of a consistent and enduring moral vision of ambiguity and complexity underpinning and informing the developing political ideology reflected in them.[55] The felt, monolithic weight of a ruthless and apparently unshakeable apartheid hegemony has been a constant in her life over the four decades in which the novels were written, and the young writer's response to the radical injustices of the situation she found herself in, and began to articulate a sense of in her work, was premised from the beginning on the moral convictions she formed in her earliest years: convictions which were overlaid but not contradicted by her subsequent rapid politicisation. Within the essentially unchanging immoral framework of apartheid it is not surprising to find some of her most direct and passionate protest articulated in those early works in which she first established her voice and style. A study of the first three novels in particular, works composed over a period of ten years during Gordimer's early maturity (she was thirty at the end of the year in which *The Lying Days* was published, and forty in the year *Occasion for Loving* appeared), is especially illuminating in revealing the dimensions of the vision which underpins the later works, and which is finally subsumed in the triumphantly imaginative rendering of not only a political but also a psychological liberation from apartheid in *A Sport of Nature*. This novel offers a summary, a resolution of, and a conclusion to the issues the preceding eight have confronted in various ways. The radical shift to the representation of a post-apartheid future, prefigured by the tentative foray into historical transition represented by *July's People*, is perhaps most clearly marked in the contrast between Rosa Burger's and Nomzamo Kgosana's respective responses to their inheritance of radical activism. Whereas Rosa can paradoxically free herself from the imperatives of her past only by succumbing to its demands and returning to her father's fold, Nomo, the last of apartheid's children, is allowed to go free, to disappear into the political irrelevance of a private life as an internationally successful fashion model, while her mother stands on the platform at the Independence celebrations of Nomzamo's fatherland – 'Whaila's country' (*A Sport of Nature,* 341). In the power of her black beauty – 'coloured', mixed-race – to triumph over the prejudices against miscegenation which had, as we have seen, caused other relationships across the colour bar to founder in earlier novels,[56] Nomzamo may be seen as Gordimer's small but potent symbol of hope for a New World whose hall-marks will be not only a non-racial community of men, but also, perhaps more significantly, a society in which the individual will be liberated from the stranglehold of the imperative to radical political action. In such a future, the political may perhaps at last be subsumed into the private in the life of the individual, and the 'conspiracy against keeping apart' be brought to a triumphant conclusion.

Chapter 6

Landscape Iconography

*History cannot happen – that is, men cannot engage in
purposive group behaviour – without images which simultaneously express collective desires and impose coherence on
the infinitely numerous and infinitely varied data of experience. These images are never, of course, exact reproductions
of the physical and social environment. They cannot motivate
and direct unless they are drastic simplifications.*

Henry Nash Smith[1]

*Was sind das für Zeiten, wo
Ein Gespräch über Bäume fast ein Verbrechen ist,
Weil es ein Schweigen über so viele Untaten einschliesst!*

Bertolt Brecht[2]

From very early on in Nadine Gordimer's career, her ability to
capture with great precision the texture of the landscapes around
her, and to inscribe the details of place into her narratives with a
freshness of response rare in South African fiction at the time,
was widely recognised even by those critics who were in the main
hostile to her work. Yet even in this area of her work there have
been critics who have claimed that her 'determinedly harvesting
eye' and the 'pellucid precision of her observation and description' amount to no more than the provision of mere 'local colour'
and 'verbal photography'.[3] Woodward gave voice to the early
and continuing dissatisfactions of some readers when he argued
in 1961 that Gordimer's work offered only 'an ultimately meaningless accretion of surface vitality to conceal a hollowness of
content', and claimed that hers was a 'poetic exhibitionism'
which did nothing to advance theme, plot and atmosphere.[4]

Yet such dismissals of this aspect of Gordimer's fiction, and
the widespread preference among her critics for a focus upon the
political and ideological content of her work, have given rise to a
significant gap in critical consideration of the achievement of the

novels. An examination of her treatment of place and its function as a signifier in her work will uniquely illuminate the ways in which public and private concerns intersect in the novels, and allow us some further insight into the passionately subjective origins of her disaffection with her world. The extent to which that disaffection has its roots in a generously emotional response to place, one which precipitated her original 'love affair with Africa', is already hinted at in the wryly self-deprecatory tone of Gordimer's confession in 1965 that she should be understood to be

> a romantic struggling with reality; for surely this very engagement implies innate romanticism? Do realists question the meaning of reality and their relationship to it?[5]

This intriguingly perceptive description of herself serves to significantly focus her account of her own sense of the ways in which her treatment of place has developed in the fiction, an account which traces the shift away from an original mimetic intent to simply give some 'life' to what she felt was the terrible 'ordinariness' of her colonial background,[6] to her later practice, in which the representation of place finds itself firmly yoked to the ideological project: the early concern with 'catching the shimmer of things' modulates (in her own words) into a preoccupation 'not with the how, but the why'.[7] A fuller examination of the complex origins of that element of romantic realism which has shaped these trends will extend our grasp of the private emotional and subjective pressures out of which the work has grown and which underlie its tensions and contradictions.

Such an examination should not be conducted in a vacuum; Gordimer's achievements need to be firmly placed within the framework of our developing sense of a South African tradition of landscape representation, as variously sketched out in an as yet limited number of critical studies.[8] These have variously attempted to suggest the extent to which the settler experience of Southern African space was, for a considerable period in the literary history of the country, filtered through and articulated by sensibilities whose aesthetic expectations were typically formed by European, and not African, 'ways of seeing' – that is, the land was represented in anything but 'innocent' ways by writers who often found it difficult to identify themselves fully with a country seen through the perspective of a typically colonial sense of exile from a metropolitan culture located elsewhere, in the 'mother-country'. (The feminisation of the idea of 'home' in the latter term betrays the extent to which the speaker implicitly expected to be nurtured by a source necessarily other than the current context in which he found himself.)

Two interrelated thrusts thus informed the initial construction of landscape in settler fiction: on the one hand, an emphasis on the land's inhospitability in the eyes of its new immigrants, and, on the other, an attempt to view and 'place' the alien landscape through the more familiar – but ultimately inappropriate – perspectives of a distant metropolitan culture.

The first of these perspectives quickly produced a controlling image of Africa as almost exclusively characterised by the 'empty' and stony barrenness of the Karoo landscape[9], the 'Karoo condition' becoming the dominant landscape trope in South African literature, in preference to the gentler paradigms which might have been expected to emerge from early settler contact with the acknowledged beauties of the Cape peninsula.[10] Schreiner, Smith and Millin offer us landscape as a metaphor of alienation, exile and isolation, largely refusing to celebrate it as a richly promising 'New World' as American writers did with their continent during a similar period in their country's cultural development. Indeed, whereas in early American literature the mythologising process enriched the landscape immeasurably, in South Africa it stripped the landscape bare.[11] Gray implicitly makes this point when, in tracing the iconology of aridity back to Schreiner's *A Story of an African Farm*, he claims that it is 'virtually a cliché of Southern African fiction' that it should depict

> vast natural forces at work on puny beings in a way which is degrading and humiliating to human ambition . . . The land dries the vital juices out of its inhabitants, stunts them, and . . . disallows the desire to take root in the land and belong.[12]

The perceived hostility of the landscape to various forms of settler human need soon came to symbolise not only the individual dilemmas of an unsuccessful transplantation, but also the harshness which was the corollary of the racist premises on which the newly established society based itself. Thus Paton, despite the extraordinary glow of his evocations of the green fecundity of the rural Natal landscape, typically reverted to organic metaphors of 'rock and stone'[13] in order to suggest the intransigence of the racism he was attacking. In more recent fiction, André Brink extends this metaphoric emphasis in his novel *A Chain of Voices* (1982), in which he develops a subtle contrast between the way in which the land is perceived by its indigenous inhabitants, on the one hand, and by its settler-exiles from Europe on the other. His Khoikhoin 'Hottentot Eve', Ma-Rose (deeply rooted in an inalienably African ancestral context), characterises her world as one 'hemmed in with stone', yet celebrates the harshness of the land, in a persuasive twist to the metaphor of aridity, as a symbol of the ability of its indigenous peoples to endure and survive even the white man's inroads, and, like the rock of the mountains, to outlive his temporary invasion. She muses:

> Indeed, our mountains are old, stretching like the skeleton of some great long-dead animal from one end of the Bokkeveld to the other, bone upon bone, yet harder than bone: and we all cling to them. They're our only hold . . .
> We of the Khoin, we never thought of these mountains and plains, these long grasslands and marshes as a wild place to be tamed. It was the Whites who called it wild and saw it filled with wild animals and wild people. To us it has always been friendly and tame. It has given us food and drink and shelter, even in the worst droughts. It was only when the Whites moved in and started digging and breaking and shooting, and driving off animals, that it really became wild.[14]

In sharp contrast, the rock and stone which hem in the white farms come to represent the harshness of the oppressor's heart. Yet Brink's bleak point is that the legendary brutality and intransigence of the Boer is itself, in its own paradoxical way, a deformed survival mechanism, a crippled version of the Khoi will to endure: for only a devastating hardening of the heart will enable the white man to suppress and evade the destructive impact of his guilt at the exploitation of the land and its people. J.M. Coetzee has recently developed this point in an intriguing way, by suggesting, in his 1988 conclusion to *White Writing*, that a corollary of such guilt is the urge to self-justification, an urge which expresses itself, in his view, in the emphasis in early South African poetry on the pervasive silence and emptiness of the landscape. He argues that the image found there of a land both uncompromisingly hostile to the frail European spirit and also empty of 'Others' who might challenge the white man's right of annexation, not only reflected the white settler's *psychic* alienation from his physical context but also might well have served to convey what might be termed a *political* subtext. 'It is hard', he writes,

> not to read a certain historical will to see as silent and empty a land that has been, if not full of human figures, not empty of them either; that is arid and infertile, perhaps, but not inhospitable to human life, and certainly not uninhabited . . . Official historiography long told a tale of how until the nineteenth century of the Christian era the interior of what we now call South Africa was unpeopled. The poetry of empty space may one day be accused of furthering the same fiction.[15]

On the one hand, then, the felt personal and ideologically determined need to develop metaphors of exile, alienation, oppression, endurance and survival may be seen to have characteristically shaped the representation of landscape in English-language South African fiction. But there are other, related strains of response with which the fiction experiments which equally, though perhaps in a less direct way, serve the psychic needs of an uneasy colonising intention. For example, that early settler writing which attempted to subsume Africa into the category of the exotic was also, as both Gray and Coetzee have attempted to show, far from innocent in its manipulation of image and symbol in constructing an implicit opposition between 'us' and 'them'. Gray has suggested that two images in particular may be seen to gather into themselves the complexity and ambivalence of ambiguous white responses to Africa.

Firstly, there is that legendary symbol of old Africa developed in *The Lusiads* by the Portuguese poet Luís de Camõens: Adamastor. Gray examines the subtext embedded in the myth of this terrible but decaying giant and suggests that references to Adamastor served to communicate a diffuse perception of archetypal Africa seen not only as both strange and threatening, but also as reassuringly (if also tragically) weakening towards death in the face of the overwhelming force of European imperialism. Yet, in an extrapolation into the future, such reassurance could only be a temporary comfort: for a sense of the possibly transient nature of the European impact upon an ancient and alien continent served to undermine the victor's enjoyment of the fruits of his conquest, and necessitated a continuing self-protective oppression of the 'Other'. Gray indeed suggests that

> "the figure of Adamastor is at the root of all subsequent white semiology invented to cope with the African experience".[16]

The degree of discomfort engendered by an alien continent perceived as possibly *irremediably* physically and spiritually hostile to European appropriation, and whose ancient powers therefore have to be represented as being in decline in proportion to the fear they arouse in the conquerors, is given a symbolic focus in the myth of Adamastor; it is a discomfort which, in various forms, arguably permeates the entire literature.

Secondly, Gray goes on to suggest that the paradoxical mingling of both attraction and fear at the heart of the essentially ambivalent European response to Africa implicit in the Adamastor myth also informs the construction of other symbolic figures, notably that of the 'Hottentot Eve'. She possesses a similarly disturbing, amoral and primitive power; in particular her unrestrained sensuality which, within the conceptual framework of the frontier myth, comes to symbolise 'both the attractions and the intractabilities of inland, that unknown terrain',[17] offers us another version of the 'heart of darkness' allegedly at Africa's core. Gray suggests that here, too, in the intermingled strains of attraction and repulsion which characterise the depiction of this primal Eve, the fiction encodes an emotional and moral unease with the fruits of conquest which remains a constant in white English-language South African writing to the present day. Although such an unease is articulated in more recent times within the context of a concern with the political complexities surrounding the maintenance of white hegemony within the country, the original sense of the ineluctable nature of the divide between 'us' and 'them' which fundamentally underpinned the idea of the

exotic and the 'Other' survives at the heart of European responses to the idea of Africa, and continues to fundamentally
shape the metaphoric construction of the South African landscape.

Such images of an alien Africa of rock and stone – arid, harsh,
and resisting imaginative appropriation by conqueror and coloniser alike – are not significantly erased or modified by other
superficially more positive perspectives which have emerged in
the literature at various points. For example, Paul Rich (1982)
has argued that the late nineteenth century evolutionary perspective encoded, for example, in Schreiner's emphasis on a natural
hierarchy into which life forms are ordered, both ironically serves
to entrench a racist construction of relative levels of human inferiority and superiority in a novel concerned with the need for
liberation from narrow cultural stereotypes, and encourages that
identification of physical with psychological frontiers which becomes a powerful signifier in South African literature. Coetzee
(1988) extends the point in suggesting that Schreiner's Darwinian
emphasis on the landscape as primarily identified with rock – in
which unimaginably ancient prehistoric forms are embedded –
rather than with foliage, articulates a sense of the continent's
utter indifference to the petty fates of temporary sojourners in the
land: European civilisation on African soil remains irremediably
inappropriate and alien to the land.

Various other alternative European modes of constructing
landscape were imported into the colonies at different times and
created their own unintentional effects of a misplaced exoticism.
Coetzee discusses the presence of residual elements of English
Romanticism in those depictions of landscape which presented
'nature' as 'the source of truth',[18] and goes on to suggest that the
idea of the picturesque controlled the structure and perspective of
many early descriptive passages.[19] Gray argues that pastoralism
in, for example, Pauline Smith's work, was defiantly deployed to
articulate and defend the moral values of an isolated and
despised rural Afrikanerdom as a way of criticising the larger,
corrupt, socio-political forces of the time: he suggests that the
pastoral emphasis attempted to contextualise in muted form the
idea of an epic heroism into the literature.[20] These various strands
in the treatment of landscape are drawn together in Rich's claim

(1982) that the South African writer's tendency to impose upon the landscape the multiple forms of symbolic significance offered by such paradigms as romanticism, pastoralism, the exotic, the picturesque, and evolutionary theory, ultimately simply served to express the settlers' need to anchor themselves in a strange land by imposing on it already familiar conventions and thought patterns. Landscape representation cast within one or other of these paradigms offered colonialists a way of naturalising an alien and unknown wilderness which urgently needed to be tamed and domesticated by the imported culture. At the core of these critical discussions of landscape representation, of course, lies a further issue: that of voice. Coetzee goes to the heart of the problem in querying whether it is in fact conceivably possible for a white, English-language writer to develop an authentically African voice for the African experience which will not be undermined by its inscription of foreign cultural perspectives: he eloquently implies the magnitude of this issue in speaking of 'the burden of finding a home in Africa for a consciousness formed in and by a language whose history lies on another continent'.[21] Although post-colonial theory has fruitfully engaged with this problem, partly by defending the processes of hybridisation, syncretism and multi-culturalism[22] as routes to meaningful integration, criticism of South African landscape representation has by and large failed to confront the essentially political issues embedded in this approach.

Such insights have contributed towards the development of an understanding of the *iconology* of South African landscape representation. Argan, following Panofsky, defines an iconology as one which "reconstructs the development and continuation of traditions of images",[23] in contrast to more traditional approaches to the analysis of place in fiction which have attempted to dissect the various ways in which specific descriptive elements are linked to thematic intention.[24] Argan's argument that every literature develops a *tradition* of images (often most obviously deployed and clearly discernible in inferior work) which is constructed out of a conjunction of sensory experience, the cultural heritage, and those codes and conventions which have been found to be useful tools of the writer's trade. Such traditions consciously and unconsciously determine image patterns, both in literature which operates within the framework of conventions, and that which reacts against them. Argan of course accepts that, without the ability to refer to codes and conventions common to both writer and reader, the work would be indecipherable. Nevertheless, he stresses that the relationship between an image and its iconic predecessor is often far from straightforward and might indeed be located in the unconscious, and he claims that it is the province of the literary iconologist to cover and illuminate such hidden connections. A fundamental corollary of the concept of iconology is its emphasis on the fact that the description of place in fiction is never innocent. Not even apparently transparent passages of landscape representation will be free of the ideological content encoded in complex ways in the iconology which shapes and forms them. Clearly, a developing iconology will embody not only a 'tradition' but also the ideological perspectives which have shaped and formed that tradition.

Thus landscape representation must be seen as not only a tool of thematic intention, but also as rooted in and giving expression to conventions, codes and stereotypes which operate as convenient 'shorthands' for communicating both overt and submerged ideological perspectives. Indeed, given the nature of codes and stereotypes as expressions of often outdated or submerged perspectives, it may happen – as Bertelsen (1982) has pointed out in an analysis of Doris Lessing's *The Grass is Singing*, that the burden of a novel's political and ideological themes may, in fact, be expressed in imagery which derives its potency and impetus from traditional 'ways of seeing' at variance with or even explicitly rejected by the novel itself. It is this potential tension between convention and intention, between submerged code and ideological thrust, between tradition and the revolutionary impulse, which needs to be examined in any discussion of Gordimer's treatment of the South African landscape. What iconography does she draw on, what iconology does she consciously develop in her manipulation of landscape in the fiction, and in what ways does her work reflect both overtly and subtextually the characteristic iconologies encoded in South African literature as such?

'a company of strangers in a place without a past'

We may begin by noting that Gordimer was, of course, well aware of the stereotypes about Africa disseminated in popular literature about the continent, and she vigorously countered them in their more obvious forms in the fiction. In particular, she explicitly rejected those 'exotic' images of Africa to be found in the work of Rider Haggard and John Buchan, and in innumerable boys' adventure stories. This is made clear in an early auto-biographical sketch for British readers which she wrote in 1954, and in which she observed that

> I suppose it is a pity that as children we did not know what people like to talk of as "the real Africa" – the Africa of proud black warriors and great jungle rivers and enormous silent nights, that anachronism of a country belonging to its own birds and beasts and savages which rouses such nostalgia in the citified, neigh-bour-jostled heart, and out of which a mystique has been created by writers and film directors. The fact of the matter is that this noble paradise of "the real Africa" is, as far as the Union of South Africa is concerned, an anachronism.[25]

It is a passage which echoes a few lines in *The Lying Days*, published a year earlier, in which Helen says of her life on the mine that it was not

> even anything like the life of Africa, the continent, as described in books about Africa; perhaps further from this than any. What did the great rivers, the savage tribes, the jungles and the hunt for huge palm-eared elephants have to do with the sixty miles of Witwatersrand veld that was our Africa? (96-97)

Here already, in her first novel, 'exotic' Africa is explicitly re-placed by the earnest truthfulness of her attempt to capture the particularities of the debased and ravaged peri-urban landscapes of the partially industrialised East Rand mining world in which she grew up. In her second novel, *A World of Strangers*, she significantly offers us images of an Africa in thrall not to the myth of the great white hunter but to (white) historical and socio-political concerns. The opening passages of this novel ironically focus on the reality behind the myth of Africa, in their reduction of notions of a luxuriantly decadent colonial lifestyle to the actu-

ality of the frantic, unromantic boredom to which a woman
trapped on a bleak bushveld farm is reduced; all that remains of
'exotic' Africa here are the superficial and decaying tourist pleasures of a Mombasa caught within the framework of an unthink-
ing, pompous, self-righteous and doomed colonial imperialism.
Similarly, the stereotypical hunter's world of 'Boy's Own' stories
is explicitly stripped of any residual mystique in Gordimer's contemptuous dissection of the guinea-fowl hunt in the Bushveld
which Toby is invited to join. The hostile, thorny landscape yields
only death – the death of the birds and of the faithful dog, Gracie,
on the hunt itself, and the collapse of two relationships during
Toby's absence: one with Steven Sitole, who is killed in a car accident while Toby is away, and the other with Cecil Rowe, who
effectively betrays his faltering faith in her by failing to inform
him of her intention to marry the wealthy businessman, Guy
Patterson. In addition, Toby's decision *not* to accept the opportu-
nity to return to England at the end of the novel, and to commit
himself instead to a life which will honour Steven's memory,
ironically makes of him, as Cooke has pointed out, the very antithesis of the traditional African adventurer who plunders and
goes home.[26]

Toby's choice is made possible not only by his identification
with Steven Sitole and with the vibrancy and tragedy of the latter's township world: it also reflects a newly discovered sense of
connection with an unfamiliar 'Africa' emptied of the accretions
of meaning which have accumulated around it over centuries in
the European mind. Toby's moment of epiphany occurs, ironically enough, within the context of the simple, crude brutalities of
the hunting trip, a mundane modern version of an African adventure which yields only one experience of emotional significance.
When for a short space of time towards the end of the hunt Toby
finds himself lost 'in a fog' (245) in the bush with a dying dog and
one of the black trackers, he is strangely relaxed by an intuitive
sense of inarticulate identification with 'the ancient continent'
which penetrates and overwhelms his consciousness as he sits on
a rock waiting to be found. In these moments he senses a natural
world temporarily stripped clean of external associations and
conventional meanings, a world of Conradian indifference to the
European sensibility imported into it, present to his senses simply

as a series of natural phenomena within which he moves, and which elicits in him 'that sudden, intense sense of my own exist- ence that is all I have ever known of a state of grace' (*A World of Strangers*, 239).

The link here between, on the one hand, Toby's perception of an unmediated, archetypal Africa as both inviolable by and indif- ferent to the flow of human affairs and, on the other, the over- whelming spiritual impact of such an intuition upon him – one which allows him to make that contact with his own authentic flow of inner life which he experiences as 'a state of grace' – alerts us to the true significance of 'Africa' in Gordimer's own psychic life. In 1961 she made an attempt to articulate her personal sense of the continent as one whose impact on the Western imagination may be both redemptive and utopian: its power is to be measured in spiritual rather than in political or material terms:

> The problem of Africa, the idea of Africa and what she stands for imaginatively; the mixture of the old legendary continent and the new one drawing its first breath when the rest of the world is tired – this abstract Africa is becoming an element of the spiritual consciousness of the peoples of the modern world. As Donne could write of his mistress – "O my America, my Newfound- land", so, today, the European or American can conceive of his Africa – not a physical concept of jungles and desert and wild beasts and black men, but a state of regeneration an untapped source in himself to which he wants to find the dangerous way back; another chance for, perhaps, another, other civilisation that draws its sustenance from very deep, very far back. This Africa is a fearful place, but in the danger lies the hope of virtue. This Africa is, of course, really only a new name for an old idea – man's deep feeling that he must lose himself in order to find him- self.[27]

Gordimer's emphasis here on Africa's symbolic significance to Western man not only attests to the continuing extraordinary impact the continent has made upon the European imagination but also reveals the extent to which the older Western sense of Africa as exotic and 'Other' survives in contemporary paradigms. Doris Lessing articulates a similar vision in an eloquent passage written in 1981:

> I believe that the chief gift from Africa to writers, white and
> black, is the continent itself; its presence which for some people is
> like an old fever, latent always in their blood; or like an old
> wound, throbbing in the bones as the air changes. That is not a
> place to visit unless one chooses to be an exile ever afterwards
> from an inexplicable majestic silence lying just over the border of
> memory, or of thought.[28]

Central to such a vision are the outside origins of the observer
sensibility, which situate it within the poignant emotional contexts of potential loss and exile. It is, indeed, a characteristically
white colonial perspective which makes of Africa both here and
in Gordimer's imagination a regenerative force as set against the
decaying and tired civilisations of Europe. It is the romantic
idealism which fuels this vision which gives rise to that excoriating contempt for all which undermines such identification which
is an insistent undertone in her work: and in particular it is in
terms of this ideal image of Africa that she appears to measure
and find unworthy the perceived hypocrisies of the current liberal
attitudes of her day. It is a vision which lies at the heart of what I
have called Gordimer's 'love affair with Africa', one which
emerges into the forefront of the fictional project in the final,
symbolically loaded, triumphant pages of *A Sport of Nature*,
where political salvation is once again equated to spiritual redemption. The celebrations take place, ironically, in the 'mother
city' of the white settlers, as described in a passage in which logic
gives way to the hyperbole of romantic excess:

> For hours the great swell of singing and chanting has been carried
> back and forth between the mountain and the sea by the south-
> easter. When the band of gold, green and black leads in the mili-
> tary escort and motorcade with the first black President and
> Prime Minister of the country . . . the swell rises to a roar that
> strikes the mountain and jets above it to the domain of eagles,
> ululating shrills of ecstasy. The mountain may crack like a great
> dark glass shattered by a giant's note never sung before. (339)

That Gordimer's repudiation of the exotic paradoxically expresses itself in a utopian romanticism both illuminates the specific uses to which landscape description is put in the novels
(which will be discussed later), and reminds us of her debt to the

particular philosophical and literary influences which have shaped not only those uses but also the construction of a public iconography out of her powerful private apprehension of landscape. In a number of comments scattered throughout the nonfiction Gordimer has made it plain that those influences came primarily from her voracious adolescent reading of the classics of European and English literature. Although she began to read southern African and African writers in her early adulthood, the formative influences on the development of her eye for the significance of place came from such writers as Woolf, Fitzgerald, Conrad and D.H. Lawrence, all writers whose voices are clearly discernible in the early novels. Lawrence in particular not only encouraged her focus on the extra-rational stream of intuitive sensual and sexual response in human relationships,[29] but also, as Gordimer writes,

> influenced my way of looking at landscape and the natural world
> in general – his sensuousness dilated my senses and brought up
> close to me rocks, petals, and the fur of animals around me.[30]

Clearly, Gordimer's first and deepest response to Africa was a sensual one,[31] and initially her most immediate goal in her writing was to communicate, as precisely as possible and with a Lawrentian eye for detail, the kaleidoscopic sensory impact of the environment upon her.[32] Particularly in the early novels her sheer delight in her ability to capture the precise modulations of light and atmosphere led her to interpolate descriptive passages into the developing narrative which fulfilled no especial thematic or symbolic function. At such junctures, the sometimes obsessive need to document her world overwhelmed art, and the charge that her work incorporates mere 'verbal photography' acquired some weight at points where the sheer accumulation of detail ran counter to or even contradicted thematic development. An example is to be found in *The Lying Days*: in a passage which deals with Helen's state of suspended discontent after her return from her holiday at the coast, her dissatisfaction with the impoverished contexts of her home is neatly symbolised in her action of pulling back the 'thin curtains' of her room only to reveal 'the dusty, clipped jasmine bush, the patch of neat grass, the neighbour's hedge' (85). She longs to be back at the coast in order to pursue her overwhelming attraction to the son of her hostess, who had aroused her nascent adolescent sexuality in a long-drawn-out and sensitive seduction. But it turns out that Ludi had simply been 'playing' with her, as his name ironically implies, and, as she struggles to avoid realising this, she falls into a period of despair which the passage of time at first does nothing to alleviate. Although both dusty yard and oncoming winter suitably symbolise her mood, the fine description of the season which follows functions simply as an inconsequential digression, offering the reader a confusion of images and similes which bear only the most tenuous relationship to both the African and the psychological contexts within which thay are situated:

> The quiet, steeped autumn days passed, as if the sun turned the earth lovingly as a glass of fine wine, bringing out the depth of glow, the fine gleam; the banks of wild cosmos opened like a wake, with the cream and pink and gilt of an early Florentine painting, on either side of the railway cutting from Atherton to Johannesburg and spattered intoxicating bees with plenty. (5)

Here the felt desire to 'paint a picture' is so strong that it gives rise to those discontinuities which have prompted the complaint that landscape is used 'unreliably' in Gordimer's work; such digressions do no real work in the novel. If we accept, as Welty has suggested, that 'the question of place resolves itself into [that of] point of view',[33] then point of view is arguably not always stable in these early works.

This is so for two interrelated reasons. Such characteristic digressions express Gordimer's life-long sense of the shaping importance of what is generally thought of as the

> inconsequence of daily life, in the fluid of which are suspended all stresses, the jagged crystals of beauty, the small, sharp, rusted probes of love, the hate that glints and is gone like a coin in water. (*The Lying Days*, 88-89)

The felt need to attempt to capture this complex, multifaceted and undifferentiated flow of life in its very inconsequentiality frequently absorbs her energies to the point where it at times unintentionally interferes with the New Critical ideal of perfect

artistic coherence and consistency to which she in general sub-
scribes. More importantly, however, such interpolations, and the
frequent proliferation of detail generally in Gordimer's descriptive passages, are a necessary consequence of the specific project
she consciously set herself, and which (particularly in her early
work) quickly took on a central importance in her work: that of
finding a 'voice' for her unique experience of Africa. She was
aware that she needed not only to find a way of articulating her
own deep sensory connections with the country in which she had
grown up, but also to discover what meanings to attach to the
landscapes she found herself in.[34] Gordimer initially knew herself
to be hampered in this search for a 'voice' by the extent to which
she perceived herself to be a victim of a typically colonial cultural
deprivation which effectively deprived her of an indigenous tradition to emulate and learn from; in 1963 she spoke of the impact
upon her childhood and adolescence of the fact that at that time
she had found 'no books about the world I knew'.[35] That the
substitution of 'foreign' reading material to fill the gap left by the
absence of such books had as its corollary a significant distortion
of vision for young colonials is illuminated in a passage in Doris
Lessing's short story 'The Old Chief Mhlanga' in which the protagonist's response to her African homeland is sensitively delineated:

> A white child, opening its eyes curiously on a sun-suffused land-
> scape, a gaunt and violent landscape, might be supposed to ac-
> cept it as her own, to take the msasa trees and the thorn trees as
> familiar, to feel her blood running free and responsive to the
> swing of the seasons. This child could not see a msasa tree, or the
> thorn, for what they were. Her books held tales of alien fairies,
> her rivers ran slow and peaceful, and she knew the shape of the
> leaves of an ash or an oak, the names of the little creatures that
> lived in English streams, when the words 'the veld' meant
> strangeness, though she could remember nothing else.[36]

The awakening of this child, first to a love of the African landscape she learns to claim as her inheritance as she grows older,
and then to a slow and painful realisation that she is to be implac-
ably and permanently excluded from this inheritance because of
the sins of her fathers, closely parallels Gordimer's own develop-

ment, as indicated both in her autobiographical sketches and in the changing thematic intentions of the sequence of novels. The dimensions of this disinheritance are made explicit in a passage in *The Lying Days*, in which Helen tells us:

> In nothing that I read could I find anything that approximated to my own life; to our life on a gold mine in South Africa. Our life was not regulated by the seasons and the elements of weather and emotion, like the life of peasants; nor was it expressed through movements in art, through music heard, through the exchange of ideas, like the life of Europeans shaped by great and ancient cities ... We had no lions and we had no art galleries, we heard no Bach and the oracle voice of the ancient Africa did not come to us, was drowned perhaps. (96-97)

Gordimer's implicit assumption here, that it is chiefly through imaginative literature that our responses to the world we inherit are shaped and given value and significance, informs her sense of being stranded both in relationship to metropolitan culture from whose imagined riches she felt herself cut off, and in relationship to the actual experiential world she physically inhabited but which had acquired no recognisable presence in the books she read. She also of course felt that, as the inheritor of a settler culture with its roots in another country, she had no access to that 'oracle voice of the ancient Africa' mentioned above. Accordingly, from a typically colonialist base, she defined her situation as one of being entrapped in a spiritual and cultural no man's land between, on the one hand, a European culture of which only a debased version remained available to the self-absorbed colonial mining world of her parents, and, on the other, the only dimly perceived and disappearing 'indigenous' Africa of the black man, unsatisfactorily reflected in the writings of the anthropologist and the hunter-explorer, to which her entry was barred by virtue of her race, language, sex, politics, and position in history. It is entirely in keeping with her white South African heritage that she should at first have attempted an escape by identifying herself with the more accessible of the two poles, and we initially find her deeply in thrall to the metropolitan culture of those sophisticated Romantic and pastoral nostalgias to which the books that were available to her gave her access.

The depth and importance of these metropolitan influences upon the imagination and expectations of a writer who nevertheless has steadfastly refused the option of exile is interestingly revealed in various little-known asides in her early writings. For example, in 1954, she wrote of weekend visits to her mother's family in Natal in terms which suggest the firmly implanted vision of the expatriate: 'there, with the "English" side of the family, in the green, softly-contoured hills and the gentle meadows of sweet grass near Balgowan, we might almost have been in England itself . . . [it was] a paradise of sorts'.[37] And in a 1965 interview a long line of English pastoralism implicitly underpins the rider to her comment that 'I shouldn't like to leave Africa; if I did, I think I could live happily in England, *in the country*'.[38] Such passages suggest that her early education in the classics of European and English literature shaped not only her moral but also her aesthetic sensibilities: her sense of what a thing or place should be in order to be considered beautiful was clearly initially determined by this literature of another hemisphere. Thus, although Gordimer herself grew up on the semi-arid Transvaal highveld, we find that natural beauty in the novels is discovered and celebrated in all that possesses the vivid greens of luxuriant growth, wetness and fecundity characteristic of England and subtropical Natal but extremely rare in the highveld landscapes of her childhood, while most of what is repudiated or found lacking in the novels is contextualised within metaphors of drought, bleakness, barrenness, colourlessness and ugliness – the elements she felt to be common in the East Rand environment she knew first and best. It is significant in this context that the novels do not offer us images of the vast grasslands of the Orange Free State, despite the fact that Gordimer spent some holidays away from the Witwatersrand here too, on visits to her father's Jewish relatives. Although she wrote briefly with some sensitivity of the 'miles and miles of sienna-red plowed earth . . . [and the] miles and miles of silk-fringed mealies standing as high as your eyes on either side of the road'[39] in an early autobiographical essay, it is a region whose absolute absence from the novels should perhaps be at least partially ascribed to its lack of that green fecundity whose symbolic resonances become so important in the work. Clearly, then, both personal experience and her typically colonial education shaped Gordimer's aesthetic values into conformity with the characteristic paradigms of English South African landscape iconography, well before political and ideological allegiances developed and deployed the metaphors already established to their own ends.

In an interesting twist however, the contrast between the aesthetic barrenness of the environment Gordimer grew up in and the fecundity of the less familiar landscape both of her holidays and of the English and European literatures she had read encoded itself in an unexpectedly paradoxical form in her landscape iconography. Although the child's initial pragmatic acceptance of the ugliness of the mining environment was countered and shaken – both by the imaginary landscapes to which her reading introduced her, and by family excursions and holidays away from the Reef which showed her that there were real alternatives to such aesthetic barrenness available, even within South Africa – the mature writer's metaphor for *reality* has remained the dry, colourless bleakness of the winter highveld world. The 'paradise of sorts' of the Natal holidays and, by extension, of English greenness, represents an ideal which for her, by definition, can have little connection with the bleak realities of ordinary, everyday life. Moreover, her response to what she perceives as aesthetic ugliness is clearly connected to her sense of exile and loss as a colonial, as is suggested in a passage from *On the Mines*, in which she writes of her childhood Reef contexts that they were peopled by

> a company of strangers in a place without a past, with nothing to quiet that certain spiritual hunger whose bread is memory . . . We who were born into [this landscape] in the Twenties and Thirties opened our eyes not so much on God's creation as on our father's bold rearrangement of it. This was very different from the hedgerows and fields that domesticate the earth . . . It was ugly. Rusted iron, a three-day beard of prickly khaki-weed, the veld burned off and the sand blowing in the season that passes for spring, in Africa.[40]

She goes on to claim that this was a landscape in the process of being dismantled, a symbolically entirely appropriate emphasis in the iconography of the novels as she sensed the apartheid era to be drawing to its close. What is significant here as well is the connection between 'reality' and a certain barren bleakness of the spirit, which is already established in an early essay in which Gordimer offers us an illuminating insight into the emotional and aesthetic worlds of herself and her sister as children on the mines: the two rapidly came to perceive this landscape – described with the cold detachment and precision of an absolutely disenchanted familiarity – as the very type of ugliness:

> All around us the shafts went down, and the gold came up; our horizon was an Egyptian looking frieze of man-made hills of cyanide sand, called 'dumps', because that is what they are . . . In the dusty month before spring – in August, that is – the sand from the dumps blew under the tightly shut doors of every house in the town and enveloped the heads of the dumps themselves in a swirling haze, lending them some of the dignity of cloud-capped mountains. It is characteristic of the Witwatersrand that any feature of the landscape that strikes the eye always does so because it is a reminder of something else; considered on its own merits, the landscape is utterly without interest – flat, dry, and barren.[41]

The passage goes on to capture the children's melodramatic magnification of the perpetually burning coal dumps as an 'Evil Mountain', which shared 'with the idea of Hades its heat and vague eternity'; it was forever dully smouldering in its depth, like 'a beast of prey', and had burnt to death one careless boy who had fallen into its crevices, and hideously disfigured another girl who had sunk into its hot ashes but lived. 'We children simply took it for granted,' adds Gordimer in an illuminating comment, 'that beauty – hills, trees, buildings of elegance – was not a thing to be expected of ordinary life.'[42]

Two important points emerge from these passages. Firstly, the pervasive imagery of dust and ugliness, and the implicit emphasis on the landscape as a dumping ground for an industrialised (capitalist) greed which poisons and lays waste the countryside, presents the environment as a kind of Hell. It is an idea which is lent an added pathos by the child's fanciful imagination which interprets the dust-enswathed dumps as the 'cloud-capped mountains' she knows of only through her reading. Indeed, Gordimer's emphasis in her early work on the sheer man-made ugliness of the Reef landscape suggests that, for her as for the activist lawyer, Anna Louw, of *A World of Strangers*, her revolt against her narrowly provincial and racist inheritance began as a simple, aesthetic 'revolt of *taste*' (181) against what her people had made of an originally pristine Africa. The impulse to generalise and universalise the particular unique components of such a landscape points us towards the developing moralising impulse of the fiction: an impulse which constructs out of the accumulated details of individual experience that idea of the 'typical' which will reveal the submerged 'Truth' about things[43] that the daily routine obscures.

Secondly, we should recognise that it is deeply significant for the fiction as a whole that, for the child that Gordimer was, natural beauty was something which was, on the whole, to be sought and found *elsewhere*: it was not expected to be a component of 'home'. Her sharply perceptive insight into the extent to which such a mind-set is characteristically a product of colonialism is directly articulated in a passage from *The Lying Days*, in which Helen evaluates the childish conclusions she drew from her clandestine visits to the mine's Concession Stores:

> Now, as I stood in this unfamiliar part of my own world, [I knew] and flatly [accepted] it as the real world because it was ugly and did not exist in books (if this was the beginning of disillusion, it was also the beginning of Colonialism: the identification of the unattainable distant with the beautiful, the substitution of 'overseas' for fairyland . . .) (21)

Clearly, then, to escape the charge of colonialism would paradoxically entail an acceptance of home as it is, in all its harsh inadequacy. And this is, indeed, the direction in which Gordimer moves; not, however, in the form of valorising the Transvaal landscapes of her childhood, but rather in her decision to focus her creative talents upon the task of inscribing a specifically South African reality in the fiction a reality understood to be irremediably bleak and harsh. The colouring it acquired in childhood is transmuted into the adult pattern of symbolic significance with which Gordimer's landscapes are increasingly invested as her political and ideological commitments take on an ever clearer form. Thus in much of the fiction beauty remains a quality vested in *other* landscapes and lifestyles: while South

Africa remains in the grip of oppression, its spiritual bleakness and barrenness must be symbolised by an emphasis on physical ugliness in the environment. The man-made ugliness of the Reef is seen simply to parallel the man-made ugliness of apartheid. Only when apartheid itself is defeated can those who both willingly and unwillingly colluded with it be returned to an enjoyment of the true archetypal Africa, whose beauties have so long been obscured and kept in thrall by the racist régime.

The pairing of actual and metaphorical aesthetic and spiritual deprivation is already implicit in Helen's comment to Joel at the end of *The Lying Days* that 'in a way it seems right that one shouldn't be happy in South Africa, the way things are' (358).[44] What Helen only intuits at this stage is that liberation from colonial mind-sets is not so much to be achieved by a jettisoning of metropolitan standards of comparison as by resisting the temptation to escape to greener pastures and, instead, committing oneself to the task of bringing about change. Although Helen's decision to eventually return to South Africa after her trip overseas expresses as yet only an inchoate sense of identification with the contexts which have hitherto shaped her, later protagonists such as Rosa Burger signal their acceptance of their moral responsibilities by refusing the option of a permanent flight to more hospitable contexts elsewhere. Indeed, in a logical development of the attitudes delineated above, Gordimer argued in 1980 that the impulse to flee uncomfortable South African realities by opting for voluntary exile in England's greener pastures was itself an expression of a colonial mentality. She criticised in particular those South African writers, such as Olive Schreiner, who attempted to settle overseas, on the grounds that

> the general motivation was a deep sense of deprivation of the world of ideas, living in South Africa. Underlying that incontestable fact . . . was a reason some had a restless inkling of, as the *real* source of their alienation at home, but – each more or less imprisoned by the consciousness of their times – all could express only negatively: by the act of taking the Union Castle mailship to what was the only cultural 'home' they could conceive of, much as they all repudiated jingoism – indeed, it was part of the philistinism they wanted to put at an ocean's distance.[45]

At one level, then, Gordimer's overt repudiation of colonial mind-sets which still long for an English 'home' coexists in some tension with her growing tendency to inscribe an image of South Africa as a land lacking the actual and metaphorical beauties vested in the mother-culture, and in terms of whose values and standards the colonial culture is found to be wanting.[46] This submerged, but powerfully present subtextual emphasis in her work ironically reflects an attempt to *integrate* her particular (parochial/colonial) thought and work with the wider concerns of the transnational 'world of ideas' to which she aspired; the implicit encoding of the latter's perceived values in her work represents an outward-reaching which promises a form of escape from her own individual 'prison-house of colonialism'. For the life of the imagination can transcend all boundaries, she suggests:

> From the day I learnt to read, British writers provided my vision of the world: for it seemed, reading what living in that world was like, that I lived outside it – until later, when British literature introduced me to the world of ideas, and made me realise that to *this* our life belonged just as much as the life of Europe: the only difference was that so little had been thought about or written of our life in Africa.[47]

Gordimer's identification with the struggle for liberation in South Africa thus logically necessitates a repudiation of the allure, the temptation of 'elsewhere', not because the beauties of home are an adequate substitute, but because a moral puritanism dictates the necessity of a paradigm of suffering and reward which powerfully skews and redirects her original sensitivity of response to the nuances of the physical world she inhabits. Her characters are therefore consigned to an indefinite sentence of spiritual and actual exile from beauty until the regenerative and redemptive millennium which *A Sport of Nature* celebrates is achieved. Consequently, although the attractions of 'elsewhere' are fully acknowledged, Gordimer-as-moralist repeatedly returns her characters, as we shall see, to that highveld environment whose harsh contours appropriately convey her sense of the depredations of apartheid upon the human community. Within such a paradigm, landscape iconography takes on a powerfully moral and thematic resonance in the novels.

'nothing was innocent, not even here'

As we have seen, Gordimer solves the problem of giving a 'voice' to Africa in two ways: firstly, by establishing a powerful vein of *private* sensory connection with the landscape in her early, minutely detailed and often finely perceptive and evocative descriptions of a context which she assumes will be unfamiliar to her readers overseas (hence the elements of exposition, explanation and generalisation interpolated into almost every such passage), and secondly, by making her landscape iconography reflect and underpin the *public* political thrust of her work. The barren contexts of the Transvaal highveld metaphorically articulate the harshness of life within an apartheid context; the absence of physical beauty in the surroundings both suggests the extent of black oppression and constitutes a form of symbolic punishment for the white oppressors; and for those who commit themselves to the struggle against apartheid, such barrenness suggests the need to defer all forms of private pleasure until the public realm has been liberated. The ramifications of such solutions now need to be considered in greater detail.

Firstly, the growing centrality of the political consciousness which informs the work has as its corollary the gradual subordination of the original, intensely felt, sensory response to landscape to the political ends the novels increasingly serve; the imagery generally becomes harder, more spare and more clearly thematically focused in the later works. Landscape largely disappears as a private sensory icon as Gordimer develops and refines her sense of the bizarre nature of the public socio-political realities around her: she herself lamented in 1985 that, after the first three novels, she had 'lost the eye that sees everything for the first time, sensuousness, a dancing nervous tension that I shan't find again'.[48] The early novels inscribed a fresh and extraordinarily vivid sensory apprehension of their African contexts: in *The Lying Days*, *Occasion for Loving*, and residually in *A Guest of Honour* and in ironic passages in *The Conservationist*, landscape has the force of a vast presence, penetrating, diverting and redirecting consciousness. In *July's People*, however, it has come to be reduced to mere scaffolding, simply sketched in as a symbolically laden backdrop to a narrative in which the political theme shapes and directs every detail. Already in *The Late Bourgeois World* the original, quasi-autobiographical, sensory experience at the heart of the earlier evocations of setting is replaced by the spare discipline of a landscape wholly conceived of in terms of the metaphorical burden it must be made to carry. The bleak colourlessness and arid lifelessness of the Transvaal winter highveld in this novel is emphasised specifically to symbolise the spiritual and political 'dry white season'[49] with which the novel is concerned. Even the extraordinary beauty of the region's winter sunsets no longer has the power to uplift the human spirit: its radiant colours are ascribed to pollution (the result of atomic bomb testing or volcanic eruptions which spread dust through the upper atmosphere), and its luminosity is given portentous significance as a harbinger of apocalypse rather than a source of solace. Nor can Elizabeth gain any inspiration from her contemplation of men on the moon in the novel's final section. For her, imperialism has culminated in a religion of technical conquest in which not only the planet's landscapes but space itself is to be colonised.

The relative decline of landscape as a focus of attention in the novels is perhaps most strikingly evident in the concluding passages of *A Sport of Nature* in which the narrative voice offers a bird's-eye view of the independence ceremony that takes place in Cape Town. The eye is directed to the crowds, the dais, the figure of Hillela on that dais, and finally to the rising flag of the new country at its moment of birth. However, the reader-as-spectator is not, even here, in the profound solemnity given to the moment, allowed more than a momentary glimpse of the magnificent natural setting which is the clearly ironically chosen physical context of the ceremony, being inextricably linked with the history of the beginnings of white settlement and exploitation which has been hammered into every white South African schoolchild. It is an omission even more noteworthy when we bear in mind an early autobiographical passage in which Gordimer showed herself to be entirely responsive to the beauties of the region. She wrote in 1954 that, 'like most South Africans, once I had been to Cape Town I wondered how I had ever thought Durban beautiful . . . it is something splendid, an almost superhuman experience, to see the tip of a continent alive at your feet [from the top of

Table Mountain]'.[50] That this splendour appears in none of the novels suggests a degree of repression and redirection of Gordimer's spontaneous response to landscape which attests to the strength of her need to subordinate its representation to her ideological concerns.[51]

Such an observation will alert us to a second characteristic of Gordimer's work not yet commented upon by the critics: the extent to which she has made of herself an essentially *regional* writer, typically restricting her settings to the specific contexts within which she has spent her childhood and the bulk of her adult life. For example, the Natal Drakensberg, the Eastern Transvaal, the Transkei, Swaziland, Lesotho, the Cape Peninsula, and that archetypal South African landscape, the Karoo, do not provide her with settings in the novels. Indeed, this much-travelled and highly urbanised writer refuses to inscribe (for largely political and ideological reasons, as we shall see) all but one of the regions of Southern Africa particularly noted for their natural beauty – the Natal South Coast. In effect, Johannesburg and its environs constitute the dominant setting throughout the work.

This voluntary restriction in Gordimer's range is cultivated for very particular purposes: to facilitate the development in the novels of what amounts to a dialectic between 'inside' and 'outside'. In this paradigm the 'real' world of Johannesburg is conceived of as the core environment, and we find contrasted to it – with varying degrees of symbolic significance – a series of other landscapes which are significant precisely because of the extent to which they exist *outside* (and, although appealing to the imagination, are finally irrelevant to) the inner world of the Reef. Not only are these environments sharply 'different' from one another, but they are also experienced as fundamentally separate, hermetically sealed off from one another to a degree possible only within a world in which the very structures of the imagination have been distorted by the insidious penetration of a divisive apartheid ideology. Thematic intention therefore clearly shapes the contrast between the lush Natal South Coast and the wintry Witwatersrand in *The Lying Days* and *Occasion for Loving*, while in *A World of Strangers*, similar significant oppositions are set up between the seedy exoticism of tourist Mombasa, the indifferent semi-wilderness of the Transvaal lowveld, the wealthy ease of the city's northern suburbs, and the vitality and deprivation of the inner city and townships of Johannesburg itself. The city is also the 'reality' against which the nightmare of exile in the African village in the northern Transvaal is measured in *July's People*. In all but two of the remaining novels it is the rest of Africa, England and the Continent which variously operate as the 'other pole'. Only in *The Late Bourgeois World* and *The Conservationist* (which, together with *July's People*, must count as the most disenchanted and alienated of the novels) do we not leave the Witwatersrand area at all. Here however, the opposition is to be located in an emphasis on an ironic anti-pastoral contrast between country and city which is implicitly present in the more wide-ranging fiction as well.

In these patterns of opposition, the 'real world' of the Witwatersrand is presented not only as the antithesis of 'exotic' Africa but, in a metaphor drawn from Fitzgerald and T.S. Eliot, as a man-made 'Valley of Ashes'[52] whose desolation is made only more poignant by such details as the brief splendour of flowering cosmos which Helen notices in *The Lying Days* along the railway line between Atherton and the city. Gordimer's iconography makes of the Transvaal landscape a metaphor for that 'felt state of zombiehood'[53] which Gray identifies as the characteristic condition of the English-speaking South African colonial in English South African fiction: a state which Gordimer mercilessly dissects in her critique of that impotent and failed liberalism which is characteristically located within the boundaries of the Johannesburg environment. In this way Gordimer reinscribes the early stereotype of an arid landscape, making the Witwatersrand another Karoo, and entrenching a metaphorical desert yet again as a dominant symbol of the actual spiritual malaise underlying the apparent privilege of white lifestyles: the 'real' world of desolate Reef landscapes highlighting the equivalent 'reality' of alienation and *anomie* among its white inhabitants.

Such a pattern of oppositions also reveals a third characteristic of Gordimer's manipulation of landscape, for which our consideration of the escape motif in the novels has already prepared us: the peculiarly South African twist given to the symbolic resonances of the inside/outside dichotomy by her political convictions, transforming it into a dialectic between reality and de-

sire. It is clear that, at a subtextual level, 'inside' must be understood to represent a form of imprisonment which the spirit (often
impotently) resists, whereas 'outside' beckons as the longed-for
alternative to a burdensome daily reality. The theme of rebellion
against colonial values is first introduced in the narrative of
Helen's secret visits to the Concession Stores in *The Lying Days*,
and first articulated in Gordimer's valorisation of the African environment as it most immediately impacts upon the senses. In the
later novels, in a neat corollary, 'inside' and 'outside' are reversed
– whereas Helen moves from imprisonment *inside* the white,
English-speaking, mining enclave into the larger outside South
African world represented by her growing identification with
African realities, first on a sensory level and then as an idea, later
characters such as Maureen find themselves uncomfortably excluded from, *outside* the mainstream of African life by virtue of
their white skins. *Inside* then becomes the world to which first
Rosa and then Hillela must earn their admission, both in the
ironic metaphor of the prison (which Jeremy Cronin has also recently fully exploited in his collection of prison poetry entitled
Inside), and in Hillela's final status as a metaphorical cornerstone
of the Independence celebrations. The one imprisoned inside
longs to escape to the outside; the excluded outsider yearns for
the reassurance of insiderdom; in both cases it is desire which
inspires the restless search for a way out of impasse.

Hence it is significantly only when the narrative voice leaves
the Witwatersrand, understood as the symbolic heart of bleak
white alienation, that colour, light, spontaneity, ease and gaiety
re-emerge as qualities warming the lives of Gordimer's characters
both when characters cross the boundary into the black world
and when they escape temporarily "overseas". Indeed that desire
to escape from the oppressive responsibilities of a social and
political conscience which haunts Gordimer's characters is perhaps most clearly reflected in such sidelong glances at the luxuriant possibilities for a fullness of life outside South Africa's arid
contexts. Consequently, as Gordimer's symbolic construction of
the South African landscape takes on an increasingly bleak and
implacable quality in the later novels, it is the 'outside' world
whose appeal is paradoxically most powerful to the imprisoned
and beleaguered imagination.

That imagination in fact appears to be liberated into its original fullness of response to the multi-faceted sensory beauties of the natural world *only* when the setting shifts *outside* the boundaries of the main arena of action. We find such a pattern particularly powerfully encoded in *Burger's Daughter*, in which Rosa's frustration at her own moral impotence when she comes across the donkey which is being beaten – in a landscape described as a hellish wasteland between city and township – is strikingly juxtaposed to the opening images of the following section in which Rosa initially feels herself to be liberated into the light and colour of the French Riviera after her long psychological imprisonment in South Africa. Flying over the Mediterranean coastline, she sees from the aeroplane 'the silk tent of morning sea tilted, pegged to keyhole harbours where boats [nose] domestically like animals at a trough' (214). The fragile sheen caught in the image of the silken tent delicately captures Rosa's sense of immense relief at her entry into a state of beauty, ease, and the comfortable, nurturing domesticity which quickly envelopes her under Katya's maternal care. The following passage, which attempts to define by implication the precise nature of the *difference* between the world Rosa has left behind and the one she enters, concentrates on her overwhelming sense of wonder at the marvellous possibility of safety and anonymity and community in such a society. In a sense she has 'come home', for here she knows her white skin is neither a symbol of a negatively constructed identity, nor can it betray her as the settler/foreigner/oppressor she cannot escape being seen as within an unliberated South Africa. Gordimer stresses how extraordinary the inhabitants' assumption of total security in this new world seems to be at first to the fugitive:

> awnings bellied; leaning people were dreamily letting the car pass across their eyes ... Laughter and chatter trailing behind or bursting ahead. [Madame Bagnelli] came and went, preparing food, between rooms vague and dark with objects not yet seen as more than shapes, and the radiance, the sweet hum of the village, on the terrace. The innocence and security of being open to lives all around was the emotion to which champagne and more wine, drunk with the meal, attached itself. All about Rosa Burger, screened only by traceries of green and the angles of houses, peo-

ple sat eating or talking, fondling, carrying out tasks – a man planing wood and a couple leaning close in deep discussion, and the susurration of voices was as little threatened by exposure as the swish of the shavings curling. People with nothing to hide from, no one to elude, careless of privacy in their abundance: letting be. (*Burger's Daughter*, 217-24)

The rich sensitivity of Gordimer's writing here betrays her own susceptibility to the manifold pleasures expanded upon in such a scene, which the novel's political project cannot condone. Her conviction that it is necessary to suppress the temptation represented by such beauty and ease of community perhaps explains why her narrative voices so seldom follow her characters into that exile which is always an option for South Africans, and only then when a return is ensured – in Rosa's case to the actual imprisonment which is all that apartheid South Africa has to offer her, and which is merely staved off by her brief sojourn in Europe.

The contrast between 'inside' and 'outside' also illuminates with some complexity and precision the tensions between the sensory and the intellectual worlds which lie at the core of Gordimer's complex consciousness. On the one hand there is her powerful sensual and emotional identification with the land in which she has grown up; on the other hand she is consumed by her conviction that, in her case, it is not merely a Wordsworthian loss of innocence in the adult which has robbed her of her inheritance, but the inexorable forces of historical injustice which have tragically 'exiled' her from a land which she feels each white South African must – like Rosa – *earn* the right to repossess. Since for Gordimer the need to oppose apartheid quickly became the single overwhelming reality in terms of which all else was simply self-indulgence, the desire to escape from this imperative was understood as a form of selfishness, the tempting nature of which must be resisted. Flight in the novels is therefore seen as essentially irresponsible, and at most can be allowed a role only as a brief holiday from the sombre pressures of daily life within the apartheid state. Nevertheless, Gordimer's resentment of this bleak imperative and her sense of its destructive invasiveness are strongly encoded in the novels in those passages in which the writing warms to the beauties of contexts as far removed as possible from those industrialised landscapes of the Reef which metaphorically come to represent the negative impact of apartheid in its ugliest forms.

The origins of Gordimer's decision to make of a particular landscape an icon of the drive to escape untenable pressures are clearly to be located in her childhood experiences. In the early novels she chooses to contrast the sub-tropical vitality and beauty of the Natal South Coast to the sharp, bleak clarity of the everyday world of the Transvaal highveld. Her choice of Natal as one of her two poles is in no way arbitrary; it was the locus of her childhood holidays, and it was here that she first understood that there were alternatives to the narrowness of the Reef, that its ugliness need not be accepted as all the world had to offer. The extent to which the child was overwhelmed by the beauty of the South Coast is clearly documented in an early autobiographical passage, in which she writes of the family's holiday destination as

> beyond the reach of even the little single-track railway. In this village, the hotel was a collection of thatch-roofed rondavels, the water was free of refuse, and the beach – ah, the beach lay gleaming, silent, mile after mile, looping over flower-strewn rocks . . . There were indeed many beaches, and always one where for the whole day there would be no footprints in the sand but my sister's and mine. In fine weather, the village was, I suppose, a paradise of sorts. In front of the little hotel was the warm, bright sea, and, curving around behind it, hill after hill covered with the improbable green sheen of sugarcane, which, moving in the breeze, softened every contour like some rich pile, or like that heavy bloom of pollen which makes hazy the inner convolutions of certain flowers. Streams oozed down from the hills and could be discovered by the ear only, since they were completely covered by low umbrella-shaped trees (these are seen to better advantage on the hills around Durban, where their peculiarly Japanese beauty is unobstructed by undergrowth), latticed and knitted and strung together by a cat's cradle of lianas and creepers.[54]

Stylistically, this sensitive evocation of a kind of earthly paradise already introduces us, in its multi-faceted rendering of the minutiae of place, to the unique characteristics of Gordimer's voice. The almost Romantic excess of pleasure in a natural world whose impact is primarily perceived through the senses, the sharp analytic eye which takes intellectual note of botanical phenomena, the precise discrimination in the adumbration of detail, the felt need to include metaphors which will refer to a wider Western culture beyond the confines of a narrow provincialism, and the attention paid to her audience's need to be familiarised with the peculiarities of an unfamiliar colonial environment, all come together in a passage as yet untouched by the tensions of moral purpose or ideological responsibility which quickly come to shape the fiction.

Only in Gordimer's first novel, *The Lying Days*, will we find elements of so politically innocent and untrammelled an evocation of natural beauty again. But the early experience of the seaside recorded above forms the raw material out of which Gordimer soon fashions an iconography which gives shape and significance to her perception of the Africa she has inherited, and which will metaphorically focus the ideological perspectives of the novels. In particular, the imagery of water, lake and ocean will play a crucial role in communicating the indefinable and mysterious essence of that private life which must be subsumed to public ends.

In disentangling the ramifications of the symbolic resonances of this group of images we should first note the extent to which beach and sea in the early novels are predictably deployed to delineate the boundaries of an archetypal natural world unsullied by the sordid impact of human civilisation. It is primal wilderness which Helen responds to in *The Lying Days* as she gets off the train at Katembi River and sees, 'at the end of the strip of coal-grit, like a short carpet abruptly rolled, thick bush, green and black, green and hard with light reached up and closed in high, singing with hot intimacy far within and dead still to the eye' (*The Lying Days*, 48). Such a landscape appears to offer itself as a place of contemplation and retreat, a source of spiritual wholeness, in which the fragmented urban psyche will be able to recover its health. This level of symbolism is most fully developed in *Occasion for Loving*, in which Jessie flees the complexities of life in Johannesburg by holidaying in her dead stepfather's beach cottage. As she wakes and looks out on the first morning, she feels that 'the sea moved towards her shiningly out of the night; it was immortality, it had been there all the time' (185). That im-

plicit sense of a spiritual home-coming is further developed in the
description of the beach-cottage:

> The walls . . . were not grown thick with layer on layer of human
> personality, but were thin and interchangeable as the shells that
> gave shelter to various sea animals, first holding the blob of ani-
> mate mucus, then inhabited by one crab or another. And all the
> time, as the sea washes in and out of all shells, sand, wind, damp,
> warmth entered and flowed through these houses; ants streamed
> over them as if they were part of the continuing surface of sandy
> earth, bats lived in them as they lived in caves, and all the silent
> things, the unnoticed forms of life mould, verdigris – continued to
> grow as they did on natural forms. (186)

This is the archetypal ideal shelter, perfectly fusing form and
function and offering a possibility of integration at the most fundamental ontological level possible. In so far as the seaside is a
site of intuitive sensory integration, it answers to the innermost
needs of the self, beyond the control of intellect and ideology.
Thus it is also the site of the quintessentially private life: the sensual, the immediate, the instinctual and the arational, beyond the
claims of both society and history. Jessie, like the house she inhabits, finds that

> she was no longer contained by walls but had a being without
> barriers moving without much change of sensation from hot sun
> to cool water, from the lap and push and surge of water to the
> damp, blowy air. When her eyes were open they followed the sea;
> when they were closed the movement was in her blood. (188)

All conventional barriers dissolve as the beach landscape becomes a kind of living room; the rocks, furniture. Jessie moves
into a paradisaical state of intuitive harmony with the natural
world where she communes with its elements at a level beyond
the conscious or the rational, as suggested in her response to the
porpoises:

> Every day, no matter what she was doing, she looked out at the
> sea and saw the porpoises passing. She had no idea that they were
> going to be passing, but when she looked out, there they went.

> She had this. It had survived. Neither petrol fumes or phenobar-
> bital, book-keeping nor all-night drinking parties had finished it.
> Living creatures came by out there in the wide water and she was
> able to know it. She never thought about it. But there they
> were . . . She had no means of communicating with them except
> whatever it was that made her know when they were there; there
> was no reason to suppose that they did not have the same sort of
> knowledge about her. (191)

Within this iconography it is entirely appropriate that it should
be at the seaside that Helen first awakens to the depths of her
own sexual being; and, though Ann and Gideon pursue their
affair during excursions into the countryside around Johannesburg and consolidate their relationship in 'the innocence of one
of these Edens' (*Occasion for Loving*, 134), it is, predictably, to
the seaside that they flee when they seek a larger space for their
love affair within apartheid South Africa. It is also there that both
Ann and Jessie acquire a necessary and determining degree of
self-knowledge.

    The centrality of water imagery is elsewhere apparent in the
novels too. Toby's first experience of a sensual and emotional
connection with an Africa beyond the political and economic
concerns of his socialist English parents' world emerges when, on
his way to South Africa, he swims in the sea off Mombasa. He
seems 'to feel an actual physical melting as if some component of
[his] blood that had remained indissoluble for twenty-six years of
English climate had suddenly, wonderfully, dissolved into free-
flowing', and he gazes 'in lazy physical joy at the lovely smooth-
patterned boles of the coconut palms waving . . . above our
heads, the water, and the white beach' (*A World of Strangers*,
14). Similarly, in *Burger's Daughter*, Rosa, fleeing from the
wasteland of South African politics, experiences a renewed sense
of the fullness of her physical being in her first afternoon in
Katya's house by the sea on the French coast. In a passage which
echoes Jessie's earlier response to the sea, she finds her

> sense of herself was lazily objective. The sea, the softly throbbing
> blood in her hands lolling from the chair-arms, time as only the
> sun-dial of the wall's advancing shadow, all lapped tidelessly
> without distinction of within or around her. (222)

It is at the seaside that she is reintroduced to sensual pleasures in her affair with the Frenchman, Bernard, which tempts her anew to abandon the burden of her inheritance entirely. An earlier lover, Conrad, who also represents the temptation of an apolitical cynicism in Rosa's life, builds a yacht in a Johannesburg backyard as part of a fantasy of escape, and Rosa later imagines that she no longer hears from him because he is lost at sea (as, metaphorically speaking, is her own instinctual, sensual self at this point in the novel). In *The Late Bourgeois World*, Max can find release from his tortured conscience only by driving his car into the waters of Cape Town harbour, an attempt at a final expiation in an act of ultimate irrationality, in which he seeks in the depths of the sea itself some form of psychic relief from his guilt and confusion. In *A Guest of Honour,* Rebecca and Bray first make meaningful contact with each other on the island in the lake, where Bray feels 'time has no meaning, human concerns are irrelevant – an intense state of being takes over' (231). The lake seems to Bray to be a 'radiance of water and sky, a kind of explosion of the two elements in an endless flash . . . One couldn't remember anything so physical. It couldn't be recaptured by cerebration; it had to be experienced afresh' (110). The lake becomes the site of a sensual privacy which later provides metaphors for Bray (now deeply committed both sexually and emotionally) as he watches Rebecca lying in the bath, her body an 'underlake landscape, white rock flesh, garden of dark weed, clinging snails of nipples' (444).

The emotional colouring given to aspects of landscape in this novel changes significantly as Bray gradually detaches himself from his wife, Olivia, and the England in which they have made their home, and commits himself to the uncertainties of a life with Rebecca and in Africa. The England in which the novel opens has a mellow tranquillity whose dimensions are caught in the image of the gun used only to shoot partridges: 'Sometimes before the dusk wavered the wood away into the distance, he went out into the sunlight that collected like golden water in the dip of the meadows and shot a partridge. There was no one to bother about shooting rights' (9). But tone and mood here are in sharp contrast to Bray's memories of England shortly before his death: as he thinks of returning to England, he remembers with distaste that 'winter was beginning there . . . Cold damp leaves deadening the pavements and the sweet mouldering grave-smell muffling up against the face. England. A deep reluctance spread through him, actually slowing his steps' (455). Africa, on the contrary, comes to be symbolised by the vast fig tree under which Bray sits with his friends or does his work:

> The multiple trunks of the tree, twisted together forty feet up, made the shape of a huge wigwam under the spread of its enormous, half-bald branches. How old was it? As old as the slave-tree? He had found thickened scars where at some point or other in its life there had been an attempt to hack it down. A reassuring object, supporting life even in the teeming parasites whose purpose of existence was to eat it out from within; an organism whose heart couldn't be got at because it was many trees, each great arterial trunk rotting away in the embrace of another that held still the form of sap and fibre; a thing at once gigantic and stunted. (481)

Gordimer, heavily influenced at this time by her reading of West African post-colonial literature and concerned with the phenomenon of neo-imperialist decadence and corruption in newly independent black countries, significantly chooses to make this enormous natural object – in the vast complexity of the life-forms it supports so similar to the sea – a symbol of her romantic conception of an archetypally African ability to endure and survive: one which will eventually have the power to transcend all temporary political setbacks.

Gordimer invests water imagery with an additional level of significance in *The Conservationist*: here water is not only destructive but becomes a force which compels self-questioning and holds out the possibility of redemption for the oppressed, death for the oppressor. Water as a purifying natural element floods the land and washes up the buried body on Mehring's farm, thus finally forcing him to confront the hidden corruption of his inner psychic self. In a similar trope in *July's People*, Maureen's desperate self-preserving flight from husband, children and village at the end of the novel entails wading through a river 'like some member of a baptismal sect to be born again' (159), and it is out of the sea at Dar-es-Salaam that Whaila emerges at Hillela's side, the 'god from the sea' who transforms her life by engaging her at the fullest sensual level, causing to emerge in her that 'new being' who becomes the ultimate symbol of hope for Africa.

We may understand the sea, then, and the natural world in general, to represent not only 'the oceanic',[55] the power of the unconscious, the instinctual and the sensual, but also an archetypal site of withdrawal and of self-discovery. As a temporary refuge or retreat it fulfils a central function in Gordimer's iconography. But we should note again that she does not allow a communion with nature to offer her characters a permanent solution to their dilemmas. In so far as such a communion represents, as Ward suggests, 'the wish-fulfilment of a desire to evade human complexity', and symbolises 'the attractions of a defection from humanity',[56] its temptations must be rejected. Indeed, already in *Occasion for Loving*, its promise that it can provide the jaded spirit with a refuge from ugly reality is shown to be illusory, for, as Jessie discovers, no retreat is safe from invasion. Upon her return from the store in which she has heard talk of plans to introduce beach apartheid in the village, she goes out onto the terrace and stands

> looking with a kind of disbelief at the wild, innocent landscape; the rain-calmed sea, the slashed heads of strelitzia above the bush almost translucent green with the rush of sap. The sun put a warm hand on her head. But nothing was innocent, not even here. There was no corner of the whole country that was without ugliness. It was no good thinking you could ever get out of the way of that. (259)

In a parallel movement a few moments later, meeting Ann down on the beach, Jessie makes the related climactic discovery that Ann unconsciously fantasises that fate, in the form of a death by drowning, will release her from the impasse she finds herself in, and bring to a conclusion the relationship between herself and Gideon in a way which will absolve her from moral responsibility. Ann's confusion and moral cowardice put an end to Jessie's fantasy that a love is possible between a white woman and a black man which can permanently transcend the barriers created by apartheid, and thus symbolically negate and cancel out the evil power of racism. The realities of the South African situation invade and destroy illusions of the possibility of escape, and, as a

significant corollary to this bleak insight, the landscape correspondingly loses its power to comfort and reassure.[57] The absence of a significant Lawrentian perspective in a later novel such
as *July's People*, which is set almost wholly within a rural environment that Maureen and Bam reluctantly experience as a refuge from the war raging in the urban centres, expresses this
insight with some power. From very early on in her career,
Gordimer insists that the pastoral idyll – that 'theme of withdrawal into an idealised landscape . . . [into] a state in which
there is no tension within the self or between the self and its environment'[58] – is untenable within an apartheid context. White
South Africans will have to *earn* their right to the indulgence of
that 'private' inner life which the pastoral mode celebrates. It is,
she suggests, a life which, in the end, only history can restore to
them.

There is another reason, however, why both the idea of the
pastoral and the Romantic impulse to escape into a communion
with 'nature' are rejected in Gordimer's *Weltanschauung*. A close
examination of her descriptive passages reveals what we might
call a powerfully Conradian element at the core of her view of the
natural world which makes it difficult for her characters to take a
simple solace in nature. Conrad's influence is indirectly acknowledged in, for example, *Occasion for Loving*, in which we are
explicitly told twice that Jessie is reading *Victory* while at the
beach (197, 219). The choice of author is not accidental, for the
idea of a vast, cosmic indifference in the natural world to the
petty flow of human affairs, which is so prominent in a novel like
Nostromo, is a muted *leitmotif* of accumulating significance in
Gordimer's work as well. Already in *The Lying Days*, Helen
speaks of her sense of Ludi's 'intimacy' with

> the large, impersonal world of the natural, which in itself surely
> negates all intimacy; in its space and vastness and terrifying age,
> shakes off the little tentative human grasp as a leaf is dropped in
> the wind. (56)

Toby in *A World of Strangers* is lost in the Bushveld in 'the indifference of the empty afternoon' (235), in which human aesthetic
standards and needs become irrelevant: there is 'no beauty, nothing ugly' there (230). Bray, in *A Guest of Honour*, passing by his

house in Gala while the town centre is engulfed in riots, sees that, in his garden,

> the old fig wrinkled in its skin of dust was fixed as Eternity. The midday peace of heat enclosed in the garden beneath it was unreachable indifference. (464).[59]

Other elements of Conrad's ethical perspective are also clearly reflected in Gordimer's work. For example, at the end of *Occasion for Loving*, Jessie's son, Morgan, reflects that 'grown-up ethics' constitute a 'private moral structure that each man must work out to hold himself together if he abandons or breaks down the ready-made one offered by school, church, and state' (284): a formulation which echoes Conrad's distinction between 'principles' and 'a deliberate belief'.[60]

Gordimer, however, deploys the Conradian concept of 'indifference' in ways which give it a uniquely characteristic resonance in her work. Her images of the natural world endow it with an unassailable independence of the puny affairs of men quite free of that element of hostility to human needs with which Conrad invests his jungle and sea. His sense of horror at the possibility of a God-less and meaningless cosmos which contemptuously negates the human need for significance and moral order is epitomised in his imagery of 'darkness'; his jungle possesses 'the stillness of an implacable force brooding over an inscrutable intention' whose significance is 'too dark – too dark altogether'.[61] But Gordimer's Natal bush, in what may be read as a specific rejection of this thrust, 'was not jungle, it made no darkness' (185-6). In a brief gloss of the Conradian perspective, Gordimer marks her divergence from it in a passage in *Occasion for Loving* in which Gideon experiences the beach as having

> the feeling – of all fecund, tropical places where plant and insect life is so profuse – not of hostility to human beings but of the indifference that man feels as hostility. Here was no account taken of anyone who walked upright on two legs ... A dead seagull on the sand was busy as a factory with the activity of enormous flies, conveyor-belts of ants, and some sort of sand-flea that made a small storm above and about the body. Butterflies fingered the rocks and drifted out to sea. Dead fish washed up among smashed shells were pulled apart and dragged away to

their holes by crabs. There was not nothing here, but everything. (219-20)

Such passages alert us to two primary and related characteristics of Gordimer's natural world. On the one hand, it is one imbued with a complex order, in which the shapes of the 'minute and dependent life of the sea' lining each rock crevice on the beach give Jessie 'the pleasure of pure form . . . they were order, perfect order at the extreme end of a process' (194-95). On the other hand, Jessie's wonder is qualified at other points by both a bracing and slightly alienated sense of the sheer, immutable *otherness* of the African landscape. In an early piece of travel-writing on the Congo, for example, Gordimer speaks of human beings as suffering from 'a natural pariahdom' in the world of beasts.[62] Later, in *A Guest of Honour*, Roly Dando's African garden at first appears slightly threatening in its violently unmediated life forms to the eyes of one accustomed to the domesticated and comfortingly decorous contours of England:

> Coarse and florid shrubs, hibiscus with its big flowers sluttish with pollen and ants and poinsettia oozing milk secretion, bloomed, giving a show of fecundity to the red, poor soil running baked bald under the grass, beaten slimy by the rains under the trees, and friable only where the ants had digested it and made little crusty tunnels. A rich stink of dead animal rose self-dispersed like a gas . . . It was the smell of growth . . . the process of decay and regeneration so accelerated, brought so close together that it produced the reek of death-and-life, all at once. (18).

Following closely upon the evocative description of Bray's gentle English country garden, and connected in its images of a fecund rawness of life to the enormous fig-tree in his African garden, such a passage is clearly intended to mark the sheer 'otherness' of an Africa entirely self-absorbed in its own processes. The indifference to the particularities of human existence, conceived of here by implication as only another manifestation of Africa's protean variety, ultimately suggests not only an archetypally indomitable African vitality, but also liberated black Africa's essential indifference to the fate of the white intruder. In the element of alienation which informs the imagery of the passage, we are reminded of the extent to which Bray, as a white man, is locked within his status as a foreigner at this juncture, in a politically and socially constituted world in which, because he has no particular place or role in it, he must reconstruct his identity 'from scratch' if he wishes to 'belong'. His deilemma is symbolic of that of white men as such in Africa.

Gordimer in fact suggests that the colonial invasion not only placed 'Africa' in its multiple levels of being under siege, but also made its essence inaccessible, even invisible, to those who embrace colonialist perspectives. In ironically reversing the issue of integration by suggesting that it is the white man who must find a way to meld with Africa and not the black man who must struggle for acceptance in white society, she implies that the process of white integration must *begin* with a sensitivity to the land and its unique sensory impact; that is, the senses and the emotions must be 'Africanised' before the intellect can respond to the political and ideological demands Africa makes upon it.

In a logical extension of this view, Gordimer suggests that her black South Africans may take a shorter route to political activism than that delineated for white colonials. No processes of emotional adjustment need precede the commitment to the struggle for them. Indeed, in *Occasion for Loving* (in which we find Gordimer's first intermittently sustained attempt to represent the consciousness of a black South African), her conviction that the claims of the public political life must oust the pull of private emotional ties is given uncompromising expression in her insistence that Gideon Shibalo *choose* between his private life as a painter and a lover of Ann, and his public commitments as a black activist. Within the established trope which marks the city as the site of reality and the arena of struggle, and the seaside as the site of fantasy and escape into a private world, it is significant that Gideon should be represented (in a deliberate inversion of the stereotype of the tribal and 'bush' African) as belonging

> to town life in a way that no white man does in a country where it is any white man's privilege to have the leisure and money to get out into the veld or down to the beaches . . . Neither had he known the white child's attachment to a pastoral ancestry fostered from an early age by the traditional 'treats' of picnics and camping. (220)

Gideon feels trapped in his unsought 'holiday' at the beach as he watches the white women in their 'abandonment to the natural world . . . with some kind of alienation and impatience – it belonged to a leisure and privilege long taken for granted' (220). Here differences in response to landscape become an index of the gulf that separates the privileged from the oppressed. Once again, the emphasis is on the claim that indulgence in a 'communion' with 'nature' is not only a private luxury inappropriate for those already committed to the city-based political struggle, but also inaccessible by definition to those most immediately affected by apartheid. Gideon demonstrably takes the wrong path in opting to abandon his political activism for the affair with Ann, and in the process both loses his old identity as a participant in the struggle and fails to acquire a new one as Ann's second husband. His unease at the beach suggests the self-destructive nature of his choice of the private over the public life and, finally, abandoned by Ann, he sinks into a state of embittered alcoholism from which Gordimer refuses to rescue him. At the end of *Occasion for Loving* it is, significantly enough, not Gideon but Jessie who, on her return to the city and in her dawning commitment to radical revolutionary struggle, is shown as 'beginning to slip into the mainstream' (274). Immersion in such pure states of being as she enjoyed at the beach is for *her* a necessary prelude to political commitment; but Gideon's choice of a retreat into a private relationship is uncompromisingly represented as a kind of defection into a side-stream – indeed, as an index of political irresponsibility.

'A farm in Africa? How he must love Africa'

Political irresponsibility is of course the temptation Gordimer's white characters repeatedly battle against or, in the case of *The Conservationist*, embrace out of a generalised indifference to the fate of the 'Other'. Any reading of the pastoral theme in Gordimer's work must ultimately consider the central significance of its ironic treatment in this novel, arguably one of her finest. Gordimer's protagonist, Mehring, whose name and origins suggest a play on the German word 'mehr', meaning 'more' –

greed is his primal sin and will be his downfall – acquires four hundred acres of land south of Johannesburg which he intends to occupy as a 'gentleman farmer'. A number of questionable motives lead him to buy the farm, none of them very firmly connected to that view of Africa encapsulated in the exclamations of his foreign business associates, whose words significantly echo Karen Blixen's sentimental romanticisation of colonial Kenya in *Out of Africa*:[63] 'A farm in Africa! How he must love Africa. And were there any wild animals there?' (40). Instead, there is Mehring's inarticulate desire to publicise his financial success by taking possession of a chunk of that land from which he has made a fortune by exploiting its resources as a pig-iron dealer. The farm embodies his fantasy of the possibility of a retirement into a rural gentility which only money can buy in South Africa. It is 'a place to get away to from the context of stuffy airports, duty-free drinks and cutlery cauled in cellophane' (23) – a Sunday retreat where those picnics scorned by Gideon can be enjoyed. It provides him with tax relief and will eventually make him even more money when it is expropriated by the government to allow for the expansion of the neighbouring township, whose dimly intuited degradation functions as a muted reminder of social realities Mehring chooses to ignore. And, initially, it seems of value to him as 'a place to [which to] bring a woman' (42). Such a stereotypically sexist motive is given short shrift in the novel, as the narrative charts the progressive disappointment of each of his expectations. To the extent to which they arise out of Eurocentric pastoral clichés, they are granted no validity in the overall thrust of the work. Far from enjoying a pastoral idyll, Mehring eventually finds himself besieged by the pervasive presence of those the novel regards as the 'true' owners of the land – the farm workers who run it and, by extension, the township inhabitants whose labour has made Mehring's wealth possible. The hint of inherent pathos in Mehring's confused desire to 'make contact with the land' (22) is, indeed, progressively negated by the accumulating evidence of that sheer insensitivity to human needs which characterises his tenancy of the farm in the first place.

The corpse buried so unceremoniously on Mehring's property by the police is an immediate and inescapable reminder of the brutalities of the world Mehring represents. The body is that of a township man, a stranger to the workers on the farm, but, as we have seen, their acceptance of their brotherhood with and responsibility towards this anonymous figure significantly elides the theoretical gap between the rural and the urban black experience, and attests to their common brotherhood in oppression. The corpse may be understood to function symbolically on a number of levels: it represents the violence which oppression and poverty have made a daily fact of black life under apartheid rule; it suggests the reality of a festering corruption below the quiet surface of white South African privilege; it symbolises Mehring's collusion with the apartheid authorities which he professes to despise in his acquiescence to its illegal burial on his land; it functions as Mehring's 'conscience', as it comes to represent both the black African 'Other' on whose exploitation he (and all of white South Africa) has built his fortune, and the hidden dimensions of his corrupted desires whose possible exposure eventually haunts him into a kind of insanity; and in its final appearance and reburial, it signifies the regenerative return of the ancestors, who will put the intruder to flight and repossess their own.

In addition, at the level of political signification, the corpse ironically contextualises Antonia's mocking comment to Mehring that he has 'bought what's not for sale: the final big deal. The rains that will come in their own time, etcetera. The passing seasons. It's so corny, Mehring' (176). Antonia's words mean to emphasize the conviction that, at a metaphysical level, the pastoral paradise cannot be recovered and that its ideal images of harmony and wholeness are no more than childish illusions. That this is intended, however, to apply specifically only to the *white* colonisers of the country, and that their exile from the land is to be understood as a punishment for their specific misdeeds, is made evident in Gordimer's willingness to grant the rural *black* community a renewed sense of wholeness, unity and purpose which is denied Mehring at the novel's end. Antonia is also making a prophetic point. She suggests that it is not possible for Mehring to be more than simply a tenant of the land, its temporary coloniser, within the larger historical context in which he finds himself: 'That bit of paper you bought yourself from the deeds office isn't going to be valid for as long as another generation . . . the blacks will tear up your bit of paper. No one'll remember where you're buried' (177). Antonia's words neatly foreshadow the eventual reversal of the roles of the anonymous dead man and the landowner, but not before we have come to understand that Mehring's inner corruption and spiritual emptiness symbolise a death-in-life which metaphorically reduces him to the level of the corpse. His macabre sense of identification with the putrefying body below his soil has its roots in his repressed guilt and fear of exposure, and his eventual flight from the land is as much a flight from an individual and private truth as from an inexorable historical process.

Within such a context, Mehring's initial delight in the land as 'innocent' (199) becomes increasingly an index of deliberate self-delusion. The land repeatedly escapes his notion that it requires a paternalistic response from him, protection and conservation. As it endlessly and seemingly effortlessly renews itself after the devastations of drought, fire and flood in its own time (as do the farm-labourers in their own fashion, by drawing upon their particular ancestral sources of spiritual regeneration, despite the extent to which they are under siege by white colonisation), so it typically again shows itself to be entirely independent of and indifferent to both Mehring's needs and his efforts on its behalf. He is as dispensable and ultimately irrelevant as the oaks and chestnuts he begins to plant and which, he understands, will fall to the axes of those of the meek who will inherit his earth. He has also mistakenly embraced a misguided conception of the land's 'indifference' which Antonia correctly senses and articulates for him: 'The famous indifference of nature really sends you, doesn't it?' she mocks. 'It's the romanticism of *realpolitik*, the sentimentalism of cut-throat competition' (200). What she suggests here is that the capitalist mentality naturally welcomes a philosophy premised on the maxim of the survival of the fittest in a God-less universe. Instead, the novel articulates a sense of nature-as-life-force which fails to privilege the hierarchical paradigm which informs all evolutionary theory, and also highlights the sheer arrogance of Mehring's conception of himself as a 'conservationist'.

Mehring is indeed revealed to be not only arrogant but also at times grossly insensitive. For example, while irritated with the children who contribute to the decline of the guinea-fowl flocks by collecting their eggs, he gives no thought to the needs and conditions of life of the people who live on his land and work it for him. The bizarre nature of his tenancy of the land is aptly symbolised in the image of his early morning walk into his dew-drenched fields, incongruously dressed for a day in the city in his business suit, and glorying in the full, sensuous beauty of this 'fair and lovely place' (183). The rich evocation of the morning's beauty is symbolically bracketed by the description of the ragged 'army' of labourers which accosts him as he leaves the house, and by his cynical, self-seeking insensitivity towards his old servant, Alina, shortly thereafter. Nowhere does Gordimer more force-fully suggest by careful juxtaposition and development of imagery the essential immorality of such an indulgence in the pri-vate delights of a sensory immersion in the natural world. In a reverse movement to the pastoral pattern, such 'civilised' plea-sures have the effect of radically diminishing Mehring rather than redeeming him.

The price of such self-indulgence is abandonment: by his son, Terry, who does not wish either to 'conserve' or to exploit this potential inheritance; by his mistress, Antonia, who simply uses his money to escape imprisonment and leave the country; and by his overseer, Jacobus, who fails to come to keep him company on New Year's Eve and prefers instead to reaffirm a communal black identity of his own. The reader, too, will eventually abandon him, although at first we find ourselves deliberately seduced into a partial identification with Mehring as 'one of us', not only by the sporadic, first-person stream-of-consciousness narration, but also by the misleading emphasis on Mehring's reassuringly fami-liar concern for conservation policy, which has been a hallmark of white interaction with the continent; and by the inherent attractiveness of Mehring's moments of wryly ironic humour at his own expense: a humour which betrays the extent to which he can lay claim to neither innocence about nor ignorance of his position. But the reader begins to realise how misdirected such an identification is as the gulf between Mehring's dominant 'false consciousness' and reality is progressively revealed. Gordimer de-velops her indictment of capitalist and 'liberal' South Africa to the point where the novel's ironic intent makes inevitable Mehring's (and the reader's) sordid epiphany in the eucalyptus grove under the shadow of the mine-dumps. As a paternalistic landowner who fails to father his own son successfully, as a 'conservationist' whose politically conservative and racist values undermine his efforts, and as a self-proclaimed expert in husbandry who is husband to no one, Mehring's manifold failures finally overwhelm him. His fate suggests the truth of Kolodny's observation that

> the illusion of ownership, control, mastery, call it what you will, is the final illusion, and makes him who falls prey to it incapable of knowing the real meaning of the landscape and man's relation to it.[64]

The incomplete seasonal cycle which represents the time-frame underpinning the narrative structure of the novel may be read as symbolically representing the abrupt truncation of Mehring's efforts to achieve that wholeness and harmony, both internally and with the external world, that the completed circle might well have symbolised. His sojourn on the land is fittingly concluded by a symbolic death, in which his fear of exposure locates itself in a betrayal of the extent to which he has fundamentally internalised the dominant racism of the country despite his claims to an enlightened liberalism. Fearing himself about to be exposed, goaded and ridiculed like a bear at the bottom of a bear-pit, he in effect flees the country, while at the beginning of the novel's final episode his labourers bury a corpse which Gordimer neatly causes the unwary reader initially to assume is that of Mehring.

Gordimer's assessment of the nature of the white man's options in South Africa is brutal in its implications in *The Conservationist*. She presents us with a vision in which it is assumed that it is inevitable that history will pass the white man by as he fails to realise that the colonial era has already come to an end, and as the black masses, phoenix-like, resume control of their land. Her romantic argument is that the black man, regardless of the effects of urbanisation and detribalisation, is rooted in the land as no coloniser-exploiter can ever be; from it he continues to gain an even renewed strength and resilience despite what Gordimer recognises to be his current degradation and spiritual fragmentation, and Adamastor will rise again. Within this scenario the African landscape plays a dual role: in addition to the emphasis placed on its independence of and Conradian indifference to the white man's attempts at control, Gordimer suggests a parallel between its regenerative powers and the black community's ability to find ways to renew itself. Critics have connected landscape iconography in this novel with a larger South African iconology in which the landscape is

> seen as a moral agent that destroys the weak and wicked [white] but purifies and nurtures the good and the strong [black] in the beauties of its bosom.[65]

Clearly, then, Gordimer's European and English literary and philosophical heritage, which, as we have seen, includes not only a respect for genuine liberal values but also an internalisation of pastoral and Romantic attitudes to nature, survives in her novels not only in the anger which informs her dissection of the degraded and impotent liberalism of ostensibly anti-racist white South Africans, but also in her focus upon the failure of pastoral and Romantic perspectives to provide that refuge and solace to the bruised and questing spirit that tradition told her she had a right to expect of them. Nevertheless, although the pastoral idyll is presented as increasingly untenable within a context in which institutionalised racism is found to be the root of all evil, the fiction seems to suggest that the South African post-apartheid millennium will restore us to those pastoral pleasures which have had to be deferred until a more just dispensation is achieved. Indeed, by the time Gordimer came to write *The Conservationist*, it was precisely her acute sensitivity to place and its centrality in her own subjective life which determined her decision to make a *misdirected* pastoralism the ultimate symbol of white capitalist corruption and alienation. Within this paradigm it is not the hostility of the African landscape which makes what Christopher Hope calls 'the shapely categories of European pastoralism and romanticism'[66] invalid in the work, but the hostility of the political dispensation to the realisation of such yearnings.

The process whereby the treatment of place is linked to the formation of an ideology[67] emerges quite clearly in an analysis of Gordimer's work. In summary, her attempt to find a 'voice' for Africa causes her to initially employ a realist technique in which the sheer accumulation of detail will provide 'local colour' and a sense of the 'quality of life'. She begins by documenting with enormous evocative skill the sheer sensory impact of this world for both herself and a reader who is very early conceived of as likely to be non-South African, in an attempt at imaginative appropriation significantly and strongly shaped by the presence both of Lawrentian and Proustian models. Proust's influence is particularly apparent in Gordimer's emphasis on the connection between the sensory and the sexual in such passages as that in *A Guest of Honour* in which Bray smells woodsmoke on his first morning in Gala after years of absence in England, and is instantly overwhelmed by a sense of Africa that 'came back to him – all, immediate, as with the scent of a woman with whom one has made love' (102). (There is a similar emphasis on the evocative power of smell in the repeated reference to the 'warm potato smell' of some unidentified African shrub which emerges several times in the fiction as a counter to the stereotype of savage bush and jungle.[68]) Gordimer's own powerful identification with the land predictably expresses itself in her inscription of her early protagonists' responsiveness to landscape as an indicator of their search for an inner wholeness and integration with Africa which will prepare the way for their redemption via a genuine political commitment. The beginnings of an African identity for the white man are clearly vested in the sensitivity of his sensory response to the landscapes he inhabits.

As, however, the hope of integration comes to appear less and less tenable, Gordimer is caught up in conflicting responses: on the one hand, the original innocence of response can no longer be sustained as awareness broadens, and, on the other, a retreat into such subjective delights appears increasingly inappropriate. A focus upon 'place' therefore survives only in so far as it can be made to take on an overtly symbolic function, and landscape description in general is both annexed to and attenuated by the ideological programme. By the time Gordimer comes to write *A Sport of Nature*, the complex shifts in narrative voice and point of view encoded in this novel communicate the extent to which she has learnt to suspect the privileging of that subjective consciousness in which her original evocation of landscape had been grounded. A necessary consequence of such a shift is that landscape representation loses its central place in the fiction as she concentrates increasingly on dissecting the complex states of alienation and *anomie* to which her characters fall prey. This all-consuming focus is no doubt what leads Dennis Brutus to complain of a lack of warmth and feeling, and of a cold detachment in her work,[69] but such a criticism ignores the many moments that surface even in the later fiction in which the original intensity of Gordimer's personal responses causes the landscape to blossom once more, despite her conscious need to subordinate it to a specific symbolic function. As she pointed out early in her career, the intermittent survival of this element in her work illustrates the extent to which her 'private preoccupations remain, running strongly beneath or alongside or intertwined with the influence of the political situation'.[70]

Nowhere is the extent to which European and African influences inextricably interpenetrate and permeate each other more evident than in Gordimer's landscape iconography: her work is firmly linked into both metropolitan and colonial iconologies which she modifies and varies rather than abandons entirely. 'Exotic' Africa is implicitly resuscitated in the Edenic landscapes of coastal Natal, while the basic elements of Schreiner's archetypally alienated Karoo are reinscribed in the arid landscapes of the Transvaal highveld.[71] Although the metropolitan pastoral and Romantic impulses are ironised in their overt manifestations, they survive both in the early emphasis on the redemptive potential of sensitivity to the natural world, and in the use Gordimer makes of the typically pastoral opposition between the country and the city.[72] Gordimer is, in fact, caught up in complex tensions between the immediacy of that intensely subjective experience which negates all stereotypes and those inherited stereotypes which help to shape and organise inchoate experience. In a final irony, her insistence that Africa 'belongs' to its indigenous black inhabitants may itself be seen as a late version of the old stereotype of exoticism she has been at pains to counter in its cruder and more overt manifestations, and its corollary is her reversal of the negative implications of the old colonial trope of 'going native' in her defiant insistence on the need to abandon white contexts in order to be accepted in black Africa.[73] The essential romanticism underlying the ideological aim is perhaps most clearly evident in *A Sport of Nature*, in which alienation and

spiritual exile are shown to be at last resolved in the transformative impact of that utopian vision of an ultimate acceptance
by and integration into 'the beloved country' which the novel
celebrates. In the hopeful naïvety of this final triumphant articulation of her hopes for the future, Gordimer does not so much lay
to rest the ghost of colonialism as demonstrate the extent to
which she has remained in thrall to its residual stereotypes, and
which it will be the task of the post-colonial literature she has
inaugurated in South Africa to transcend.

Chapter 7

Conclusion: *My Son's Story*

Writers brought up in Africa have many advantages – being at the centre of a modern battlefield; part of a society in rapid, dramatic change. But in the long run it can also be a handicap: to wake every morning with one's eyes on a fresh evidence of inhumanity, to be reminded twenty times a day of injustice and always the same brand of it, can be limiting. There are other things in living besides injustice, even for the victims of it.

Doris Lessing[1]

There is a tendency among critics to patch up flaws, to make connections which may be there for other readers ... [but] however unified a work may be in intention, it is sadly fragmented in effect ... This is what I have called the concept of availability: just as all of his experience is not available even to the most gifted creative writer, so all of the writer's work is not available to even the most interested reader.

Philip Hobsbaum[2]

Gordimer's most recent novel, *My Son's Story*,[3] published as this study was nearing completion, illuminates once again both the extent and the limits of her achievement as a novelist in South Africa. In particular, it confirms in a variety of ways the centrality in her work of the twin impulses to generalise and to romanticise, which have as their corollary that tendency to both succumb to and construct stereotypes which we have traced through the body of the work. The interconnectedness of these two impulses is perhaps best demonstrated by turning again to Gordimer's somewhat self-deprecating but insightful description of herself in 1965 as 'a romantic struggling with reality',[4] a phrase which is of central importance in any consideration of her work for several reasons. It reminds us that her need to construct models of typicality is rooted in an originally romantic idealism which expresses itself in that characteristic undercurrent of earnest moral didacticism which is so powerful a directive force in the fiction. It also alerts us again to those subjective continuities of response which so firmly knit the ten novels together into a coherent *oeuvre*, and shape their themes, attitudes and perspectives in ways which allow the uniquely personal vision, which underlies and informs her shifting public political stance over four decades, to emerge.

It is continuities in the works which have emerged with particular clarity in this study. One of the fiction's most persistent tropes is represented in Gordimer's enduring conviction that only a 'new' type of white South African will be accepted in the emergent societies of post-colonial Africa, an idea which shapes both the early characterisation of Ann Davis in *Occasion for Loving* and the later idealised representation of Hillela in *A Sport of Nature*. In *My Son's Story*, the decision to make her protagonists South African 'coloureds', of mixed race, suggests that Gordimer may well have decided at this point in her development that the 'new African' is best found among those who fuse the European and African traditions in their very blood. The *central* white character of the novel, Sonny's lover Hannah Plowman, has come from outside South Africa, and is returned to that wider and more impersonal world of international humanitarian endeavour from which she has come at the end of the novel: her role in 'the struggle' remains merely that of observer and advisor, and it is entirely symbolically apt that when she finally leaves the country it is Sonny and his family, and not the white activists of earlier novels, who will continue the struggle to take possession of what is theirs by right of their history of blood and oppression.

In addition, Gordimer's consistent representation in the fiction of South Africa as 'a binary-option, single-vision country where one must choose between happiness and freedom'[5] shapes the dialectic between the personal and the political which lies at the core of every one of her works. In February 1991 she rearticulated in a muted form the central insight which directs the fundamental thematic thrust of her entire body of work:

> I think people are torn by the different pressures put on them in their lives. And it is very rare, I would say, almost never, that the personal doesn't give up without a tremendous struggle.[6]

This struggle has characteristically been largely represented as taking place within the framework of the relationship between mentor and disciple, or more particularly, between parents and their children. As we have seen, the truly adult consciousness, in Gordimer's view, is one which has succeeded in disciplining itself into an acceptance of the need for self-sacrifice in the interests of the greater good, thus demonstrating a moral maturity which is the goal of the *Entwicklungsroman* at the core of each of the novels. *My Son's Story* also follows this pattern. The ambiguously (Faulknerian) personal pronoun of the title alerts us to not one but three separate histories of moral growth offered in the novel: Sonny's tale of decline and rehabilitation, told by the son-as-antagonist; Aila's story of emancipation and fulfilment, told by the son-as-impotent-lover; and Will's own account of his growth to an uneasy and angry maturity of purpose. At the heart of this novel then, as in *Burger's Daughter* and a number of other works, we have the archetypal tale of the child's attempt to escape its parental inheritance and achieve the freedom to make different (and more selfish) life choices. However, in a characteristic move, freedom is shown to be most surely found in the subordination of the self to those larger ideals to which the parents have already committed themselves. Instead of succeeding in freeing themselves from parental influence, the children are reluctantly brought to an acknowledgement of the validity of their parents' commitments as models for their own lives. Within this paradigm, which also informs, for example, Toby's relationship with both his parents and his mentor and one-time lover, Anna Louw, in *A World of Strangers* (as well as such shorter pieces as the story 'Letter from his Father'[7]), Gordimer introduces a subtextual emphasis on the need for respect for the elders whose strongly conventional thrust supplements and may be said to give a paradoxical respectability to the revolutionary theme of the novels. Such an emphasis seems, in fact, strangely anomalous within the historical context of the 1976 Soweto uprising, when the strength and energy of the *children* of Soweto, who courageously confronted the enemy in the face of their parents' impotent despair, became a beacon of hope in the struggle against apartheid and a central symbol in much black protest literature. Gordimer's insistent valorisation of parental models of action, however, reminds us once again of her submerged but powerful commitment to those thoroughly conventional and traditional liberal-humanist values which she consistently deploys as the standard against which reality is to be measured,[8] even as she demolishes liberalism's pretentions as a force for change within the context of political life in South Africa. Thus Will, in *My Son's Story*, who chronicles with adolescent rage, bitterness and despair his father's sexual infidelity to his mother, and his mother's perceived emotional infidelity to the family, finds his obsessive prurience and politically cynical resentment ultimately discredited. The feverish tone of his first-person inserts is neutralised by a dispassionate and somewhat gently romantic third-person narrative voice whose contrasting balance of tone suggests the inevitability of the final defeat of his rebellion against the adults' example. At the end of the novel he is implicitly brought into the parental fold, won over despite himself by the unassuming heroism of his elders' painful and complex commitment to their ideals. Within such a framework, there is an obvious irony to Will's rebellious and childish desire to become a clown, and his father's contrary dream that he should become a writer: Will's anger does indeed have a clownish element to it, while it is, significantly, his father's wishes for him which are ultimately fulfilled.

In this latest novel, then, Gordimer's characters once again travel the well-worn path from political *gaucherie* to a redemptive conversion to 'the struggle', from an undefined and misdirected youthful idealism to an earnest commitment to a disciplined and effective pragmatism in the service of revolutionary principle. Here, too, we find again the movement towards commitment implicitly equated to the experience of religious conversion, a pattern in which the moral demands of political struggle replace the discarded forms of a discredited Christianity, but in which the intensity of that emotional idealism which informs religious faith is put to the services of political activism. Thus Gordimer obliquely suggests that Hannah's political commitments are to be understood as channelling those energies which would, under other circumstances and in different times, have informed a missionary zeal, and her political idealism is placed within a framing vision of South Africa as

> a centripetal force that draws people, in the region, not only out
> of economic necessity, but also out of the fascination of commit-

ment to political struggle. The fascination came to her in the mud-brick and thatch of the mission, the dust that had reddened her Nordic hair and pink ears: from her grandfather's commitment to struggle against evil in men, for God. For her the drive was to struggle against it for man – for humans. (88)

The path to political redemption is, of course, fraught with difficulties: Gordimer's work is caught in the complex tensions between her vision of ideal possibilities in both the private and the political life, and the brutal realities around her. Indeed, the inherent idealism which simultaneously informs her exploration of the possibilities of absolute emotional and sexual fulfilment in personal relationships, the utopian inclination of her political imagination, and her uncompromising rejection of apartheid, may be understood as paradoxically constituting an emotional defence against those realities and their corollary of white guilt. The unique difficulty of bridging the gap between the ideal and reality in contemporary South Africa, and the impossibility at the same time of escaping the consequences of being white in a racist society, which has constrained Gordimer (in her own words) 'to identify only with [her] colour' – giving rise to that 'split consciousness' identified in a variety of forms by her critics[9] – have imprisoned her to an unusual degree within her historical situation, redirecting her artistic development and imposing on her what is at times a numbing narrowness of vision.

The view that apartheid has had the effect of stunting the imaginative and creative powers of those South African artists who have felt themselves compelled to respond to the imperative to be *engagé* has been eloquently put forward by Albie Sachs, in his influential criticism in 1990 of South African apartheid literature as so

> narrowed down [that] . . . the only conflict permitted is that between the old and the new, as if there were only bad in the past and only good in the future . . . [with] good people on the one side and the bad ones on the other.[10]

It is a claim which implicitly echoes JanMohamed's assertion in 1983 that the Manichean oppositions on which not only apartheid ideology but the colonial mentality as such is based are too deeply entrenched to allow post-colonial writers such as

Gordimer to escape their effects.[11] In Gordimer's *oeuvre*, the 'us' versus 'them' paradigm informs the fiction in its various permutations to the present moment: a generally faceless 'System, out there', is designated as the source of all the evils against which those comfortingly united in the warmth of the struggle wage their continuing battle for the victory of good. Within such a context the intense emotional and sensory connections with the African landscape which first made of her a writer were to a degree pushed aside by her developing response to the perceived demands made upon her work by the historical period in which she found herself caught[12] – a response which the inherent idealism of her liberal-humanist orientation made inevitable. Consequently, the emotional connections from which the politics originally sprang have become increasingly obscured as the political agenda has gathered impetus in the work, while the clichés current in the public political arena have emerged refracted through the fiction as a body of stereotypes encoded both in reaction to and as an unconscious reflection of the perceptual strait-jacket imposed by apartheid.

Ideology has had a further clearly definable impact upon the fiction in encouraging the tendency towards generalisation in Gordimer's work. As we have seen, Clingman has interpreted this as an application of the Lukacsian theory of 'typification', in which the extent to which the particular can be made to stand for the general becomes the bearer of the ideological message. However, this interpretation of Gordimer's construction of stereotypes alerts us not so much to a strength in the works as to the distorting power of ideology upon the original creative impulse. Not only is Lukacsian theory in this area problematic as such (as has been suggested in Chapter 3), but its adoption as an explanatory model in assessing Gordimer's achievement simply serves to illuminate the extent to which some of Gordimer's major strengths as a writer are subverted by the ideological agenda which the fiction increasingly serves. In particular, her ability to construct with consummate precision the unique dimensions of a thoroughly individualised consciousness, in all the variety and richness of its idiosyncratic and transient subtleties of mood and response, is contradicted by her insistence upon elevating the uniquely particular into the typical: her fundamental sensitivity is significantly obscured by such politically didactic thrusts. In general, the tendency to 'typification' does little more than over-simplify and distort the complex realities to which she is otherwise so sensitive, giving a misleadingly absolutist status to the delicate flux of shifting temporal perceptions.

The assumptions embedded in the generalisations on which a sense of the 'typical' are based can be at times, as we have seen, disturbingly offensive. In _My Son's Story_, for example, we are confronted with the gratuitous, anti-white, class-conscious sneer contained both in the description of the 'plaster pelican' in Sonny's suburban garden, which was 'no doubt left behind by the white owners as the shed cast of any creature exactly reveals itself' (90), and in the contemptuous reductionism of the comment that 'the black ghettos were army encampments, and police dogs with their gun-carrying handlers replaced white ladies with poodles in the shopping malls' (97). A similar degree of falsification and simplification colours Will's comment that Sonny had 'the facility for picking up incidental knowledge that only intelligent people whose formal education is limited, possess' (35). The characteristic 'voice' of such asides is to be heard throughout the fiction, and reveals both the didactic impulses which shape much of the work and the ideological perspectives which direct those impulses.

Such moments of excess alert us to the exacerbated tension in the work between, on the one hand, Gordimer's continuing focus upon the art of 'seeing' a moment, an event or a mood as fully as possible, and, on the other, her political didacticism which determines that the passion for finely tuned detail shall expend itself all too often upon the stereotypical. For example, the thematic predictability in late anti-apartheid literature of the description of the unprovoked police attack upon the mourners at the graveside in Alexandra township in _My Son's Story_, however precisely observed, cannot escape an element of the banal and the clichéd. Gordimer's true strengths as a novelist emerge here not in her recapitulation of the outworn themes of the anti-apartheid struggle, but in her delicately precise and detailed analyses of the complex web of tensions and loyalties, passions and sympathies which knit together the human fabric. In this aspect of her work we have the art of 'seeing' put to persuasive use, in which her unerring eye for the savingly human and the telling or comic detail, and her ability to reduce the pompous, the portentous or the potentially tragic to the level of the touchingly ordinary are entirely in agreement with the European narrative traditions in which the work is grounded.

That Gordimer is herself aware of the various ways in which the political imperative has distorted her work is suggested in her very recent comments on the extent to which the South African writer's creative freedom has been curtailed and crippled by the historical situation in which he has found himself: not only by the operations of the censorship system, but also by the demand that literature align itself in the struggle. In 1990, in the midst of renewed hope that the apartheid era was coming to a close, Gordimer addressed a Writers Day conference sponsored by PEN in London, in which she is reported to have said that

> release from censorship is like a removal of a vice from a writer's head, leaving behind "a cramped and distorted imagination". Censorship necessitates that the writer of moral conscience "cut and weld his work into a weapon". And with the removal of that necessity, "accustomed to the obsessive demands of selecting every situation and word for its trajectory against apartheid, South African writers will have to open themselves to a new vocabulary of life . . . The real writers . . . will have the . . . wonderfully daunting task of finding ways to deal with themes that have been set aside in second place while writing was in battle-dress – the themes of humanity in all its forms, human consciousness in all its mystery, which demand not orthodoxy of any nature, but the talent and dedication and daring to explore and convey freely through individual sensibility".[13]

Here at last we have an implicit acknowledgement from Gordimer that her own writing too (for she would surely count herself among the 'real writers' mentioned above) has been 'in battle-dress', forced into that *engagément* which the tensions encoded in the fiction suggest she has at times struggled against as passionately as her frequently reluctant revolutionaries are shown to do.

Such an admission, of course, also again highlights the problematic character of Gordimer's continuing denial of an ideological tendentiousness in her novels, and of the concomitant charge of moral didacticism: for example, she asserted again in an interview in 1991 that she did not write 'from an ideological position. I am a writer, not a propagandist'.[14] However, her revealing equation of 'propaganda' with 'ideology' here should alert us to her continuing deployment of a reductionist version of the concept of ideology. She clearly understands it to refer simply to a particular socio-political programme or platform, eliding its wider application as a term referring to the entire body of established beliefs and assumptions which underlie and inform the construction of the relationship between Self and Other, and whose main purpose has been defined by JanMohamed, following Jameson, as 'self-validation' via 'strategies of containment'.[15] It is in this sense of the term that JanMohamed is able to claim that ideology should be defined as the subtext buried within the text, and that Jameson defines it as the active repression of underlying historical contradictions.[16] JanMohamed goes on to argue that

> the writer, by unconsciously attempting to valorise the position of self and his group in the face of an antagonistic alterity, is most often unable to proceed beyond the limited (and limiting) *real* economic and socio-political interests of his class and group . . . to the extent to which a text valorises any aspect of a class ideology it *lives* – it actively engages in a *political*, albeit a symbolic *act*.[17]

The entire discussion of ideology is highly relevant to Gordimer's work, particularly in so far as it argues that ideological discourse is made up of both overt cognitive structures and covert emotional structures, whose conjunction will produce a tension between conscious textual intention and unconscious selectivity and closure, between 'communal obligation' and 'subjective desire'.

It is within the parameters of these definitions that Gordimer must be understood to express both conscious and unconscious ideological biases, despite her claims to the contrary. Even at the overt level of party politics her commitments to a particular political ideology have been clear. During the period in which the ANC was banned, her representation of an impotent white liberalism, set in strong contrast to positive images of the black struggle, encoded but did not obscure her covert political allegiances; they emerged most unambiguously in the Charterist bias of *A Sport of Nature*, which took as its subject the history of the ANC in exile. Subsequent to its unbanning she publicly announced her membership of the ANC[18] and took on a leading role in one of its cultural organisations, the Congress of South African Writers (COSAW). Such long-standing and clear-cut commitments have inevitably also informed the fiction, despite her express desire to keep the artist and the citizen apart.

It is, however, as we have seen, within the context of the relationship between (white) self and (black) other that the unconscious link between submerged ideology and stereotypes becomes particularly clear. Gordimer's inscription of stereotypes in her work is indeed the clearest indicator available in the fiction of the nature and dimensions of her ideological commitments. Her fundamentally romantic and idealistic temperament, necessarily at odds with the reality within which it has found itself, has been peculiarly susceptible to the temptation to succumb to that 'admixture of myth and unconscious deformation of reality' which Gilman claims gives rise to stereotypes,[19] and which may be said to represent the negative side of the gulf between Self and Other. Although on the one hand she consciously demolishes the crude racist stereotypes current in her time, she simultaneously encodes, on the other hand, not only alternative and more positive tropes but also, at a subtextual level, as we have seen, the mental perspectives and particular mind-sets which underlie the prejudices she overtly rejects. Gilman's definition of stereotypes as 'palimpsests on which the bi-polar representations [of 'us' and 'them'] are still vaguely legible'[20] goes some way towards accounting for such paradoxes in the work. His assertion that 'each society has a distinct "tradition" . . . that determines its stereotypes'[21] echoes JanMohamed's emphasis on the impossibility of freeing oneself from those particular definitions of difference which are entrenched in the society into which one happens to be born. Such an insight allows us to recognise the inevitability of Gordimer's continuing construction of a sense of difference around the specifics of race and colour, given her particular background and historical context.

Gordimer has been acutely aware of critical response to her work, and its impact upon the fiction is often visible. For example, her sensitivity towards accusations that her work has been theoretically reductionist and simplistic is reflected in *My Son's Story* both in a new tendency to offer a more complex view of resistance politics and in her defiant intensification and at times overt justification of elements criticised in previous works. Thus having been accused of presenting the 'liberation movement' in *A Sport of Nature* as monolithic and morally unassailable, she chooses in *My Son's Story* to make something of the emergence of disaffected cadres within the ranks. However, the inherent romanticism of her imaginative thrust into revolutionary politics and her powerful ideological commitment to the ANC ensure that, in the novel, the threat is smoothly overcome in impeccably democratic fashion by a leadership invariably wise, moderate and pragmatic. Here again we may see the extent to which Gordimer's work reflects rather than advances political discussion; the novel refers to topical issues but does not run the risk of attempting to suggest resolutions to the dilemmas debated. Thus Sonny and Hannah discuss the ethics of violence (as Whaila and Hillela did in *A Sport of Nature*), and briefly delineate the challenges posed by the collapse of the Eastern European Communist régimes, but neither topic elicits more than a tentative assertion of the complexity of the issues at stake. Gordimer's characteristically fragmented dialogues, so carefully attuned to the incompleteness and hesitancies of actual speech patterns (the preference of the dash over the inverted comma to demarcate direct speech suggests something of the hesitancy of the spoken word), merely record the most general delimitations of each debate rather than offering further ideas and developing positions of substance. Documentation of issues of this kind frequently entails the insertion of the clichés of revolutionary rhetoric in her work: in a characteristic move, Gordimer chooses to justify rather than apologise for or delete this element in the fiction: both in *Burger's Daughter* (328) and in *My Son's Story*[22] she vigorously defends her practice by claiming that the cliché functions as a symbolic shorthand upon which the transformative energies of the individual psyche will work to construct those powerful meanings which are the necessary ground of disciplined and purposive action.

In *My Son's Story* she also attempts to respond positively to recent feminist criticisms of her work (see Chapter 4) by fore-grounding female strength, and in implicitly recognising the re-cent move towards an affirmation of the importance of female contributions to 'the struggle'. Despite her choice once again of a male first-person narrator as the dominant voice, she not only presents Hannah (with only residual irony) as 'a feminist, careful of genders' (88), but also shows us Aila, a direct descendent of Mrs Bamjee in the short story, 'A Chip of Glass Ruby' (1965)[23], as fully capable of outdoing her men at every level in her quiet embrace of an emancipation simultaneously emotional and political. Aila overtakes the faltering efforts of Sonny (ambushed and eventually made politically impotent, as Gideon was before him, by his relationship with Hannah), and proves herself to be finally more powerful and effective than her husband precisely because, Gordimer suggests, as a mother she possesses a more urgent intuitive grasp of the extent to which, in the world into which she will send her children, the private and the political are indissolubly intertwined and must be addressed as one. The novel therefore offers us a series of significant contrasts: whereas Sonny talks and Will watches and rages, Aila acts; whereas Sonny be-comes obsessively aware of 'needing Hannah', first Aila and then Hannah free themselves of needing Sonny; whereas Sonny and Will stay behind, Aila, Hannah and Baby move into the wider arena of the struggle in exile. It is, indeed, a novel which cel-ebrates female rather than male heroism, despite – or perhaps, given the conceptually idealised nature of heroism, because of – its refusal to enter deeply into the female consciousness.

Such a refusal reminds us that, notwithstanding the evidence of Gordimer's muted responsiveness in *My Son's Story* to reac-tions to her earlier works, it is the continuities of interest and purpose (in all their contradictory complexity) rather than any marked development which reveal most fully the assumptions, attitudes and values on which the works are based and which they encode at both conscious and unconscious levels. *My Son's Story* fails to offer its readers a change of direction or a renewed freshness of vision; indeed, each of the motifs dealt with above may be found to be at least marginally present in earlier works. The key to such continuities, as I have suggested, is to be found in Gordimer's fundamental romanticism, which predisposes her to that ultimate utopianism whose centrality in the individual's spiritual life is so passionately defended by Sasha in *A Sport of Nature* (187), and whose value she has recently reasserted in 1991 in her comment that

> I am all for a dash of idealism . . . If there is no idealism there is no hope of ever changing the world. We must cling to our idealism and fight for it. If only a tiny bit of it is realised every time, every 100 years, that is important. Idealism is not something that hundreds of thousands of people can display consciously except for an hour or two at a rally or in times of crisis. But I am still amazed – and it is one of the things which made me write *Burger's Daughter* – at how extraordinary it is to live and have lived in a country where there are heroes, where there are people who go off to jail for 10, 20 years out of a belief in democratic ideals.[24]

As noted already, Gordimer's passionate belief in and admiration for such heroism informs that contempt for those who remain satisfied with mere gestures which has so frequently steeled her tone into the chilliness which has repelled critics such as Dennis Brutus. The living heroes of the above passage suggest to her that it might be possible to close the gulf between ideal conceptions of what is possible and the reality around her, and betray her into that romantic Messianic sentimentality which colours her depiction of both Whaila (in *A Sport of Nature*) and of Sonny. Indeed, at one point in *My Son's Story*, Sonny's overwhelming *goodness* – so repeatedly stressed – is illustrated by the implicit comparison with the Holy Family which is embedded in the suggestion that the history of himself and his family can be summed up as 'the love of a schoolteacher for a Virgin, the happiness of the first Baby, and then the son named for genius' (99). Within such a paradigm a degree of sentimentality clearly triumphs: intentions are shown to be pure, however flawed their consequences; 'the leadership' is worthy of absolute respect, whatever disaffections might temporarily arise in the ranks; and self-indulgent passions are dislodged in favour of an unreserved dedication to the Cause, whose significance as a religious *icon* in the individual's spiritual life is marked by its connection with notions of sin and redemption. Thus the meaning of life is to be found once again in selfless service to the struggle, which will bring with it the absolution of acceptance into the community of the oppressed: the whites who attend the 'cleansing of the graves' ceremony in Alexandra township find black hands eagerly reaching out to greet them, and gratefully receive 'the blessing of the hands, the healing touch' (108).

Such telling emphases also once again reveal the shaping impulse behind such idealised depictions: the need to find *a way to belong*, to escape the pain of exclusion, marginalisation and superfluity. Commitment to the Cause will eventually allow the emancipated white South African to share in the inheritance of the land of her birth and rescue her from alienation and despair. The essential romanticism and implicit meliorism of this vision is everywhere apparent in what Gordimer omits from rather than includes in her narrative in *My Son's Story*: in her reductive representation of imprisonment as primarily a bonding experience during which the concomitant impeccable revolutionary credentials may be forged; in her representation of the townships as places of teeming human warmth, vitality, affection and colour; and in the imagery of such passages as that describing the funeral of young activists shot by the police, in which the freshly covered graves are represented as 'beds, the shape of sleeping bodies with a soft cover of this red woolly earth drawn over their heads' (109). Not only do such passages take no account of torture in South African prisons, of townships riven by internecine warfare in which 'necklacing' had become endemic during the period in which the novel was being written, or even of the sheer lack of even the most basic amenities of life which makes Alexandra township perhaps one of the bleakest places on earth. They also once again implicitly represent 'the struggle' through the lens of those essentialist, liberal-humanist values encoded in the novel's insistent references to the great icons of Western culture, such as Shakespeare, Van Gogh and Kafka, who are each significantly singled out for mention as Sonny's spiritual guides and mentors to the exclusion of those figures who have been elevated as particular inspirations to revolutionary politics in Africa in this century.

Perhaps, in the final analysis, the contrast between Gordimer's reputation overseas and at home can only be addressed within the general parameters of a reader-oriented criticism. It is clear that a domestic audience intimately familiar with conditions entirely strange to an international readership may find merely banal what the outsider finds illuminating and reassuringly accessible through the shared values which underpin the works. Indeed, many of the clichés and stereotypes embedded in the works can only be identified by what Stanley Fish has called 'interpretive communities'[25] made up in this case either of those immersed in the situation from which such myths have arisen or of those entirely familiar with the indigenous literary contexts within which the works must be situated. Thus Coetzee's observation, that 'those South African writers who make the grade [internationally, do so because] . . . they are seen to have privileged access to a theme of compelling importance which we may loosely call "the South African situation" ',[26] emphasises the inevitable gap between those who desire such access and those who are trapped within 'the situation' itself. What Foucault has called the 'author-function'[27] may also be seen to have played a part in the construction of Gordimer's reputation overseas, in so far as it has diverted attention from the fissures and contradictions in her work and has made it possible for the *oeuvre* to be represented as 'required background reading for anyone who wants to know what it was like in South Africa in the late twentieth century'.[28]

Gordimer herself has been keenly aware of the gap in her work between theory and practice, intention and reception. 'Nothing I say here will be as true as my fiction,' she wrote in 'Living in the Interregnum';[29] while her awareness of not only the political but also the ontological restrictions under which she has written is suggested by her comment that 'the real dangers lie in the hidden places close to you'.[30] That she has not been altogether successful in the immensely difficult task that she set herself illuminates not so much 'what it was like in South Africa' as what it was like to be an affluent, white, English-speaking woman with liberal sympathies and a passionate desire to write responsibly of the bewildering tensions endemic to her world 'in the late twentieth century'. Indeed, although our admiration for her willingness to bear witness to her own particular segment of experience of life under apartheid during difficult decades must be qualified by an awareness of the manifold ways in which her vision has been limited and even deformed by her personal and historical con-

texts, we should not ignore the overwhelming symbolic significance of the fictional project in Gordimer's own spiritual and
emotional life. Its unique centrality is suggested by analogy in the
closing passages of *My Son's Story*, in which Will (named after
William Shakespeare in a moment of parental prescience) tells us
that what his father did has made the son a writer – not merely a
chronicler of domestic dramas, but one whose task he conceives
it to be to record 'what it really was like to live a life determined
by the struggle to be free' (276). It is deeply significant that he
believes that it is through the fulfilment of this task that he will be
rescued from exclusion and marginalisation both in the family
and in society as such. In assigning himself the role of historian
and interpreter of his parents' politically committed lives, he
finally discovers a place for himself, too, within 'the struggle'.
Those who have questioned Gordimer's own credentials as interpreter of a struggle in which she has largely been an observer only
may find here an implicit response to such criticisms. Will's
defence of his choice may be read as Gordimer's assertion of the
personal value of the role she herself has filled in South Africa's
cultural life over the last forty years – one which suggests that, in
the pursuit of her art, she has achieved a kind of triumph over the
multiple marginalisations of sex, language, class and colour into
which she was born, and has earned for herself that right to
'belong' in the emergent new Africa,[31] whose boundaries it has
been the fiction's task to construct prophetically as the ultimate
object of Desire.

The Novels:
Gordimer's Chronology

The Lying Days	1953
A World of Strangers	1958
Occasion for Loving	1963
The Late Bourgeois World	1966
A Guest of Honour	1970
The Conservationist	1974
Burger's Daughter	1979
July's People	1981
A Sport of Nature	1987
My Son's Story	1990

Full information on the editions used is given in the Bibliography.

Notes

Epigraphs

1. Stephen Watson, *Selected Essays*, 1990: 181.
2. D.H. Lawrence, *Studies in Classic American Literature* (1924), excerpted in *The Oxford Dictionary of Quotations*, 1980: 311. The New Criticism's 'intentional fallacy' resurfaces repeatedly in contemporary literary theory; see for example Weedon, who writes that 'authorial intention, even when apparently voiced in aesthetic theory, is no guarantee of the actual meaning of the fictional text' (*Feminist Practice and Post-Structuralist Theory*, 1987: 162).

Preface

1. Ralph Ellison, *Shadow and Act*, 1972: 27, 44.
2. Lewis Nkosi, "A Keynote Address" in G. Davis (ed.), *Crisis and Conflict*, 1990: 26.

3. See Michael Wade, *Nadine Gordimer,* 1978, who has extensively examined the theme of 'Europe-in-Africa' in Gordimer's work.
4. Stephen Clingman, *The Novels of Nadine Gordimer,* 1986.
5. Nadine Gordimer, 'A Writer in South Africa', 1965: 25.
6. Nadine Gordimer in interview with Pat Schwartz, 1984.
7. Sections of this text have appeared in various publications in a slightly different form. An early paper entitled ' "History from the Inside?": Text and Subtext in some Gordimer Novels', and published in G. Davis (ed.), *Crisis and Conflict: Essays in Southern African Literature*, 1990, has supplied material for the present Introduction and the chapter on 'Stereotypes' in Gordimer's work. A paper entitled ' "Both as a Citizen and as a Woman?": Women and Politics in Some of Gordimer's Novels' included in A. Rutherford (ed.), *From Commonwealth to Post-Colonial*, 1992, has also supplied material for the Introduction and forms the basis of the chapter on 'Gordimer's Women'. Two articles on J.M. Coetzee's novel *Foe* (see the bibliography) have been drawn upon in a brief discussion of post-structuralist thrusts in South African fiction in the chapter on 'Gordimer's Women'. The chapter on 'Images of Blacks' is an expanded version of a paper entitled 'The "Conspiracy Against Keeping Apart": Some Images of Blacks in Nadine Gordimer's Novels' which appears in E. Reckwitz, L. Vennarini and C. Wegener (eds.), *The African Past and Contemporary Culture*, 1993. A shortened version of the chapter on 'Landscape Iconography' in Gordimer's novels has been published by Macmillan in a collection of essays edited by Bruce King, *The Later Fiction of Nadine Gordimer*, 1993.

Chapter 1: Introduction: South Africa's Conscience

1. Czeslaw Milosz, letter, *The New York Review of Books*, 1988.
2. Excerpted from Derek Walcott, 'The Muse of History'; 1979, in Tim Brennan, "Cosmopolitans and Celebrities", 1989.
3. See Robert Haugh, *Nadine Gordimer*, 1974; Michael Wade, *Nadine Gordimer*, 1979; Christopher Heywood, *Nadine Gordimer*, 1983; John Cooke, *The Novels of Nadine Gordimer*, 1985; Stephen Clingman, *The Novels of Nadine Gordimer*, 1986; Judie Newman, *Nadine Gordimer*, 1988.
4. See 'Gordimer – South Africa's Conscience', a review by Julian Symons, 1984. A recent version of this assessment is to be found in a review of *My Son's Story* in which Penny Perrick writes: 'If one were never to read any other literature about South Africa, Gordimer's work would be enough . . . As a literary keeper of records, she has no peer' (1990). Superlatives abound in foreign assessments of South African writers: thus André Brink is reminded that he has been called 'the white giant among South African writers' by Dieter Welz in the NELM interviews (see Welz, 1987: 55).
5. Nadine Gordimer, 'A Writer in South Africa', 1965: 22.
6. Clingman's subtitle (1986). It is a phrase he draws from Gordimer's comment in *The Black Interpreters* (1973: 7) that 'if you want to read the facts of the

retreat from Moscow in 1815, you may read a history book; if you want to know what war is like and how people of a certain time and background dealt with it as their personal situation you must read *War and Peace*'. In an interview with Diana Cooper-Clark in 1983 Gordimer said that 'the historian can tell you the events and can trace how the events came about through the power shifts in the world. But the novelist is concerned with the power shifts within the history of individuals who make up history' ('The Clash', 54).

7. Clingman, 1986: 244. Gordimer herself presents her role as that of 'interpreter, both to South Africa and the world, of a society in struggle' ('Living in the Interregnum', in *The New York Review of Books*, 20 January 1983). For contemporary perspectives from some South African writers upon many of the events and issues which Gordimer's work is concerned with, see, for example, the useful contributions from Abrahams, Rive, Butler, Ebersohn, Schoeman and Gwala in M. Daymond *et al.* (eds.) *Momentum*, 1984. The concept of history, however, has been problematised in ways Clingman does not take into account. See, for example, David Elliot's comment that 'not only in South Africa but across the world "history" has become a plural noun as it is recognised that the story you now tell says as much about your life as it does about the past . . . The issue of "whose history" necessarily supplants "a unitary view"' (in *Art from South Africa*, 1990: 7). We might also note Napoleon Bonaparte's definition: "History is a set of lies agreed upon" (epigraph in Ronald Wright, *Stolen Continents*, 1991: 3).

8. Data given in several telephone conversations with Ann Cronjé, Marketing Manager of Longman-Penguin S.A., May–June 1988. Longman-Penguin on average recorded sales of only about one thousand units a year across ten available titles in South Africa, and claim to distribute Gordimer's works in South Africa mainly in 'academic' bookshops as a 'duty' to the South African public rather than for reasons of profit. This data remained essentially unchanged when Ann Cronjé was contacted for further information in January 1991.

9. Es'kia Mphahlele, in conversation with the author in 1983, commented curtly that "we don't read her": an interesting brush-off, given Mphahlele's discussion of 'menacing servants' in Gordimer's fiction in *The African Image*, 1962: 133-34.

10. See, for example, Arnold Abramowitz, 1956: 13-17.

11. A. Woodward, 1961: 12.

12. Excerpted in N. McEwan, *Africa and the Novel*, 1983: 132.

13. Heribert Adam, "Reflections on Gordimer's Interregnum", 1983.

14. Tony Morphet, 1984: 2.

15. K. Parker, 1989: 222.

16. D. Enright, 1984.

17. Don Maclennan, 1989: 33.

18. Brenda Cooper, 1988: 4.

19. Robert Haugh, 1974: 162.

20. Ravan Press's *Staffrider* editor, Andries Oliphant, was reported as saying at Gordimer's official 1990 birthday party that 'it is sad that Gordimer has been unsung in her own country because of apartheid' (*The Weekly Mail*, Johannesburg, 23-29 November 1990: 23). One of the purposes of this study is to demonstrate the degree to which such an assessment is simplistic and unsatisfactory.

21. Tony Morphet, 1984: 2.

22. Stephen Clingman, 1986: 222.

23. Nadine Gordimer.

24. See Gordimer, 'Living in the Interregnum' (1982), in Stephen Clingman (ed.), *The Essential Gesture*, 1988: 226. Apartheid of course affects all South Africans, regardless of colour, in subtle and not always easily understood ways. See, for example, Deon Viljoen, writing on the *Cape Town Triennial 1985* Art Exhibition. He suggests that 'the awareness that isolates and separates and categorises, born for instance of the élitism of the Avant-garde, found a fertile breeding ground in South Africa's sensitivity on issues of division and social separation. The Apartheid mentality may have a stronger grip on our lives than we suspect. It has affected our lives far more profoundly than mere laws promulgated in the name of Apartheid. An art that wishes to make a significant contribution to the South Africa of the 21st century will have to begin by burying that set of attitudes'. Martin Trump makes a similar point when writing on the practice of tertiary education in South Africa over the past few decades: 'Academics stand firm guard over their areas of expertise, while students are left to put together the pieces of a diffuse, fragmented education. It is interesting to note the ideological parallels between this situation in tertiary-level humanities education and that prevailing in the broader social and political structures of South Africa . . . a tendency towards division and separation – in short, towards the fostering of an apartheid mentality' (1989: 164).

25. See, for example, the comments on this head by Martin Trump in his paper, 'The Short Fiction of Nadine Gordimer' (1986: 342) in which he quotes Clingman in his claim that Gordimer is in a 'split historical position'.

Chapter 2: Liberalism, Ideology and Commitment

1. F.R. Leavis, excerpted in K. Parker, *The South African Novel in English*, 1975: 2.

2. Doris Lessing (1958), quoted in D. Ward, *Chronicles of Darkness*, 1989: 1.

3. June Jordan, quoted in a review by Jenny Turner, 1993: 28. Jordan is quoted as going on to say that South Africa could not be imagined by outside observers as being 'beautiful or large or bright or able to grow peaches; there could not be people laughing there, or music'.

4. Tony Morphet, quoted by Mike Nicol, 1992.

5. See, for example, a recent anonymous review of *My Son's Story* (in the *Sunday Star*, Johannesburg, 2 December 1990), in which the reviewer

complains that Gordimer is 'a writer revered here, but read elsewhere. This is in part because her writing has a constantly explicatory quality to those who live here. The reader feels like a dull child having a lesson explained that is known only too well by rote'. Stephen Gray has claimed in a review of André Brink's *Mapmakers* that dissidence has become a 'commodity' for South African writers, and 'a very saleable one right now' (1984: 9), while Christopher Hope, in a 1988 talk to students at the University of the Witwatersrand, spoke dismissively of South African literature as 'a single-issue literature' with 'a dependable cowboy-movie value system'. J.M. Coetzee, in a more sympathetic comment in 1983, said in an interview that 'I know something of the insidious pressures faced by South African writers to simplify and explain for a foreign audience' (see Tony Morphet, 'Two Interviews with J.M. Coetzee', 1987: 459-60).

6. Nadine Gordimer, 'The Essential Gesture' (1984) in Stephen Clingman (ed.) *The Essential Gesture*, 1988: 245; and in interview with Boyers *et al.*, 1984: 9.

7. Tim Brennan, 1989: 8. The term 'post-colonial' has been unsatisfactorily defined as covering 'all the culture affected by the imperial process from the moment of colonisation to the present day'. 'Post-colonial *literatures*', on the other hand, are defined as literatures which 'emerged in their present form out of the experience of colonisation and asserted themselves by foregrounding the tension with the imperial power, and by emphasising their differences from the assumptions of the imperial centre' (B. Ashcroft *et al.*, 1989: 2).

8. Lewis Nkosi, 1990: 20-1.

9. See Nadine Gordimer, 'Notes of an Expropriator' (1964); also 'Leaving School – II' (1963).

10. Nadine Gordimer, 'Notes of an Expropriator' (1964).

11. *ibid*.

12. Nadine Gordimer, 'Where Do Whites Fit In?' (1959), in *The Essential Gesture*, 1988: 27, 30. The figure of Hillela in *A Sport of Nature* may be understood as a realisation of the desire to 'find a society . . . where . . . white skin will have no bearing on [her] place in the community', a desire at last ideally consummated within an African context.

13. Nadine Gordimer, 'Leaving School – II', 1963: 64.

14. Gordimer's early resistance to the pressure to be *engagé* foreshadows, in a curious historical reversal, current debates in South African left-wing circles on the cultural role of the artist. This issue was given prominence in an influential paper by Albie Sachs prepared for an in-house ANC seminar (see 'Preparing Ourselves for Freedom' (February 1990) in I. de Kok and K. Press, 1990: 19-29). Sachs opposed the inscription by art of 'the multiple ghettoes of the apartheid imagination', and suggested that 'our members should be banned from saying that culture is a weapon of the struggle' (1990: 19). Stephen Watson had already called the requirement to be *engagé* an 'unexamined dogmatism' and had quoted Kundera in insisting that art should be protected from the 'mindlessness of politicisation' ('Poetry and

Politicisation' (1985), in *Selected Essays*, 1990: 13, 14). Gordimer's recently articulated view of herself as a 'cultural worker' (1984) (see this chapter) seems outdated in the light of such perspectives.

15. Gordimer said in 1961 that 'I think I am the sole example of a South African who has chosen that other new theme – the decline of a liberalism, black-and-white, that has proved itself hopelessly inadequate to our historical situation' ('The Novel and the Nation in South Africa' (rep.), in G.D. Killam, 1973: 51).

16. Es'kia Mphahlele, 'South African Literature versus the Political Morality', 1983: 9. It is by and large this version of liberalism which is castigated by Gordimer in the novels. See, for example, Helen's rejection of Paul's attempts to 'change the system from within' and give it a human face' in *The Lying Days*.

17. See D. Ward, 1989: 120.

18. Nadine Gordimer, 'The Fischer Case', 1966: 30.

19. R. Boyers *et al.*, 'A Conversation with Nadine Gordimer', 1984: 11. But how much further? Note that Gordimer attacks capitalism, both in *The Conservationist* and in 'Living in the Interregnum', but not in favour of a Marxist or even covertly socialist perspective. In fact, she offers only sketchy descriptions of some responses to competing economic theories, and leaves us with little more than a vague plea for the development of an 'alternative left, a democracy without economic or military terror' ('Living in the Interregnum' (1982), in *The Essential Gesture*, 1988: 237).

20. Nick Visser, 1985: 10-11.

21. These definitions are offered by Elie Kedourie, 'The Limitations of Liberalism', in *The American Scholar*, 1989: 265.

22. Tim Brennan, 'Cosmopolitans and Celebrities', 1989: 6, 8-9. In 1965, stressing that she was 'not a politically minded person by nature,' Gordimer said, 'I don't suppose that, if I had lived elsewhere, my writing would have reflected politics much. If at all . . . [earlier] I was completely uninterested in politics' ('A Writer in South Africa', 1965: 23, 27).

23. Nadine Gordimer, 'A Writer in South Africa', 1965: 22. In 1956 she is reported as having said that she had 'so far avoided political themes' – another indicator of early resistance to *engagement* (see Cooke, quoting Paton, 1976: 64).

24. Clingman (1986: 6-7) demonstrates clearly the extent to which 'Gordimer's work is by definition caught up in the major movements of South African literature' as it responded to political developments, but does not suggest that she does more than reflect opinions and positions which have been given some public prominence in her fiction. Note, too, Driver's comments (1983: 32) that Gordimer 'has on the whole translated existing political philosophies into fictional form and . . . toed a straight-forward political line. Maclennan claims (1989: 32) that Gordimer's 'main theme is her attachment to a certain ideological notion of History . . . A complex rhetoric has persuaded me to take fiction for fact: with one eye to watch the claustrophobic dance of inadequate characters in their frail humanity, and

with the other to watch an inexorable historical process that seems to be disconnected from their lives, and which yet dictates how we shall see their emptiness and futility'. See too Elaine Fido, who, in writing of *A Guest of Honour,* says that 'as a political novel [it] deals rather too much in commonplaces: neo-colonialist versus neo-Marxist; liberalism distressed by political realities; industrial action versus organised authority being treated as subversion; political thugs enjoying violent rampages in the name of the Party. It is like a collection of news reports of recent years, and not only from Africa . . . The novel reveals a stubborn and outmoded liberalism, with the dream of socialism – if we are to take Bray's ideas seriously – still over-riding the hard facts of human nature. The country Gordimer has created is just barely plausible but not nearly so politically interesting as modern Africa' (1978: 30-31).

25. Brenda Cooper, 1988: 10.
26. 'I'm a white South African radical. Please don't call me a liberal', said Gordimer, in a 1974 interview printed in *The Times* of London. However, see the discussion which follows on her continuing allegiance to fundamental liberal values at odds with the debased versions thereof which she opposes in contemporary South Africa.
27. Nadine Gordimer, in conversation with Susan Sontag, 1985: 17.
28. Es'kia Mphahlele, 1962: 67, 87.
29. Nadine Gordimer, in interview with Anthony Sampson, 1987.
30. See Eve Bertelsen, 'Doris Lessing', 1986: 156-57. Raymond Williams suggests that the term 'communism' should be connected to 'communion' as in 'Communion Table' (*Keywords*, 1976: 63). In this connection it is interesting to note that Bennie Alexander, spokesperson for the Pan-Africanist Congress, described South African Communists as 'liberals who have learned to abuse neo-Marxist terminology' (Network News, SATV, 20:00, 12 April 1990).
31. Gordimer responds to Conor Cruise O'Brien's description of *Burger's Daughter* as 'a profoundly religious book' by agreeing that Rosa was indeed struggling against 'a doctrine of suffering as a revolutionary for the redemption of a classless freedom. The imposition of faith coming from a profoundly religious background since the kind of Marxism that her parents accepted so uncritically was indeed a religion [*sic*]; it was a demand for faith' (see the interview with Diana Cooper-Clark, 1983: 58).
32. Excerpted in T. Davenport, 1987: 368.
33. See 'Living in the Interregnum' (1982), in *The Essential Gesture*, 1988: 235.
34. See for example the conclusions to *The Lying Days, A World of Strangers, The Late Bourgeois World, Burger's Daughter* and *July's People.*
35. Gordimer was asked in 1984 whether she hoped to achieve 'the drastic changes which need to be achieved in South Africa without a revolution'. Her reply is characteristically moderate and idealistic: 'I have the obstinate utopian notion – and I'm not alone in this – that we must try to achieve this revolution without the terrible bloodshed that has happened in other places' R. Boyers *et al.*, 'A Conversation with Nadine Gordimer', 1984: 15).
36. When asked why she had never been even under house arrest in South Africa,

Gordimer answered that 'first of all, I would say I'm not brave enough. I have never taken any direct political action. Someone like myself takes calculated risks. And everybody has his or her own particular ceiling of risk' (see R. Boyers *et al.*, 1984: 22).

37. Nadine Gordimer, *What Happened to 'Burger's Daughter'?*, 1980: 29.

38. R. Boyers *et al.*, 1984: 4-5.

39. Louis Althusser, 'A Letter on Art in Reply to André Daspré' in *Lenin and Philosophy*, 1971: 204-205.

40. Nadine Gordimer, 'Leaving School – II', 1963: 64.

41. Nadine Gordimer, 'A Writer in South Africa', 1965: 22.

42. Gordimer interviewed by John Barkham in *Saturday Review*, 16 January 1963: 63, quoted in John Cooke, 1976: 235; footnote 28.

43. Nadine Gordimer 'English-Language Literature and Politics', 1975: 110.

44. Nadine Gordimer, 'The Novel and the Nation in South Africa' (1961), in G.D. Killam, 1973:37. Gordimer's suggestion that Africa's conditions are unique reveals that typical colonialist perspective already discussed above, one clearly present in her implicit dismissal of South Africans as 'conspicuously lacking' in 'intellectual curiosity' (49).

45. See for example Don Maclennan, 1989: 30-33.

46. Nadine Gordimer, 'Introduction' to *Selected Stories*, 1975: 12.

47. Nadine Gordimer, 'Living in the Interregnum' (1982), in Stephen Clingman (ed.), *The Essential Gesture*, 1988: 232-33.

48. *ibid.*, 241.

49. Nadine Gordimer in interview with Diana Cooper-Clark, 1983: 58; see also her 1987 interview with Anthony Sampson. The extent to which the novel cannot escape ideology is suggested by Lennard Davis, who writes that 'the novel's fictionality is a ploy to mask its genuine ideological reportorial function' (1987: 213).

50. Abdul JanMohamed, *Manichean Aesthetics,* 1983: 263-64.

51. Nadine Gordimer, 'Introduction' to *Selected Stories*, 1975: 14-15. See too Gordimer's comments in 1961 on the subject of commitment: 'There are a number of things to be committed to in South Africa – colour groups, language groups, political groups, and so on – and to be committed to one is to find yourself in bitter opposition to one, or some, or all of the others. The novelist writes about what sense he makes of life; his own commitment to one group or another enters his novel as part of, sometimes the deepest part of, the sense he makes of life. If, on the other hand, the commitment enters the novel not as part of the writer's conception of the grand design, but as an attempt to persuade other people – then the book is not a novel but propaganda with a story' ('The Novel and the Nation in South Africa' (1961), in G.D. Killam (ed.), *African Writers on African Writing*, 1973: 38). Note that Gordimer here rejects not commitment but propaganda.

52. Nadine Gordimer, in conversation with Susan Sontag, 1985: 16. See too Gordimer's well-known statement that 'politics is character, in South Africa' ('A Writer in South Africa', 1965: 23).

53. Visser argues that 'the sense of politics as ultimately inimical to the higher aspirations of the individual is a cardinal tenet of the liberal ideology . . . What makes ideology so difficult to discuss [in fact] is that its power lies in its invisibility to those who operate within it' (1985: 17, 13). Visser interestingly claims that 'radical fiction fails so often because the political stance taken is typically contradicted and subverted in the course of the novel . . . It is not politics that betrays artistry, but artistry that betrays politics' (1985: 7).

54. Nadine Gordimer, 'English-Language Literature and Politics', 1975: 100.

55. Nadine Gordimer, 'A Writer in South Africa', 1965: 22.

56. This point is made by Paul Bailey in his introduction to the Virago edition of *Occasion for Loving*, 1983: ix; he writes that 'the idiocy, the simple-mindedness of the notion of white supremacy is so transparently obvious [to her] that she relegates it to the background of her fiction: it's always *there*, a fact of South African life'.

57. Nadine Gordimer, in interview with R. Boyers *et al.*, 1984: 27. In 'The Novel and the Nation in South Africa' (1961) Gordimer said that 'the question [South Africans] must ask of the novelist and the one he must attempt to answer is: What is the life of man?' (in G.D. Killam (ed.), 1973: 50).

58. Nadine Gordimer, 'Living in the Interregnum' (1982), in *The Essential Gesture*, 1988: 231-32.

59. Nadine Gordimer, in conversation with Susan Sontag, 1985: 17.

60. The first three novels in particular were strongly influenced by the works of Proust and D.H. Lawrence. See 'Notes of an Expropriator' and 'Leaving School – II' for Gordimer's list of the readings which shaped her *Weltanschauung*. See too Gordimer's comments to Diana Cooper-Clark on Proust's influence on her work (interview, 'The Clash', 1983: 55).

61. Gordimer calls herself Jewish in an early interview, though it was her father (and not her mother) who was a Latvian or Lithuanian Jew, and despite the fact that she says she was not given a Jewish education. Her identification with Judaism may be seen as an expression of her general sympathy with the marginalised and the oppressed, beyond the confines of race politics (see R. Boyers *et al.*, 'A Conversation with Nadine Gordimer', 1984: 11). In scattered comments Gordimer links various categories of oppressed people: thus Gideon 'forgot that he was an African, burdened, like a Jew, with his category of the chosen' (*Occasion for Loving*, 135); 'all writers in South Africa,' Gordimer said in 1979, 'are an oppressed minority.'

62. Nadine Gordimer, 'A Writer in South Africa', 1965: 21.

63. Rose Zwi's phrase, in 'Prologue', in *The Purple Renoster 8*, 1968: 5.

64. Nadine Gordimer, 'A Writer in South Africa', 1965: 28.

65. Tony Morphet, 1984: 2. In a lecture given at the University of the Witwatersrand in August 1990, Breyten Breytenbach reminded his audience that 'the artist invents only himself'.

Chapter 3: Stereotypes: Text and Subtext

1. Friedrich Engels, excerpted in A. Jefferson and D. Robey, *Modern Literary Theory*, 1982: 143.
2. F.R. Karl, *American Fictions*, 1983: 595.
3. Lionel Abrahams, letter to *The Weekly Mail*, 16-22 March, 1990: 12. Abrahams's autobiographical novel, *The Celibacy of Felix Greenspan* (1977), was a refreshingly non-political exercise in establishing an identification with a South African heritage outside the parameters of stultifying ideological pressures: a unique work in the decade in which it appeared. In 1983 Abrahams wrote that 'three years of association with political people did nothing to persuade me of the error of my individualistic-liberal ways. Instead they produced a graphic demonstration of the confusions, destructiveness, and self-destructiveness inherent in that form of power-drive which is the radical approach to things' (in M. Daymond *et al.* (eds.), *Momentum*, 1984: 4). Contrast this to Mbulelo Mzamane's argument in 1979 that 'since the most important lessons for South Africans are in the political sphere, a writer is unimportant, irrelevant, and probably alienated unless he is political' (quoted in Marquard, 'Some Racial Stereotypes in South African Writing', 1, from *Forced Landing: Africa South: Contemporary Writings* (ed. Mothobe Mutloatse), Johannesburg, 1980: 3). Gordimer has subscribed to the latter view (characteristic of black protest writing in particular) in her pronouncements in recent years.
4. See Stephen Clingman (*The Novels of Nadine Gordimer*, 1986: 9-10) who has suggested that characterisation in the later novels is to be understood as a form of Lukacsian 'typification'.
5. Webster's Dictionary (1966) defines 'stereotype' as, among other possibilities, 'a standardised mental picture held in common by members of a group and representing an oversimplified opinion, affective attitude, or uncritical judgement'.
6. Jean Marquard, 'Some Racial Stereotypes in South African Writing', 1981: 1-2, 10. Note that Parker also offers a list of common stereotypes in South African literature in his introductory essay to *The South African Novel in English*, 1978: 8.
7. Abdul JanMohamed, *Manichean Aesthetics*, 1983: 267.
8. Abdul JanMohamed, 'The Economy of Manichean Allegory: the Function of Racial Difference in Colonialist Literature', 1985: 66.
9. See for example the prologue to *A World of Strangers*, set in Mombasa; the depiction of wealthy Johannesburg northern suburbs socialites at The High House in the same novel; and the conversations conducted at Hjalmar Wentz's bar in *A Guest of Honour*.
10. Sander L. Gilman, *Difference and Pathology*, 1985: 17, 18, 27. Gilman also reminds us that 'stereotypes can and often do exist parallel to the ability to create sophisticated rational categories that transcend the crude line of difference present in the stereotype', and that the 'deep structure' of the stereotype 'reappears in the adult as a response to anxiety' (1985: 18-19).

11. As Stephen Watson has suggested in an influential essay in which he quotes from Memmi, the coloniser-who-refuses "may openly protest or sign a petition, or join a group hostile towards the colonisers. This already suffices for him to recognise that he has simply changed difficulties and discomforts. It is not easy to escape mentally from a concrete situation, to refine its ideology while continuing to live with its actual relationships" (Albert Memmi, *The Coloniser and the Colonised*, London: Souvenir Press, 1974: 20, quoted in S. Watson, "Colonialism and the Novels of J.M. Coetzee" (1985) in *Selected Essays 1980-1990*, 1990: 44).

12. Quoted from Nadine Gordimer, 'Literature and Politics in South Africa', in *Southern Review* 7 (Australia), November 1974: 226, in Abdul JanMohamed, 'The Economy of Manichean Allegory', 1985: 69.

13. Abdul JanMohamed, 1985: 67.

14. Nadine Gordimer, 'Afterword: "The Prison-house of Colonialism"' (1980), in C. Barash (ed.), *An Olive Schreiner Reader* 1987: 226.

15. Nadine Gordimer, 'The Novel and the Nation in South Africa', 1961: 522.

16. Nadine Gordimer, 'South Africa: Towards a Desk-Drawer Literature', 1968: 69.

17. See M. Horrell (comp.), *A Survey of Race Relations in South Africa, 1964,* 1965: 94-95.

18. See the biographical note on Harris in T. Karis and G.M. Carter (eds.), *From Protest to Challenge*, 1977: 37.

19. Nadine Gordimer, 'South Africa: Towards a Desk-Drawer Literature', 1968: 71.

20. Compare the link Gilman sets up between difference and pathology, in which he suggests that, in so far as health (and the good) is consistently in opposition to illness (and the bad), 'the idea of pathology [becomes] a central marker for difference . . . Order and control are the antithesis of pathology. "Pathology" is disorder – the loss of control, the giving over of the self to the forces that lie beyond the self' (1985: 23-24).

21. See for example the interviews with Ann Harris in 'Death in a Suitcase' in 'Sunday Magazine', *Sunday Times,* 22 July 1964: 8-12; 'Life with Harris – by his Wife', in *The Rand Daily Mail*, 7 November 1964; 'My last Hours . . . and my Life with John Harris', by Ann Harris as told to Margaret Smith, *Sunday Times*, 4 April 1965 (these are all Johannesburg-based newspapers).

22. In 'South Africa: Towards a Desk-Drawer Literature' (1968: 71), Gordimer said that she had wished to examine 'how this tragedy might have come about'.

23. *Katrina* (1969), directed by Jans Rautenbach; see the entry in K. Tomaselli, *The Cinema of Apartheid*, 1989, for further details.

24. See Chapter 4 for a consideration of the significance of Gordimer's choice of career for Nomzamo, and Chapter 6 for an analysis of the process of deferral which her characters are subjected to while 'the struggle' continues to be waged.

25. Ilse Fischer (Bram Fischer's daughter) revealed in 1986 that Gordimer gave

her the novel to read, prior to its publication, not to elicit her approval or secure her permission for its revelation of details about herself and her family, but simply as a courteous gesture, to make her aware, in advance of publication, of what was said in it. The extent to which this and other novels rework actual events of the time was emphasised by Ms Fischer in her comments. For example, she herself first met Gordimer when, as a teenager, she was waiting outside the Johannesburg Fort to see her mother – a moment recreated by Gordimer in her opening image of Rosa Burger outside the 'fortress' (*Burger's Daughter*, 9).

26. See Heribert Adam's comments on Gordimer's 'Living in the Interregnum' for a critique of her vision of revolutionary apocalypse. The fundamental assumptions of *July's People* are questioned by implication in this paper, since the novel, which was published just before the essay appeared, presents a fictional version of the complex of emotions about South Africa's situation with which the essay deals (Adam, 'Reflections on Gordimer's Interregnum', 1983: 3-4).

27. See Arthur Goldstuck on the subject of South African urban legends in *The Rabbit in the Thorn Tree* , 1990.

28. 'English-Language Literature and Politics', 1974: 105.

29. The tenacity of this myth is suggested by its recent reappearance in a book review by Harvey Tyson in a Johannesburg newspaper: ' "At least I can count on you to protect me if the violence comes, can't I, Cephas?" The white Johannesburg housewife, unnerved by stories of nearby riots, looked up from the newspaper at her longtime servant. "Ma'am," he replied slowly, "you're the first one I'm going to shoot" ' (*The Star*, 18 July, 1988).

30. Judie Newman in *Nadine Gordimer*, 1988, points out that the phrase may be traced to Ernst Fischer's *The Necessity of Art* (1958).

31. R. Williams, *Keywords*, 1976: 39.

32. Note Jacques Barzun's observation that 'the overwhelming majority of all anti-bourgeois artists are and have been bourgeois born and bred' (in *The Use and Abuse of Art*, 1974: 62). Previously, in a polemical passage, he had said, 'What a convenient word is bourgeois . . . and how flexible in its application . . . [The bourgeois] is not a reliable historical character. He is shifty as to chronology, status, income, opinions and activity . . . When the contemporary abolitionist gives as a reason for destroying the bourgeois world its "materialism", hypocrisy, lack of justice and oppressive arrangements, he is in fact giving reason for destroying every civilised society that has ever existed . . . [Revolutionary artists outside totalitarian régimes] do not seek the tighter regimentation they would get under dictatorship or the closer contact with the dullness of humanity. They imagine on the contrary the anarchist heaven of free spirits moving through life in easy, frictionless self-development, because no longer bound by material needs or vulgar ambition: . . . an unconditioned world' (1974: 66-67).

33. See Nadine Gordimer, 'Where Do Whites Fit In?' (1959), in *The Essential Gesture*, 1988: 29: 'No one can measure how much of colour-prejudice is

purely class-prejudice, in a country where there has been a great gap between the living standards of black and white.'

34. See Kenneth Parker, *The South African Novel in English*, 1987: 16.

35. See Nadine Gordimer *et al.*, *What Happened to 'Burger's Daughter', or How South Africa Censorship Works*, 1980. However, a number of critics have noted that Gordimer's implied audience is clearly an international one. See, for example, the frequent substitution of "segregation" for "apartheid" in her novels, and her tendency to explain terms and regulations with which a South African readership would be fully familiar.

36. Abdul JanMohamed, 1985: 65.

37. Sander L. Gilman, 1985: 23, 25. Gordimer's image of the black will be dealt with more fully in Chapter 5.

38. See S. Milbury-Steen, *European and African Stereotypes in Twentieth-Century Fiction* (1981), and Marion Berghahn, *Images of Africa in Black American Literature* (1977) for discussions of such stereotypes.

39. Stephen Watson, 'Recent White English South African Poetry and the Language of Liberalism' (1980/1983), in *Selected Essays 1980-1990*, 1990: 29. See too this chapter, note 7 above.

40. For example, note the (colour-blind) comment in a review in a Johannesburg newspaper by John MacLennan: 'In spite of popular conception, South Africa is a relatively poor country. It has a GNP only one seventh of the United States and even if existing wealth were redistributed this would do no more than expand modestly the number of privileged people' (*Sunday Star*, 10 July 1988).

41. I. Currie, review of B. Ashcroft *et al.*, *The Empire Writes Back*, 1990: 108. Currie claims that 'post-colonial discourse has discovered the opposition of margin and center as a primary structure of colonialist practices'.

42. See Derek Wright, 'Requiems for Revolution', 1989: 66-67. Stereotypes may function as 'deliberate strategies in a total satiric polemic rather than [as] an index to limitations in the author's vision and technique'.

43. Stephen Watson, 'Poetry and Politicisation' (1985), in *Selected Essays 1980-1990*, 1990: 15.

44. In ironic contrast to this view, note J. M. Coetzee's essay 'Idleness in South Africa' in *White Writing* (1988). His delineation of European distaste for what was perceived as the primitive sloth of a people whose unwillingness to place themselves at the service of the conqueror became an index of the extent to which they were seen to have failed to evolve on the evolutionary ladder is instructive. Gordimer's contempt for the leisured lifestyles of her whites may be seen to reflect just such a puritanical colonial perspective within the context of an ironic reversal of the target of such criticisms.

45. K. Parker, *The South African Novel in English*, 1987: 14.

46. Nadine Gordimer, 'The Novel and the Nation in South Africa' (1961), in G.D. Killam (ed.), *African Writers on African Writing*, 1973: 43. The full comment is: 'And when I say us, I mean exactly that – all of us of all colours who live in South Africa, not the mutually exclusive "them" and "they" of our daily lives within the South African caste system.' She is discussing the

relevance of Harold Bloom's novel *Episode in the Transvaal* to all South Africans in a piece of non-fiction marked by its earnest, didactic tone.

47. N. Gordimer, 'Living in the Interregnum', 1983, in *The Essential Gesture*, 1988: Section 5.

48. Georg Lukacs, *The Meaning of Contemporary Realism* (1955), 1963: 122-23. According to Clingman (1986: 10), Gordimer first read Lukacs in 1968 and was sufficiently impressed to make copious private notes upon *The Meaning of Contemporary Realism*.

49. Stephen Clingman, 1986: 52, 97.

50. J. M. Coetzee usefully reminds us that history should be seen as a 'pattern . . . born from chaos': in other words, as a form of discourse rather than a representation of Truth (*Life and Times of Michael K*, 1983: 216).

51. Stephen Clingman, 1986: 144.

52. Note the extent to which the opposition set up in the novel between Mehring and the farm labourers may be read as yet another stereotype, one identified, for example, in Christopher Hope's review of André Brink's *A Chain of Voices*. He writes that 'of course, the contrast between the unctuous, guilt-ridden hypocrites in the big farm house, and the resilient, fornicating, hard-drinking folk in the slave huts, conforms to a favourite South African stereotype' (in *The London Magazine* 22(4), July 1982: 78-80).

53. See John Cooke, 'The Novels of Nadine Gordimer', 1976, who makes a similar point about *A World of Strangers*.

54. Quoted in Abdul JanMohamed, 1985: 64, from Edward Said, *Orientalism*, New York, 1978: 7.

55. JanMohamed claims that, because the 'native' does not have access to these texts (on account of linguistic barriers), and since the European audience has no direct contact with the native, imperialist fiction tends to be unconcerned with the truth-value of its representation' (1985: 63).

56. JanMohamed, *Manichean Aesthetics*, 1983: 97.

Chapter 4: Gordimer's Women

1.   Ruth First and Ann Scott, *Olive Schreiner: A Biography*, 1980: 23. Gordimer quotes this passage in her 1980 review of this biography entitled 'The Prison-House of Colonialism', and reprinted, first as an 'Afterword' in C. Barash (ed.), *An Olive Schreiner Reader: Writings on Women and South Africa* 1987, and then as the 'Foreword' (with some significant changes) to a new Virago edition of the biography in 1989: 3-8. This second version differs slightly from the earlier versions (see this chapter, notes 12, 13).

2.   Nadine Gordimer, quoted in John Cooke, 'The Novels of Nadine Gordimer', 1976: 235, footnote 33; from Gordimer's "Introduction" to B. Sachs (ed.), *Trek Anthology*, Johannesburg: Dial Press, 1971.

3.   See for example Brenda Cooper, 'New Criteria for an "Abnormal Mutation"? An Evaluation of Gordimer's *A Sport of Nature*', 1988. See also Karen Lazar, 'The Personal and the Political in some of Nadine Gordimer's

Short Stories', 1988, which contains an interesting interview with Gordimer that touches upon some of the issues developed in this paper. See also her 'Feminism as "piffling"? Ambiguities in Nadine Gordimer's Short Stories', 1990. See also Dorothy Driver, 'Nadine Gordimer: The Politicisation of Women', 1983; and her ' "Woman" as Sign in the South African Colonial Enterprise', 1988. The last-mentioned essay develops observations which usefully illuminate aspects of Gordimer's work, although it does not deal directly with contemporary fiction. See also Cecily Lockett, 'Feminism(s) and Writing in the South African Context', 1989.

4.   Cecily Lockett, 1989: 27.

5.   Gordimer (1981), quoted in Driver, 1983: 33, from Susan Gardiner's 'Still Waiting for the Great Feminist Novel': Nadine Gordimer's *Burger's Daughter'*. Gardiner was herself quoting Gordimer's talk to the 'Women in Publishing' Conference, May 1981, entitled 'A Note on Women and Literature in South Africa', and published in shortened form as 'Women Who Took the Literary Lead', in *The Rand Daily Mail,* Johannesburg: 14 May 1981. See too, Driver, 1983: 45.

6.   Nadine Gordimer, in *Women Speak,* 1989: 55; a publication in which papers presented at a conference held by COSAW in Johannesburg, in November 1988, have been made available to the general public.

7.   *ibid.*

8.   Nadine Gordimer, in interview with Dieter Welz (1985), in *Writing Against Apartheid,* 1987: 40.

9.   See Martha Bayles in 'Feminism and Abortion', who writes that 'once upon a time university women had argued that scientific reason had no gender, and that aesthetic imagination was androgynous. But no longer' (1990: 85).

10. Nadine Gordimer, 'Introduction' to *Selected Stories,* 1975: 11.

11. Nadine Gordimer, in conversation with Robert Boyers *et al.,* 1984: 27-28. The point is repeated in a 1988 interview with Karen Lazar (1988: viii).

12. Nadine Gordimer, 'Afterword: "The Prison-house of Colonialism"' (1980); in C. Barash (ed.), *An Olive Schreiner Reader,* 1987: 225.

13. Nadine Gordimer, 'Foreword' in Ruth First and Ann Scott, *Olive Schreiner: A Biography,* 1989- 7.

14. Nadine Gordimer, (1981) quoted in D. Driver, 'Nadine Gordimer: The Politicisation of Women', 1983: 45. In an interview with Jonathan Paton in 1985 Gordimer stressed again that she is 'not a feminist'.

15. Nadine Gordimer, in interview with Karen Lazar, 1988; Appendix v-vi.

16. Nadine Gordimer, in conversation with Robert Boyers *et al.,* 1984: 22-23.

17. Nadine Gordimer, in interview with Jonathan Paton, 1985.

18. Margaret Andersen, *Thinking About Women,* 1983: 290.

19. Nadine Gordimer, in conversation with Robert Boyers *et al.,* 1984: 19-20.

20. Nadine Gordimer, in interview with Lazar, 1988, Appendix v.

21. See the discussion of this issue in my analysis (Chapter 5) of images of blacks in the novels. In her interview with Lazar (1988; Appendix iv-v), Gordimer again claims there is an unbridgeable gulf between black and white experience, and repeats her conviction that feminist concerns must await the

resolution of the larger political issues of the day. That her position is here overtly in line with that of black female activists is made clear in her account in this interview of the reasons for the failure of one aspect of the 'Women for Peace' program in 1976. She says that '[black women felt that what] was happening to their children could not be separated from the pressures on the liberation movement . . . And then the whites were afraid that it was becoming political, not understanding that it was always political. So, the two movements split . . . [The differences] will exist until all discriminatory laws against people are removed. Then you can think about a genuine feminism in this country'.

22. Ellen Kuzwayo has however recently articulated a view well in line with Gordimer's own anguished consciousness of an unbridgeable gulf between black and white experience. She writes that 'interest in the woman writer in Africa has focussed primarily on the white writer – especially those from southern Africa such as . . . Nadine Gordimer and Doris Lessing. [However,] when these writers refer to black women, they do so as outsiders with an even more limited knowledge of the black woman's everyday existence than the black (male) writer's . . . These writers . . . are not the ones from whom we can reasonably expect to receive a full and informed exploration of the African woman's experience, and, of course, they do not claim to offer one' ('Introduction' to *Women in South Africa*, 1988: 9-10).

23. W.D. Ashcroft, 'Intersecting Marginalities: Post-Colonialism and Feminism', 1989: 26. Ashcroft writes that 'the problem for essentialist feminisms is that, by asserting on the one hand that the Otherness of women is a construction of patriarchy and yet that it is out of this Otherness that a female language must be constructed or recovered, it falls into . . . [a] dilemma . . . [However] it is in seizing and refashioning the patriarchal language that the "silenced" voice can be heard'.

24. Nadine Gordimer, in interview with Stephen Gray, 1981: 291.

25. I cannot agree with Lazar, who claims that Gordimer's 'stringent dismissals of feminism have given way to a more subtle investigation of such issues' (1990: 17). Clingman also claims (in my view without substance) that Gordimer 'has progressed from an account of growing up as a woman to a politicised feminism adapted to the realities of South Africa' (1986: 223). The characterisation of Hillela scarcely bears out these claims, as we shall see.

26. Nadine Gordimer, 'A Writer in South Africa', 1965: 23.

27. Nadine Gordimer, in conversation with Susan Sontag, 1985: 16-17. See also Chapter 2 in this book and Gordimer in interview with Joachim Braun, 1985.

28. Nadine Gordimer, 'The Essential Gesture' (1984), in *The Essential Gesture*, 1988: 242.

29. Quoted in Lazar (1988), from Rosalind Coward, 'Are Women's Novels Feminist Novels?', in *The New Feminist Criticism*, 1986: 238.

30. Cecily Lockett, 'Feminism(s) and Writing in the South African Context', 1989: 1.

31. See Karen Lazar, 'Feminism as "piffling"?' 1990: 2.

32. Chris Weedon, *Feminist Practice and Post-Structuralist Theory*, 1987: 4 and 135. I am indebted to Weedon's excellent summary of recent feminist theory.

33. See my two studies of this novel in *English Academy Review* 4, 1987, and *English Studies in Africa* 32(1), 1989.

34. J.M. Coetzee, 'Nabokov's *Pale Fire* and the Primacy of Art', 1974: 5.

35. Compare J.M. Coetzee's use of this metaphor in *Life and Times of Michael K,* 1983.

36. See Gordimer's essay of this title, 'Where Do Whites Fit In?' (1959), in *The Essential Gesture*, 1988.

37. See this chapter, epigraph 1 and footnote 1.

38. Nadine Gordimer, 'Foreword', in R. First and A. Scott, *Olive Schreiner: A Biography*, 1989: 5.

39. Nadine Gordimer, 'Leaving School – II', 1963: 59.

40. Quoted in C. Weedon, *Feminist Practice and Post-Structuralist Theory*, 1987: 151, from Rosalind Coward, *Female Desire*, London: Paladin, 1984: 16.

41. Nadine Gordimer, 'Leaving School – II', 1963: 59.

42. *ibid.*, 62.

43. Nadine Gordimer, 'A South African Childhood', 1954: 116-17.

44. Nadine Gordimer, in interview with Karen Lazar, 1988: Appendix ii.

45. Nadine Gordimer, 'Leaving School – II', 1963: 59.

46. We might note that, in three early essays, 'Leaving School – II' (1963), 'Notes of an Expropriator' (1964) and 'A Writer in South Africa' (1965), in which Gordimer variously attempted to outline the *literary* influences which have shaped her writing and her thinking, out of some forty writers mentioned, only nine are female and only three of those (George Eliot, Virginia Woolf and Muriel Spark) are given any prominence in her accounts.

47. See Nadine Gordimer, 'A Writer in South Africa', 1965.

48. Nadine Gordimer, 'Introduction' to *Selected Stories*, 1975: 11.

49. Nadine Gordimer, 'Leaving School – II', 1963: 62.

50. See Gordimer's references to D.H. Lawrence in 'Notes of an Expropriator' (1964), and 'A Writer in South Africa' (1965).

51. Gordimer's phrase, in interview with Anthony Sampson, 1987.

52. Karen Lazar, 'Feminism as "piffling"?' 1990: 3-4.

53. See M. Bayles, 'Feminism and Abortion', 1990: 87.

54. See Elaine Fido, 'A Guest of Honour: A Feminine View of Masculinity', 1978: 34.

55. Nadine Gordimer, in interview with Anthony Sampson, 1987.

56. Note that Gordimer does not, however, normally sanction overt private power-plays within the context of a love relationship. In *Occasion for Loving* Jessie complains that 'it makes me sick when everybody's playing. People show off so much in love affairs... I sometimes get afraid that everything we think of as love – even sex is – nearly always power instead' (154). Personal integrity becomes the only defence against the urge to exploit.

57. See Tilly Olsen, *Silences*, 1980: 225.

58. Louise Yelin, 'Exiled In and Exiled From: The Politics and Poetics of *Burger's Daughter*', 1989: 400.

59. *ibid.*, 408.

60. See Fido's discussion of this in her essay on *A Guest of Honour*, 1978.

61. The sentimentality of this image is by implication sharply satirised in Christopher Hope's choice of title for his new novel, *My Chocolate Redeemer*, 1989. Note the frequency with which the adjective 'obsidian' appears. The romanticisation of the powerful black male in the fiction is discussed more fully in Chapter 5.

62. Lockett is the only feminist critic of Gordimer's work thus far who has grasped this point in its broad outlines. She writes that 'despite a history of refusing to involve herself in women's activities, Gordimer accepted an invitation to speak on the topic of "Images of Women in Literature" at a recent COSAW conference . . . Yet her discussion showed that her thinking on gender has not shifted at all . . . Perhaps it is the recognition that to speak as a woman is to speak from a position of marginality and oppression that frightens this writer who has achieved literary power by adopting the language of patriarchy' (1989: 28).

63. In *The Lying Days*, Joel is repeatedly connected with the 'non-European'. See, for example, the passage in which he teasingly responds to Helen's attempts to fix her sense of his otherness (by comparing his dark hair to that of an Indian waiter) by saying, 'yes, I know I'm black . . . Right, I'm greasy too . . .' (140). The use of the racist stereotype mocks Helen's attempt to neutralise the racist classificatory system.

64. See, for example, Gordimer's references to the difficulties which led to the dissolution of the Johannesburg PEN Centre in 1981: Gordimer in interview with Dieter Welz (1985) in *Writing Against Apartheid*, 1987: 37-40; and with Anthony Sampson, 1987.

65. Peter Horn connects racial and gender oppression in suggesting an equation between blacks and women in a recent formulation: 'All women are black. As blacks they are invisible. All blackness is constructed on the model of women: subservient, providing the background against which the whiteness of the male can be discerned without drawing attention to himself' (1989: 64). See also Gates, 1990: 21.

66. Cooper (1988) has suggested that Gordimer's apparent hatred of white women such as Maureen arises out of a deep-seated self-hatred. Implicitly acknowledged here is the impossible position women occupy in South Africa, as both victims of sexism and of apartheid. White women in particular are in an ambiguous position; they benefit from a system which oppresses other black women as domestic servants, and thus in effect find themselves allied with the male oppressor class despite themselves. See Driver (1988) on this issue as well.

67. See for example Doris Lessing's *The Grass is Singing*, J.M. Coetzee's *In the Heart of the Country*, Olive Schreiner's *The Story of an African Farm*, and, within a wider colonial context, Jean Rhys's *The Wide Sargasso Sea*.

68. Nadine Gordimer, in interview with Welz, 1985, in *Writing Against Apartheid*, 1987: 42.
69. See Heribert Adam, 'Reflections on Gordimer's Interregnum', 1983.
70. John Cooke, 'The Novels of Nadine Gordimer', 1976: 68.

Chapter 5: Images of Blacks

1. Hazel Waters, 'Introduction', *Race and Class*, July-September 1989: i.
2. Ralph Ellison, *Shadow and Act*, 1972: 28.
3. Nadine Gordimer, 'The Novel and the Nation in South Africa', 1961: 39.
4. Nat Nakasa, 'Johannesburg, Johannesburg' (1967), in Digby Ricci (ed.), *Reef of Time*, 1986: 241.
5. Gordimer's dilemma is indirectly discussed by Es'kia Mphahlele, who asserted in 1962 that the serious writer in South Africa *must* confront 'the need . . . to come to terms with himself in relationship to his position as either one of an underdog majority or as one of a privileged minority. Within this context the urges to preach, protest, hand out propaganda, to escape, sentimentalise, romanticise, to make a startling discovery in the field of race relations, to write timelessly, and other urges, all jostle for predominance in the writer' (*The African Image*, 1962: 120-21).
6. Nadine Gordimer, 'The Novel and the Nation in South Africa', 1961: 44-45.
7. *ibid.*, 44-45.
8. Nadine Gordimer, 'Apartheid' (1959), excerpted in John Cooke, 'The Novels of Nadine Gordimer', 1976: 126.
9. Nadine Gordimer, 'The Novel and the Nation in South Africa', 1961: 52.
10. Nadine Gordimer, 'English-Language Literature and Politics', 1975: 118. She goes on to say that 'the law effectively prevents any real identification of the writer with his society as a whole, so that ultimately he can identify only with his colour' (119). Athol Fugard recently made this point again in response to the charge that writers like himself 'preach to the converted': 'The gap that divides the experience of the white South African and the black South African is so colossal, so enormous, that even if you're voting for the right party you're not converted' (public lecture given at the University of the Witwatersrand, Johannesburg, 28 March 1990).
11. See Gordimer's interview with Diana Cooper-Clark, 1983: 53. Gordimer reiterates her point in her interview with Boyers *et al.*, in which she is asked to comment on André Brink's belief that 'if you're white you cannot write convincingly of the black situation, and vice versa'. She answers that 'there are certain areas of life on both sides, which each side cannot write about in terms of the other. There are areas of white life, a kind of ivory tower white life, that are so remote from black experience that I doubt if any black writer could write convincingly of them' (1984: 27). This is qualified a year later in an interview with Dieter Welz in which she said, 'I do think there is, at the end of the scale on either side, an area where white cannot write about black and black about white, but in between there are hundreds of years of – if not

common experience, in the sense that you are both experiencing it in the same way – at least common experience in the sense that you experience each other; and I think that blacks know things about whites and whites know things about blacks that are never spoken. But writers have access to these things' (1985: 40-41). In this latter formulation Gordimer's belief in the special status of the writer and her tactful sense of the impenetrability of black experience for the white observer are neatly brought together to justify her own delicately balanced practice on both a political and an aesthetic level.

12. Achebe goes on to say, 'I would not dream of constructing theories to explain "the European mind" with the same "bold face" that some Europeans assume in explaining ours' ('Where Angels Fear to Tread', in G.D. Killam (ed.), *African Writers on African Writing*, 1973: 6-7).

13. See B. Ashcroft *et al.*, *The Empire Writes Back*, 1989: 86.

14. Kenneth Parker, 'Introduction' to *The South African Novel in English*, 1978: 8.

15. Steve Biko, *I Write What I Like* (1979: posthumous), excerpted in David Ward, *Chronicles of Darkness*, 1989: 129, 182.

16. Elaine Fido argues that Gordimer 'further protects herself from having to grapple too closely with the inner lives of her black characters [in *A Guest of Honour*] by channelling all the novel's experience through Bray's until the last section', when Rebecca's point of view takes over (1978: 32). A similar point may be made about the manipulation of point of view in the other novels.

17. Gordimer praises Harold Bloom's book, *Episode*, in 1961, for presenting Africans as 'social beings, thinking people; they have other qualities than the patience, endurance, and acceptance of the stock African in our literature' ('The Novel and the Nation in South Africa', 1961: 44). Steven Sitole and Gideon Shibalo, precursors of the black political activists of the later fiction, are drawn in deliberate contrast to such stereotypes.

18. Kenneth Parker, 'Introduction' to *The South African Novel in English*, 1978: 20-21.

19. See, for example, Rian Malan, *My Traitor's Heart*, 1990.

20. Ralph Ellison, *Shadow and Act*, 1964: 181.

21. Nadine Gordimer, 'How Not to Know the African', 1967: 46-47.

22. See for example the depiction of Mehring's rural Afrikaans neighbours in *The Conservationist*. See too Chapter 1, footnote 24.

23. She herself has attempted to free the African in some small way from the silence imposed upon him by apartheid by incorporating banned material into her novels in order to make certain ideas available to the public. See Clingman's discussion of such passages in *A Guest of Honour* and *Burger's Daughter*, in which, he says, she gives 'a voice to a certain social and historical presence' (1986: 188).

24. Fanon alerts us to the extent to which the association of animal imagery with the representation of blacks constitutes a typical racist colonial stereotype: 'The native knows all this and laughs to himself every time he spots an allusion to the animal world in the other's words. For he knows he is not an

animal; and it is precisely at the moment he realises his humanity that he begins to sharpen the weapons with which he will secure his victory' (*The Wretched of the Earth*, quoted in Cooke, 1976: 20).

25. Nadine Gordimer, 'Leaving School – II', 1963: 63.

26. See Nadine Gordimer, 'Johannesburg', in *Holiday* 18, 1955: 46-51.

27. Gordimer's own Jewish heritage has been frequently commented on, and it should neither surprise us that many of her protagonists are given some Jewish blood, nor that in this first, semi-autobiographical novel the issue of anti-Semitism should be given such prominence. Note too Ward's comment that Hillela's name in *A Sport of Nature* may well refer to Rabbi Hillel, who stands for 'a liberal and humanising strain in Jewish thought' (Ward, 1989: 133).

28. See J.M. Coetzee on Sarah Gertrude Millin (1980), in *White Writing*, 1988: 138. In asserting that, before 1945 (when Gordimer was 22 years old) the discourse of racism was premised on the idea that people are most fundamentally distinguished from one another *in the blood*, Coetzee highlights a corollary to this notion, that suffering for the mixed-race individual is thus axiomatic: 'The question of whether one is for or against his suffering, for or against the mere mechanism – ostracism – through which his suffering is realised, thus becomes, in Millin's argument, as secondary as the question of whether one is for or against the suffering of Oedipus. All one's human pity may flow out to the victim. Nevertheless, his suffering was fated' (1988: 140).

29. Fanon also equates Jew and Black in his comment upon the progress of his own moral growth: 'The Jew and I: since I was not satisfied to be racialised, by a lucky turn of fate I was humanised. I joined the Jew, my brother in misery' (*Black Skin. White Masks*, 1952: 122; see also 115-23). Gordimer's internalisation of typical European stereotypes in this area is suggested by Sander Gilman's comments that 'the depth of the association of the Jew with the black enabled non-Jewish Europeans during the nineteenth century to "see" the Jews as blacks. The association of blacks with revolution, a powerful one in the late eighteenth and early nineteenth century, is carried over to the role of Jewish emancipation . . . The association of black revolutionaries with sexual excess becomes one with that of sexual aggression' (1985: 34). Gilman goes on to assert that 'the association of the images of "blackness" and "Jewishness" is a test case for the inter-relationship of images of difference' (1985: 35).

30. F. Fanon, *ibid.*, 1952: 17-18, 36.

31. Ralph Ellison, *Shadow and Act*, 1953: 106.

32. Es'kia Mphahlele points out the artificialities of such depictions: 'As long as Miss Gordimer moves among those she knows very well – those of her colour, naturally – her portrayal of people is full-blooded and capable . . . [She] herself [however] has no means of knowing the African better than she knows Steven, who is articulate and can speak her language, because of racial and social barriers. But she knows the catalyst can remain where she wants it to be' (*The African Image*, 1962: 148).

33. Dickens writes that 'Wemmick's house was a little wooden cottage in the midst of plots of garden, and the top of it was cut out and painted like a battery mounted with guns ... "That's a real flagstaff you see," said Wemmick, "and on Sundays I run up a real flag ... if you can suppose the little place besieged, it would hold out a devil of a time ... the office is one thing, and private life another. When I go into the office, I leave the Castle behind me and when I come into the Castle, I leave the office behind me"' (*Great Expectations* (1861), 1953: 193-95). Compare the description of Sam's house in *A World of Strangers*, as given by Toby: 'Sam's house was in another township ... and when we walked through the yard-smell of ammonia and wood-smoke, to which I was by then accustomed ... and through the door that opened abruptly from two uneven concrete steps, I was bewildered. I might have stepped into a room "done over" by some young couple in a Chelsea flat. Green felt deadened the floor underfoot. There was a piano, piled with music. A record player in what all cabinet makers outside Sweden consider to be Swedish style ... At the window, a green venetian blind dropped its multiple lids on the township' (*A World of Strangers*, 131-32).

34. Here Gordimer's implicit division of blacks into two categories reflects (probably unintentionally) Mphahlele's ironic assertion that there are two types of blacks in South Africa: the educated and the illiterate (see *The African Image*, 1962: 207-208). Such an echo would suggest an inherent class consciousness emerging subtextually in the works, despite Gordimer's avowedly egalitarian stance.

35. See Maughan-Brown (1983), who follows Berghahn (1977) in emphasising the 'Black Sambo' element in such a representation: the 'natural' servant, non-violent and humble, ' "justifies and thereby serves to perpetuate servitude and extreme social inequality. It is the image the white man can hold to prevent guilt from enslaving other humans. It is the image of confident racist domination" ... [and] is appropriate to the liberal-humanist ideology of colonial trusteeship' (Maughan-Brown quotes Billig in this passage) (1983: 75).

36. See Ellen Kuzwayo, 'Introduction' to *Women in South Africa: From the Heart – An Anthology*, 1988: 2; and Jacklyn Cock, *Maids and Madams*, 1980. Es'kia Mphahlele accuses Gordimer of an insensitive ethnocentricity in his assertion that 'nonwhite characters interest Miss Gordimer only as far as they throw light on the subtleties of group attitudes and pig-headedness among whites'. He claims that the novels concentrate on the 'one-way impact' of 'the white man's reaction to the presence of the black man' (*The African Image*, 1962: 135).

37. Frantz Fanon, *Black Skin, White Masks*, 1952: 17.

38. Nadine Gordimer, in interview with Anthony Sampson, 1987.

39. Frantz Fanon, *Black Skin, White Masks*, 1952: 35-6.

40. Nadine Gordimer, 'Towards a Desk-Drawer Literature', 1968: 69.

41. Ian Glenn, 'Race and Sex in English South African Fiction', 1984: 155-59. Glenn notes that Plomer gives his female protagonist, Mabel van der Horst,

who marries a black man, the title of 'Eurafrica': as an ironic variant upon 'Ur-Afrika, it is a label which would be peculiarly appropriate to Hillela as well'.

42. Excerpted in Glenn, 1984: 159, from Frantz Fanon, *Black Skin, White Masks*, Gordimer reverses this to read, 'I am worthy of black love. I am loved as a black woman'.

43. Es'kia Mphahlele offers a dismissive view of *négritude* which is worth quoting to place Gordimer's idealisation of black beauty within a larger context. 'To us in multi-racial communities, then,' he writes, '*négritude* is just so much intellectual talk, a cult . . . if there is any *négritude* in the black man's art in South Africa, it is because we *are* African. If a writer's tone is healthy he is bound to express the African in him. Stripped of Senghor's philosophical musings, the African traits he speaks of can be taken for granted; they are social anthropology' (1962; quoted in M. Cook and S.E. Henderson, *The Militant Black Writer in Africa and the United States*, 1969: 51-52).

44. J.M. Coetzee, writing on Sarah Gertrude Millin in *White Writing*, 1988: 158.

45. See Henry Louis Gates, 'Introduction: "Tell Me, Sir. . . What *is* 'Black' Literature?" ', 1990: 21.

46. Gates suggests that 'one must *learn* to be "black" in [the USA] because "blackness" is a socially produced category . . . The concepts of "black" and "white" [are no longer] thought to be pre-constituted: rather, they are mutually constitutive and socially produced' (1990: 20-21).

47. Fanon, 1952: 129.

48. Excerpted in A.A. Mazrui, 'The Patriot as Artist' (1966), in G.D. Killam (ed.), *African Writers on African Writing*, 1973: 78-79.

49. Gordimer may have drawn the phrase from Sarah Gertrude Millin, whose argument on colour-consciousness Coetzee summarises: 'Those who deny having "colour consciousness . . . are biologically speaking sports", or else deceive themselves. Colour consciousness is a "profound feeling (call it instinct or call it acquired prejudice)" and can be overcome only by another biological force such as sexual desire' (see *White Writing*, 1988: 153). Gordimer reverses the negative connotations implicit in Millin's use of the word 'sport'.

50. Nadine Gordimer, 'Johannesburg', in *Holiday* 18, 1952: 46-51.

51. Nadine Gordimer, in interview with Diana Cooper-Clark, 1983: 48-49. Her denial that such a mysticism informs her work may reflect a new sensitivity to a point Es'kia Mphahlele made a number of years earlier; he said in 1962 that, because the South African government was 'using institutions of a fragmented and almost unrecognisable Bantu culture as an instrument of oppression, we dare not look back' (*The African Image*, 1962: 193).

52. Note the prevalence of this trope of colonial literature. Neil McEwan has identified as a literary stereotype in such fiction the representation of a 'demoralised, "masochistically" self-centred Western culture . . . often presented as if in monolithic opposition to a "primitive" but "soulful" Black world' (*Africa and the Novel*, 1983: 165).

53. Denis Beckett in *Sunday Star*, 16 December 1990.

54. See D. Ward, *Chronicles of Darkness*, 1989: 135, in which he suggests that only in her celebration of the possibility of a successful transition to a non-racial South Africa that informs the end of *A Sport of Nature* does Gordimer succeed in averting 'the instinct for tragedy'.

55. Ward comments that 'the changes in ethical concerns, in fields of vision, modes of analysis of the world, of perception, of human relationship, are as great as the reach of time might suggest. The continuities are equally strong; the relationship between the continuities and the change is so complex that it can emerge only through close reading' (1989: 112).

56. See in particular Anna Louw's account of her brief 'mixed marriage' to a man she identifies only as a South African Indian. She ascribes its failure to the impossibility of their having a child within such a context (*A World of Strangers*, 176-77). See too my comments on this issue in Chapter 3.

Chapter 6: Landscape Iconography

1. Henry Nash Smith, *Virgin Land*, author's preface, 1970: ix.

2. Bertolt Brecht, from 'An die Nachgeborenen', in Peter Suhrkamp (ed.), *Bertolt Brechts Gedichte und Lieder*, 1958: 158. In translation the poem is entitled 'To Posterity' and reads as follows:

   > Ah, what an Age it is
   > When to speak of trees is almost a crime
   > For it is a kind of silence about injustice.

3. Quoted in John Cooke, 'The Novels of Nadine Gordimer', 1976: 80, 75; from R. Sands (1970) (see Cooke, note 16, p. 233), and reviews by Mona Woodward (1969) and David Hendricks (1960) (see Cooke, note 3, 232). Cooke claims that Gordimer's 'special concern with backdrops . . . coupled with an unusual native skill in representation, made her presentation of her world's surface the most impressive aspect of her early work . . . [but that] detailing the backdrop leads to some awkwardness and discontinuity of perspective' in the early novels (1976: 75).

4. Anthony Woodward, 'Nadine Gordimer', 1961: 3, 5.

5. Nadine Gordimer, 'A Writer in South Africa', 1965: 28.

6. See Cooke's citation (1976: 75), of Gordimer's comment that Europe seemed 'exotic' to her in contrast to the 'ordinariness' of her own life (in 'Writing in South Africa: Nadine Gordimer Interviewed', in *New Nation,* September 1972: 14).

7. Nadine Gordimer, 'A Writer in South Africa', 1965: 28.

8. See for example the studies by Harmsen (1958), Gray (1979), Christie *et al.* (1980), Rich (1982), Povey (1983), Cooke (1985), and Coetzee (1988). The bibliography gives full details.

9. Stephen Gray, 1979: 151; Gray adds that ' "the Karoo condition" becomes transportable to almost any area of the sub-continent . . . [such as] Gordimer's Transvaal'. Harmsen comments earlier that the Karoo 'has a

quite inexplicable power to make artists produce their most moving work' (whereas the Natal coast has inspired very little) (1958: iv).

10. See, for example, two responses by non-South African architects, Sir Herbert Baker and Sir Edwin Lutyens, who, while working in the colonies, variously extolled the beauties of both the Cape and the Transvaal in their memoirs in lyrical terms seldom matched in the fiction of the day. For example, Baker writes in 1944 of Stone House in Johannesburg that it overlooked 'the summer green and winter gold of rolling grassveld, and away to the distant faint blue Magaliesberg mountains . . . There, perched on high, 5,700 feet above the sea, we lived in pure air from all the winds that blew, and above the frosts of winter that settled in the plains below. The almost daily thunderstorms in the summer months were formidable, but glorious to behold as they gradually dissolved and drifted away eastwards in the evenings with the glow of the setting sun upon the white dome clouds fringed with the lightning flashes; the landscape below was then seen through thin-spun veils of rain . . . Gardeners on the rocky ground at that high altitude have to fight against difficult conditions: frosts of winter, the hot sun and drought in the growing months of spring, followed by the torrential rains of summer. Yet at that time the gardens of Johannesburg, of the poorer as well as the wealthier, reached a greater state of perfection than was usually found on the Cape Peninsula, which for gardeners is so beautifully endowed by nature' (1944: 48, 55). Lutyens writes of the Johannesburg area: 'O the clear bright sky, the exquisite clear softness of the light over field and sky to the east. The sunset is too colourful to be really beautiful, but the silver greys and bright blues all as clear as crystal and the purples are wonderful. Italy cannot touch it with all her mystery of the ages' (quoted in C. Hussey, *The Life of Sir Edward Lutyens*, 1950: 206).

11. In this context we should note that Gordimer evidently considered the significance of the difference between the American and the South African frontier experiences with some care, as is made clear in a passage in *Burger's Daughter* in which Rosa meets the great-granddaughter of a Canadian railway millionaire and muses that 'the Burgers were trekking to the Transvaal when the great-grandfather was laying rails across Indian territory. It's an accident of birth, that's all, whether one has a grandfather who has chosen a country where his descendants can become rich and not question the right or whether it turns out to be one where the patrimony consists of discovering for oneself by what way of life the right to belong there must be earned by each succeeding generation, if it can be earned at all' (237-38). Such a perspective lends to the novel the quality of a muted Greek tragedy, wholly consistent with the more savage and outspoken point of view of *The Conservationist* and *July's People*. See too the passage quoted from 'The Novel and the Nation in South Africa' (1961: 38, referred to in footnote 28), in which Gordimer assigns to Africa a position in relationship to Europe which America appears to have held three centuries earlier.

12. Stephen Gray, *Southern African Literature: An Introduction*, 1979: 150-51.

13. See I. Glenn, 'The Immorality Act and the Liberal Novel', 1985: 112; he cites a passage in Alan Paton's *Too Late the Phalarope* to make this point.

14. André Brink, *A Chain of Voices*, 1982: 24, 25. In contrast, Alida, the Cape Town-born newly-wed wife of the white patriarch, Piet, offers her first impressions of the interior in sharply negative terms: 'Then came the mountains, those forbidding mountains. No man could possibly scale them, I was convinced; yet there were the tracks of wagons, and tossing and swaying we crossed them, the ultimate frontier and abandonment of hope, to break into a new dimension of intractable land, Africa. After the compliance of the Cape there was this new crudeness, simple statements of stone and narrow valleys; destiny assuming the shape of a cruel geography' (69).

15. J.M. Coetzee, *White Writing*, 1988: 177.

16. Stephen Gray, *Southern African Literature: An Introduction*, 1979: 26: Gray goes on to describe Adamastor as "menacing but mimical, and seen across a barrier, he belongs to an older but defeated culture, and is likely to sink the new European enlightenment if allowed within its purlieu" (27).

17. *ibid.*, 1979: 39.

18. J.M. Coetzee, *White Writing*, 1988: 99.

19. See Coetzee's interesting discussion of the connection between the picturesque and the sublime in American literature. He suggests that the idea of the sublime served an 'expansive nationalism' which took root in the New World early in its history, and argues that the picturesque failed to develop into the sublime in South African responses to the landscape because a concomitant nationalism emerged only very much later in this country's development (*White Writing*, 1988, Chapter 2).

20. See Stephen Gray, *Southern African Literature: An Introduction*, 1979: 23. M.H. Abrams writes that, since Empson, 'we label as pastoral any work which contrasts simple and complicated life, to the advantage of the former'. The term has been extended to include 'any work which envisions a withdrawal from ordinary life to a place apart, close to the elemental rhythms of nature, where a man achieves a new perspective on life in the complex social world' (*A Glossary of Literary Terms*, 1988: 128).

21. J.M. Coetzee, *White Writing*, 1988: 173.

22. See Ashcroft *et al.*, *The Empire Writes Back*, 1989: 194-97.

23. Argan, 'Ideology and Iconography', 1975: 298; he distinguishes between this and *iconography*, which specifically refers to the actual assignment of meaning to objects. See Paul Fussel, *The Great War and Modern Memory* (1975), for an analysis of the iconology of the 1914-18 war.

24. In Philip Stevick (ed.), *The Theory of the Novel*, 1967: 313-31.

25. Nadine Gordimer, 'A South African Childhood', 1954: 128-29. Over thirty years later, this gesture in the direction of traditional stereotypes has been replaced by her sharply uncompromising rejection of anything associated with these images. For example, she attacks examples of the ubiquitous South African genre of the wildlife painting in *A Sport of Nature* as 'the toadying gifts of white visiting artists . . . subconsciously reproducing the white man's yearning for Africa to be a picture book bestiary instead of the continent of black humans ruling themselves' (306).

26. John Cooke, 'The Novels of Nadine Gordimer', 1976: 120.

27. Nadine Gordimer, 'The Novel and the Nation in South Africa' (1961), in D.G. Killam (ed.), *African Writers on African Writing*, 1973: 38.

28. Doris Lessing, 'Preface' to *African Stories*, 1981: 6.

29. See Chapter 4.

30. Nadine Gordimer, 'A Writer in South Africa', 1965: 24.

31. Stephen Clingman, *The Novels of Nadine Gordimer*, 1986: 112.

32. See Gordimer's comment on her gradual loss of this quality in her writing in 'A Writer in South Africa', 1965: 28.

33. Eudora Welty, 'Place in Fiction', 1956: 64 .

34. See J.M. Coetzee, 1988: 166, for an analysis of this typically colonial dilemma. Coetzee suggests that 'the critical question occupying South African landscape poetry [and by extension the fiction] [is]: How are we to read the landscape we find ourselves in? . . . If literary landscape is not to be secondary or inferior art, a mere verbal transcription of a scene already visually composed, it must . . . read out and articulate the meaning of the landscape'.

35. See Nadine Gordimer, 'Leaving School – II', 1963: 61.

36. Doris Lessing, 'The Old Chief Mhlanga', in *African Stories*, 1981: 47-58.

37. Nadine Gordimer 'A South African Childhood', 1954: 118. Coetzee comments that 'the European eye will be disappointed in Africa only as long as it seeks in African landscapes European tones and shades' (1988: 39).

38. Nadine Gordimer 'A Writer in South Africa', 1965: 25. Kenneth Parker has argued that, although Afrikaans literature from its inception served as a vehicle for the enunciation of political aspirations, the English felt 'their cultural heritage [to be] umbilically tied to that of the mother country'; conversely Afrikaners tried to create an 'indigenous product' (1978: 5).

39. Nadine Gordimer, 'A South African Childhood', 1954: 111.

40. Nadine Gordimer, *On the Mines*, 1973: 2, 7. The confused signification of residual metropolitan forms transplanted to this environment is suggested in another section of this passage: 'On the veld there were built the billiard rooms of the General Manager's fretted wood-and-iron Residence, the squalid concrete bunks of the Compound. Both were thought apposite to the needs – of whom? for what? A wood-and-iron version of the facilities of a Victorian house party; a cross between a military barracks, a prison, and a boy's school . . .' (1973: 2).

41. Nadine Gordimer, 'A South African Childhood', 1954: 111-12.

42. *ibid.*, 1954: 112.

43. Nadine Gordimer has said that 'my method is to let the general seep up through the individual' ('A Writer in South Africa', 1965: 23). In practice, in certain circumstances and emotional contexts, the unique moment freezes and gains the status of the typical in the subjective consciousness of a protagonist. In *Burger's Daughter*, Rosa, while still shocked by Baasie's midnight telephone call, awakens to 'another perfect noon. This spell of weather continued for a short time yet. So for Rosa Burger England will always be like that: tiers of shade all down the sunny street, the shy white feet of people who have taken off their shoes and socks to feel the grass, the sun

wriggling across the paths of pleasure boats on the ancient river; where people sit on benches drinking outside pubs, the girls preening their flashing hair through their fingers' (324). The idea that 'reality' is a subjective and individual construction underlies many such passages (see, for example, Anna Louw's description of Neksburg in *A World of Strangers*, 180-81), and alerts us to some interesting parallels between Gordimer's and Coetzee's work.

44. In contrast, note Albie Sach's comment that 'there is nothing that the apartheid rulers would like more than to convince us that because apartheid is ugly, the world is ugly' (1990: 21). Gordimer ironically comes close to endorsing such an apartheid-determined perspective.

45. Nadine Gordimer's 'Foreword' to R. First and A. Scott, *Olive Schreiner: A Biography*, 1989: 6 (a revised version of 'The Prison-house of Colonialism' (1980)). In this context it is interesting to note Schreiner's overwhelmingly negative response to Johannesburg: see, for example, R. Rive (ed.), *Olive Schreiner: Letters 1871-1899*, 1987: 333, 337, 340.

46. We might contrast Gordimer's landscape iconology to that of an Afrikaans writer, C.M. van den Heever, who, in a novel such as *Somer* (1953) inscribes an unselfconscious and intuitive immediacy of response which bespeaks an identification with the landscape which no English writer has articulated to date to a similar degree.

47. Nadine Gordimer, 'Notes of an Expropriator', 1964.

48. Nadine Gordimer, 'A Writer in South Africa', 1985: 28. See Paul Rich, who writes in 'Tradition and Revolt in South African Fiction' that Gordimer moved 'towards seeing the African landscape not as a deadening backdrop for the white segregationist imagination but the focus for a liberating African consciousness that will eventually transcend white cultural and political domination' (1982: 60). Yet Gordimer herself felt that the yoking of landscape to the political project had diminished her work in certain ways: see Boyers *et al.*, in conversation with Nadine Gordimer, 1984: 12.

49. See Mongane Wally Serote, 'To Don M – Banned', in M. Chapman (ed.), *A Century of South African Poetry*, 1981: 341.

50. Nadine Gordimer, 'A South African Childhood', 1954: 121.

51. See J.M. Coetzee's comment that 'silence in literary space . . . speaks in a different way, but it does speak: it makes sense; silence carries out a function that should always be recognised and studied . . . Silences are not hollow spaces but elements complementary to the verbal construct' (1988: 17).

52. See, for example, Toby's description of the landscape around Sam's house as a 'waste ground', a 'promontory of ashes and clinker'; 'we might have been standing on the crater of a burnt-out volcano, the substance beneath our feet gave no life to anything, animal or vegetable, it was a ghost of the fecund earth' (*A World of Strangers*, 160-61).

53. Stephen Gray, *South African Literature: An Introduction*, 1979: 154.

54. Nadine Gordimer, 'A South African Childhood', 1954: 118.

55. David Ward, *Chronicles of Darkness*, 1989: 118, ascribes this term to the sea in Gordimer's novels.

56. *ibid.*, 1989: 118, 119.
57. Jessie's despairing protest is echoed in a recent newspaper article written by Creina Alcock (1990), who ascribes her altered response to the Natal landscape of Msinga (where she farms) to the continuing violence which has torn the region apart. She writes, 'It's more than an hour's drive to Waayhoek [to which she is transporting the victim of a 'necklace' killing in a coffin], through wooded hills and flowering grass. I stare at the hills, but they've lost their strength, and there isn't enough beauty to uphold me ... The hills themselves seem different, sunken in on themselves, pockmarked with graves ... I always thought that landscapes were more important than people ... But now when I look at the landscape, it aches.' The underlying trope here is the idea that knowledge corrupts; the innocence of 'the Adamic universe before the capsule of knowledge came to infest it' (Tucker's phrase, 1967: 172) cannot be maintained in a fallen world.
58. See Leo Marx, *The Machine in the Garden*, 1964: 13.
59. Note that Clingman claims that 'nothing could be further from the vision of *Heart of Darkness* than Gordimer's theme in *A Guest of Honour*' (1986: 127). In his concern to dissociate Gordimer from the imperialist motif he discerns in Conrad's novel, however, he fails to do justice to the extent of Conrad's influence on Gordimer's work as a whole.
60. Marlow says, 'Principles? Principles won't do ... No; you want a deliberate belief' (in Joseph Conrad, *Heart of Darkness*, 1963: 37). Elsewhere I have suggested that by 'principles' Conrad means those 'ideas which can crumble quickly under pressure since they are not, for Marlow, based on a clear grasp of reality [thus representing a kind of false consciousness]; a deliberate belief, on the other hand, represents a choice shaped by experience and thought, rationally rather than emotionally held, and thus far less susceptible to revision' (see Wagner on *Heart of Darkness*, 1984: 68).
61. Joseph Conrad, *Heart of Darkness*, 1963: 34, 79.
62. 'The Congo' (1960-61), in *The Essential Gesture*, 1988: 149.
63. See Karen Blixen, *Out of Africa* (1937), 1953: 15.
64. Annette Kolodny, *The Lay of the Land*, 1974: 141.
65. Sarah Christie *et al.* (eds.), *Perspectives on South African Fiction*, 1980: 184.
66. Christopher Hope, reviewing *White Writing* (J.M. Coetzee, 1988), 1988: 15. Coetzee claims the pastoral fell into disuse in South African literature early on because it was too obviously divorced from South African realities to remain a usable genre.
67. Ricardo Gullón, 'On Space in the Novel', 1975: 15. See too Eudora Welty, who has said that 'location is the ground conductor of all the currents of emotion and belief and moral conviction that charge out from the story in its course: ... symbols in the end ... are permanent forms of focussing' ('Place in Fiction', 1956: 72, 63).
68. See *A Guest of Honour*, 14, 204, and *July's People*, 160.
69. Dennis Brutus, 'Protest against Apartheid', in C. Pieterse and D. Munro (eds.), *Protest and Conflict in African Literature*, 1969: 97. He writes that 'though Nadine Gordimer would say that she is condemning South African

society for being dehumanised, I would say that Nadine Gordimer, who is one of our most sensitive writers, is also the standing, the living example of how dehumanised South African society can become – that an artist like this lacks warmth, lacks feeling, but can observe with a detachment, with the coldness of a machine'. I have attempted to show that passionate feeling nevertheless is what informs Gordimer's anger at and contempt for aspects of her society.

70. Nadine Gordimer, 'A Writer in South Africa', 1965: 23.

71. John Cooke argues that Gordimer develops 'obvious correctives to those unfortunately resilient stereotypes of Darkest Africa' (1978: 534), but fails to note the extent to which she constructs alternative stereotypes to take their place.

72. Note in this context Jessie's observation that the city turns lively and adaptable children into 'ulcerous' and 'neurotic' adults (*Occasion for Loving*, 190), while, as we have seen, the failure of the Smaleses in *July's People* to identify in any emotionally meaningful way with the rural landscape to which they have fled becomes an index of their typical failure as both whites and urbanites to connect with an African reality, and a symbol of their irreversible spiritual alienation. Gordimer's recurrent emphasis on an opposition between country and city is derived from European models, and is paralleled in Doris Lessing's work. In a recent review of a study of Lessing's novels by M.A. Singleton, Diane Tolomeo notes in a passage which illuminates Gordimer's fiction as well that, in Lessing's work, 'the veld signifies the unity of nature, the "mythic state" in which an individual belongs to the whole, possesses instinct without reason, and participates in the repetitive cycles of nature . . . The city, on the other hand, stands for the fragmented perceptions of individuals who lead lives that are unbalanced and in conflict, participating in destructive patterns that will lead mankind to disaster' (1978: 51). Gordimer, as a thoroughly urban writer, articulates 'the country' not as 'the farm' of Smith's and Schreiner's work, but as the holiday landscapes of the leisured white classes – in itself already an index of the extent of white alienation from the land. Nevertheless, as we have seen, the opposition outlined above still functions in the novels. It is in operation, for example, in the description of MacDonald's Kloof in *The Lying Days*: 'It was as if the earth, ugly, drab, concealing great riches for sixty miles, suddenly regained innocence where it no longer had anything to conceal and flowered to the surface' (141).

73. See John Cooke, 'The Novels of Nadine Gordimer', 1976: 120, where he makes the point that, in *A World of Strangers*, Toby's final decision to remain in Africa is in effect a decision to 'go native'.

Chapter 7: Conclusion: *My Son's Story*

1. Doris Lessing, 'Preface' to *African Stories*, 1981: 6.

2. Philip Hobsbaum, from *A Theory of Communication* (London, 1970: 47ff.),

quoted in Wolfgang Iser, *The Act of Reading: A Theory of Aesthetic Response* (1976), 1978: 16.

3. Nadine Gordimer, *My Son's Story*, Cape Town: David Philip, and Johannesburg: Taurus, 1990.

4. Nadine Gordimer, 'A Writer in South Africa', 1965: 28.

5. See Ursula Le Guin, in an essay entitled 'A Non-Euclidean View of California', in *Dancing at the Edge of the World*, 1989: 98, in which she comments at length upon the utopian imagination.

6. Nadine Gordimer, in interview with Mike Nicol, in *The Weekly Mail*, Johannesburg, 22-28 February 1991.

7. See 'Letter to His Father' in *Something Out There*, 1984: 39ff., in which Gordimer adopts the point of view of Kafka's father, who is responding to his sons's criticisms: it is the *father's* perspectives which are valorised.

8. See for example Don Maclennan, 'The Vacuum Pump: The Fiction of Nadine Gordimer', 1989: 32. He asserts that Gordimer's fiction 'tells me that I must reject bourgeois humanism, and therefore all those values through which I am in fact being appealed to in order that she can make her case in the first place'.

9. See the Introduction to this study; Nadine Gordimer's comment comes from her essay 'Literature and Politics in South Africa' (1974), and is quoted by Abdul JanMohamed in *Manichean Aesthetics*, 1983: 265.

10. See I. de Kok and K. Press (eds.), *Spring is Rebellious*, 1990: 20. Note that in 1976 Cooke suggested that Gordimer should be seen as potentially a better writer than her politics have allowed her to be, and quoted Peter Nazareth as saying in 1975 that 'in another time and another place, Nadine Gordimer would have been another Jane Austcn' (1976: 230, n. 31).

11. Abdul JanMohamed, *Manichean Aesthetics*, 1983: 277; see too 65.

12. Perspective shifts significantly in Gordimer's various comments on the white South African relationship to landscape. An unmediated innocence of response is offered in her explanation to Diana Cooper-Clark that writers 'get their earliest impressions . . . from the quality of the light, the kind of mud you play with, the kind of trees you climb well. I am white but those trees and that mud were Africa, so they are inside me and they come out, I suppose, in one's work' (1983: 49). But a year later, in the Boyers interview, she offers an interpretation of white response which arises directly out of the felt pressures of a political ideology: 'the white claim to the land simply cannot carry the same weight as that of blacks because history intervenes in the construction of a white identity by insisting that what has been taken by conquest cannot be unproblematically enjoyed' (1984: 6). The dilemma represented here by the gap between innocence and experience, one inherent in the tension between the personal and the political, lends some weariness to her voice as she goes on to say that, as she has grown older and more politically aware, she recognises that she has lost 'that vividness . . . that freshness [of eye] because I've seen everything too often' (*ibid.*, 12).

13. See Alina Gildiner, 'The Human Truth' (a review of *My Son's Story*), in *The Globe and Mail*, Toronto, 1991.

14. Nadine Gordimer, in interview with Mike Nicol, February 1991. Nicol had asked her, 'Do you write from an ideological position?'
15. Abdul JanMohamed, *Manichean Aesthetics*, 1983: 266.
16. Discussed in JanMohamed, *ibid.*; see 266-272.
17. *ibid.*
18. See the interview with Mike Nicol, 1991, in which Gordimer states, 'I am a socialist – not a communist, as rumour has it . . . I am a member of the African National Congress'.
19. Sander L. Gilman, *Difference and Pathology*, 1985: 35.
20. *ibid.*, 18.
21. *ibid.*, 20. Note that Gilman insists that 'we can and must make the distinction between pathological stereotyping and the stereotyping all of us need to do'.
22. In Sonny's oration at the graveside, the narrator tells us, 'he used the vocabulary of politics because certain words and phrases were codes everyone understood . . . They expanded in each individual's hearing to carry the meaning of his frustrations, demands and desires' (*My Son's Story*, 112).
23. In *Selected Stories*, 1983: 264ff. originally published in *Not for Publication*, 1965.
24. See Nadine Gordimer's interview with Mike Nicol, February 1991.
25. See Stanley Fish, 'Interpreting the "Variorum"' (1976) in J.P. Tompkins (ed.), *Reader-response Criticism*, 1980: 182.
26. J.M. Coetzee, 'The Great South African Novel', 1983: 74.
27. Michel Foucault, 'What is an Author?' (1977), in J.V. Harari (ed.), *Textual Strategies*, 1979: 148. See too the collections of essays on reader-response perspectives edited by Tompkins (*Reader-Response Criticism*) and Suleiman and Crosman (*The Reader in the Text*), both published in 1980.
28. This judgement, ironically, comes from a fellow South African: see J.M. Coetzee, 'The Afrikaners: On the Lip of a Volcano', 1986: 69. Coetzee's generous assessment is not qualified and takes no account, for example, of the need for a black perspective on the experience of the majority of South Africans under apartheid.
29. Nadine Gordimer, quoted from 'Living in the Interregnum' by George Brock, in his interview with Gordimer, 1983.
30. Nadine Gordimer, in interview with George Brock, 1983. Note that, although Gordimer seems to be referring to the possibility of betrayal to the apartheid secret police, her comment reflects ironically upon the issue of subtexts in the fiction.
31. See Gordimer's plea in 'Where Do Whites Fit In?' (1959), in which she claims to be one of those 'who want to belong in the new Africa as we never could in the old, where our skin-colour labelled us as oppressors to the blacks and our views labelled us as traitors to the whites. We want merely to be ordinary members of a multi-coloured, any-coloured society, freed both of the privileges and the guilt of the white sins of our fathers' (in S. Clingman (ed.), *The Essential Gesture*, 1988: 25-26).

Bibliography

Nadine Gordimer: Primary Material

Novels

The Lying Days (1953), (introduction by Paul Bailey), London: Virago, 1983.

A World of Strangers (1958), Harmondsworth: Penguin, 1962.

Occasion for Loving (1963), (introduction by Paul Bailey), London: Virago, 1983.

The Late Bourgeois World (1966), Harmondsworth: Penguin, 1982.

A Guest of Honour (1970), Harmondsworth: Penguin, 1973.

The Conservationist (1974), Harmondsworth: Penguin, 1978.

Burger's Daughter, London: Jonathan Cape, 1979.

July's People, Johannesburg: Ravan/Taurus, 1981.

A Sport of Nature, Cape Town: David Philip, and Johannesburg: Taurus, 1987.

My Son's Story, Cape Town: David Philip, and Johannesburg: Taurus, 1990.

Short Story Collections

Face to Face, Johannesburg: Silver Leaf Books, 1949; 16 stories; 13 reprinted in *The Soft Voice of the Serpent* (with 8 new stories), Johannesburg: Silver Leaf Books, 1953.

Six Feet of the Country, London: Victor Gollancz, 1956.

Friday's Footprint, London: Victor Gollancz, 1960.

Not for Publication, London: Victor Gollancz, 1965.

No Place Like: Selected Stories, London: Jonathan Cape, 1975 (with an introduction by Nadine Gordimer); published as *Selected Stories*, Harmondsworth: Penguin, 1983.

A Soldier's Embrace: Stories, (1980), Harmondsworth: Penguin, 1982.

Something Out There, Johannesburg: Taurus/Ravan, 1984.

'Once Upon A Time', in *The Weekly Mail,* 23 December 1988 – 12 January 1989: 31.

Crimes of Conscience, London: Heinemann, 1991.

Why Haven't you Written: Selected Stories 1950–1972, London: Penguin, 1992.

Essays, Articles, Non-fiction

'A South African Childhood: Allusions in a Landscape', in *The New Yorker* (30), 16 October 1954: 111-29.

'Johannesburg', in *Holiday* 18, 1955: 46-51.

'The Novel and the Nation in South Africa' (first published in *The Times Literary Supplement*, 11 August 1961: 520-23); now in G.D. Killam (ed.), *African Writers on African Writing*, London: Heinemann, 1973: 33-52.

'Leaving School – II', in *The London Magazine*, 3 (2), May 1963: 58-65.

'Censored, Banned, Gagged', in *Encounter* 20 (6), June 1963; now in *The Essential Gesture*, S. Clingman (ed.), Cape Town: David Philip, and Johannesburg: Taurus, 1988: 49-56.

'Notes of an Expropriator', in *The Times Literary Supplement*, 4 June 1964: 482.

'A Writer in South Africa', in *The London Magazine*, May 1965: 21-28.

'Plays and Piracy', in *Contrast* 12, July 1965: 53-55.

'The Fischer Case', in *The London Magazine* 5 (12), March 1966: 21-30.

'How Not to Know the African', in *Contrast* 15, March 1967: 44-49.

'The Interpreters: The Theme as Communication in the African Novel' (1968); unpublished paper presented at the 1968 National Arts Winter School, University of the Witwatersrand, Johannesburg.

'South Africa: Towards a Desk-Drawer Literature', in *The Classic* 2 (4), 1968: 64-74.

'The Interpreters: Some Themes and Directions in African Literature', in *The Kenyon Review* 32 (1), 1970: 9-26.

'Themes and Attitudes in Modern African Writing', in *Michigan Quarterly Review* 9 (4), Fall 1970: 221-31.

On the Mines (with David Goldblatt), Cape Town: Struik, 1973.

The Black Interpreters: Notes on African Writing, Johannesburg: Spro-Cas/Ravan, October 1973, incorporating an earlier paper: 'African Literature', a talk given at the University of Cape Town Summer School, February 1972, and published by The Board of Extra-Mural Studies, University of Cape Town, in 1972 as 'Part I: Modern African Fiction in English'.

'A Writer's Freedom', paper read at the conference on 'Writings from Africa: Concern and Evocation', held by the South African Indian Teachers' Association, Durban, September 1975; published in *English in Africa* 2 (2), 1975: 45-49; and in *New Classic* (2), 1975: 11-16; and reprinted in S. Clingman (ed.) *The Essential Gesture*, Cape Town: David Philip, and Johannesburg: Taurus, 1988: 87-92.

'English-Language Literature and Politics in South Africa', in C. Heywood (ed.), *Aspects of South African Literature*, London: Heinemann, 1976: 99-120; a paper originally given at the Conference on 'Literature on the Conditions of South Africa', University of York, 4-7 April 1975, and published also in *Journal of Southern African Studies* 2 (2), April 1976.

'Introduction' (April 1975), to *Selected Stories*, Harmondsworth: Penguin, 1983.

'The Prison-house of Colonialism', in *The Times Literary Supplement*, 15 August 1980; republished as 'Review of *Olive Schreiner: A Biography*', in Malvern van Wyk Smith and Don Maclennan (eds.), *Olive Schreiner and After: Essays in Southern African Literature*, Cape Town: David Philip, 1983; as 'Afterword: "The Prison-house of Colonialism" ' (rev.), in C. Barash (ed.), *An Olive Schreiner Reader: Writings on Women and South Africa*, London: Pandora, 1987: 221-27; and as 'Foreword' to Ruth First and Ann Scott, *Olive Schreiner: A Biography*, London: The Women's Press, 1989.

What Happened to 'Burger's Daughter'? or How South African Censorship Works, with John Dugard *et al.*, Johannesburg: Taurus, 1980.

'Living in the Interregnum', in *The New York Review of Books*, 20 January, 1983; reprinted in S. Clingman (ed.), *The Essential Gesture*, Johannesburg: Taurus and Cape Town: David Philip, 1988.

Lifetimes under Apartheid (with D. Goldblatt), London: Jonathan Cape, 1986.

The Essential Gesture, (ed. S. Clingman), Cape Town: David Philip, and Johannesburg: Taurus, 1988.

'Censorship and the Artist', in *Staffrider* 7 (2), 1988: 11-16.

'Images of women in Literature', *Buang Basadi / Khulumani Makhosikazi / Women Speak*, a COSAW publication of papers read at the 'Conference on Women and Writing', Johannesburg, November 1988: 53-55.

'Who Writes? Who Reads? The Concept of a People's Literature', in *Staffrider* 9 (1), 1990: 36-41; paper presented in 1989 at a symposium of the UNESCO Working Group,

'Look Back and Shudder' (a review of Allistair Sparks, *The Mind of South Africa: The Story of the Rise and Fall of Apartheid*, 1990), in 'Review: Winter Books Supplement', *Sunday Star*, 20 May 1990: 1-2.

Interviews

'South African Writers Talking' (with Es'kia Mphahlele and André Brink), in *English in Africa* 6 (2), September 1979: 1-23; a Round Table Discussion, chaired by André de Villiers at Rhodes University, 17 April 1979, and sponsored by The Institute for the Study of English in Africa.

With Stephen Gray, in *Contemporary Literature* 22 (3), Summer 1981.

With Joachim Braun, 1982; videocassette: Peter A. Frense, Director; Christopher Davies, Producer; Johannesburg: Profile Productions, 1982; in the holdings of The Wartenweiler Library, University of the Witwatersrand.

With Diana Cooper-Clark, 'The Clash', in *The London Magazine* 22 (11), February 1983: 45-59.

With George Brock, 'Nadine Gordimer', in 'Today' section, *The Star* Johannesburg, 28 November 1983: 3.

With Robert Boyers *et al.*, in *Salmagundi* 62, Winter 1984: 3-31.

With Pat Schwartz on *Something Out There*, in 'Profile', *The Rand Daily Mail*, April 1984: 7.

'Nadine Gordimer: An Interview', in M. Daymond, K. Jacobs and M. Lenta (eds.), *Momentum*, Pietermaritzburg: University of Natal Press, 1984.

With Jonathan Paton, videocassette, in the holdings of The Wartenweiler Library, University of the Witwatersrand, 1985.

With Dieter Welz, March 1985; published in Dieter Welz, *Writers Against Apartheid* (NELM Interview Series No. 2), Grahamstown, NELM, 1987: 37-45.

'In Conversation' (with Susan Sontag), in *The Listener*, 23 May 1985: 16-17.

With Heather Ross, 'Profile: Gordimer: The Prickly Conscience of a Country', in *Business Day*, 24 July 1986.

With Anthony Sampson, in *Sunday Star*, Johannesburg, 5 April 1987: 17.

With Jannika Hurwitt, in *Active Voice: An Anthology of Canadian, American and Commonwealth Prose* W.H. New and W.E. Messenger (eds.), Third Edition, Scarborough, Ont.: Prentice Hall Canada 1991.

With Mike Nicol, 'Gordimer: more than "just a writer"', in *The Weekly Mail*, 22-28 February Book Supplement, 1991: 11.

Conversation with Gordimer, (eds. Nancy Topping Bazin and Marilyn Dallman Seymour), Jackson, Mississippi and London: University Press of Mississippi, 1990.

Works Cited

Abrahams, Lionel, letter to *The Weekly Mail*, 16-22 March, 1990: 12.

— *The Celibacy of Felix Greenspan*, Johannesburg: Bateleur Press, 1977.

Abramowitz, Arnold, 'Nadine Gordimer and the Impertinent Reader', in *The Purple Renoster*, September 1956: 13-17.

Abrams, M.H., *A Glossary of Literary Terms* (5th ed.), New York: Holt, Rinehart, and Winston, 1988.

Adam, Heribert, 'Reflections on Gordimer's Interregnum', in *Occasional Papers: Series No. 1*, Centre for Research on Africa, University of the Western Cape, December 1983.

Alcock, Creina, 'A Woman in Hell', in 'Review' section, *Sunday Star*, Johannesburg, 6 May 1990: 1, 6-7, and article on her and quoting her, written by Carol Lazar, in the same edition of *Sunday Star*, entitled 'In the Valley of Death a Widow Rages', 6 May 1990: 1.

Althusser, Louis, 'A Letter on Art in Reply to André Daspré', in *Lenin and Philosophy* (1966), (translated by Ben Brewster), London: N.L.B., 1971: 203-208.

Andersen, Margaret L., *Thinking About Women: Sociological and Feminist Perspectives*, New York: Macmillan, 1983.

Anonymous, 'Age of Despair' (review of J.M. Coetzee, *Age of Iron* and N.Gordimer, *My Son's Story*) in Book Reviews (eds. D. Streak and Y. Fontyn), 'Sunday Magazine', *Sunday Times*, Johannesburg, 2 December 1990.

Argan, Giulio, 'Ideology and Iconography' (translated by Rebecca West), in *Critical Inquiry*, Winter 1975: 297-305.

Ashcroft, W.D., 'Intersecting Marginalities: Post-Colonialism and Feminism', in *Kunapipi* 11 (2), 1989: 23-35.

Ashcroft, Bill, with Gareth Griffiths and Helen Tiffin, *The Empire Writes Back: Theory and Practice in Post-Colonial Literatures* (New Accents Series), London: Routledge, 1989.

Bailey, Paul, 'Introduction' to *Occasion for Loving*, London: Virago, 1983.

Baker, Herbert, *Architecture and Personalities*, London: Country Life Limited, 1944.

Barash, C. (ed.), *An Olive Schreiner Reader: Writing on Women in South Africa* (Afterword by Nadine Gordimer), London: Pandora, 1987.

Barzun, Jacques, *The Use and Abuse of Art*, Princeton: Princeton University Press, 1974.

Bayles, Martha, 'Feminism and Abortion', in *The Atlantic Monthly*, April 1990: 79-88.

Beckett, Denis, 'Judge PAC by same standards', in 'Review' section, *Sunday Star*, newspaper, Johannesburg, 16 December 1990: 2.

Berghahn, Marion, *Images of Africa in Black American Literature*, London: Macmillan, 1977.

Bertelsen, Eve, 'Doris Lessing' (interview), in *The Journal of Commonwealth Literature* 21 (1), 1986: 134-61.

Blixen, Karen (Isak Dinesen), *Out of Africa* (1937), Harmondsworth: Penguin, 1954.

Boyers, Robert, 'A Conversation with Nadine Gordimer' (interview), *Salmagundi* 62, Winter 1984; (with Clark Blaise, Terrence Diggory and Jordan Elgrably).

Brennan, Tim, 'Cosmopolitans and Celebrities', in *Race and Class* 31 (1) (special edition on *Literature: Colonial Lines of Descent*), July – September 1989: 1-19.

Brink, André, *A Chain of Voices*, New York: Willie Morrow, 1982.

Brock, George, 'Nadine Gordimer', in 'Today' section, *The Star*, Johannesburg, 28 November, 1983.

Chapman M. (ed.), *A Century of South African Poetry*, Johannesburg: Ad. Donker, 1981.

Christie, S., G. Hutchings and D. Maclennan, *Perspectives on South African Literature*, Johannesburg: Ad. Donker, 1980.

Clayton, C. (ed.), *Women and Writing in South Africa*, Johannesburg: Heinemann, 1989.

Clingman, Stephen, *The Novels of Nadine Gordimer: History from the Inside*, Johannesburg: Ravan Press, 1986.

Cock, Jacklyn, *Maids and Madams*, Johannesburg: Ravan, 1980.

Coetzee, J.M., *White Writing: On the Culture of Letters in South Africa*, New Haven, and London: Yale University Press, and Johannesburg: Radix (Century Hutchinson S. A.), 1988.

— 'The Afrikaners: On the Lip of a Volcano', in *Fair Lady* Magazine, 28 May 1986; originally published in *The New York Times Magazine*.

— 'The Great South African Novel', in *Leadership S.A.*, Summer 1983: 74-79.

— *Life and Times of Michael K*, Johannesburg: Ravan, 1983.

— *In the Heart of the Country*, Johannesburg: Ravan, 1978.

— 'Nabokov's *Pale Fire* and the Primacy of Art', in *UCT Studies in English* 5, October 1974: 1-7.

Conrad, Joseph, *Heart of Darkness* (Norton Critical Edition, ed. Robert Kimbrough), New York: W.W. Norton, 1963.

Cook, Mercer and Stephen E. Henderson, *The Militant Black Writer in Africa and the United States*, Madison: University of Wisconsin Press, 1969.

Cooke, John, 'The Novels of Nadine Gordimer', Ph.D. thesis in manuscript form, Northwestern University, 1976.

Cooper, Brenda, 'New Criteria for an "Abnormal Mutation"? An Evaluation of Gordimer's *A Sport of Nature*', unpublished paper (1988); revised version published in M. Trump (ed.), *Rendering Things Visible*, Johannesburg: Ravan, 1990: 68-93.

Cronin, Jeremy, *Inside* (Staffrider Series No. 21), Johannesburg: Ravan, 1983.

Currie, Iain, Review of *The Empire Writes Back* (Ashcroft, Griffiths, and Tiffin: 1989), in *PreTexts* 2 (1), Winter 1990: 105-10.

Davenport, T.R.H., *South Africa: A Modern History* (Third Edition), Toronto & Buffalo: University of Toronto Press, 1987.

Davis, Geoffrey (ed.), *Crisis and Conflict: Essays on Southern African Literature* (Proceedings of the 11th Annual Conference on Commonwealth Literature and Language Studies in German-speaking Countries, Aachen-Liege, 16-19 June 1988), (vol. 2 of *African Literatures in English*, eds. Elmar Lehmann and Erhard Reckwitz), Essen: Verlag die Blaue Eule, 1990.

Davis, L.J., *Factual Fictions: the Origins of the English Novel*, New York: Columbia University Press, 1983.

Daymond, M., J. Jacobs, and M. Lenta (eds.), *Momentum*, Natal University Press, 1984.

De Kok, Ingrid, and Karen Press (eds.), *Spring is Rebellious: Arguments about Cultural Freedom by Albie Sachs and Respondents*, Cape Town: Buchu Books, 1990.

Dickens, Charles, *Great Expectations* (1861), (Introduction by K. Hayens), London: Collins, 1953.

Driver, Dorothy, ' "Woman" as Sign in the South African Colonial Enterprise', in *Journal of Literary Studies* 4 (1), March 1988: 3-20.

— 'Nadine Gordimer: The Politicisation of Women', in *English in Africa* 10 (2), October 1983: 29-54.

Elliot, David, 'Babel in South Africa', in *Art from South Africa*, Museum of Modern Art, Oxford; distributed by Thames and Hudson, 1990: 6-10.

Ellison, Ralph, *Shadow and Act* (1964), New York: Vintage Books (Random House), 1972.

— *Invisible Man* (1952), Harmondsworth: Penguin, 1965.

Enright, D.J., 'Which New Era?' (review of Nadine Gordimer, *Something Out There*), in *The Times Literary Supplement*, 30 March 1984.

Fanon, Frantz, *The Wretched of the Earth*, New York: Grove Press, 1981 (originally published 1961 by Francois Maspero, editeur, Paris; and copyright 1963 by *Présence Africaine*).

— *Black Skin, White Masks* (1952: originally published in French as *Peau Noire, Masques Blancs*), translated by Charles Lain Marle-mann, New York: Grove Weidenfeld, 1967.

Fido, Elaine, 'A Guest of Honour: A Feminine View of Masculinity', in *World Literature Written in English* 17 (1), 1978: 30-37.

First, Ruth and Ann Scott, *Olive Schreiner: A Biography*, (foreword by Nadine Gordimer), London: The Women's Press, 1989.

Fish, Stanley, 'Interpreting the "Variorum"' (1976) in J. Tompkins (ed.), *Reader-Response Criticism*, Baltimore and London: Johns Hopkins University Press, 1980.

Foucault, Michel, 'What is an Author?' (1977) in J.V. Harari (ed.), *Textual Strategies*, Cornell University Press, 1979.

Friedan, Betty, *The Feminine Mystique* (1963), New York: Dell Publishing, 1970.

Fussell, Paul, *The Great War and Modern Memory*, Oxford University Press: 1975.

Gates Jnr., Henry Louis, 'Introduction: "Tell Me, Sir . . . What *is* 'Black Literature'?"', in *PMLA* 105 (1), January 1990: 11-22.

Gildiner, Alina, 'The Human Truth' (review of Nadine Gordimer, *My Son's Story*), in 'Books' section, *The Globe and Mail*, Toronto: 5 January 1991.

Gilman, Sander L., *Difference and Pathology: Stereotypes of Sexuality, Race, Gender and Sex*, Cornell University Press, 1985.

Glenn, Ian, 'The Immorality Act and the Liberal Novel', in *Africa Seminar: Collected Papers* (vol. 5, 1985), Centre for African Studies, University of Cape Town, 1988: 108-123.

— 'Race and Sex in English South African Fiction' (1983-1984), in C. Malan (ed.), *Race and Literature* (Censal Publication No. 15), Pinetown: Owen Burgess Publishers, 1987.

Goldstuck, Arthur, *The Rabbit in the Thorn Tree: Modern Myths and Urban Legends of South Africa*, London: Penguin, 1990 .

Gray, Stephen, *Southern African Literature: An Introduction*, Cape Town: David Philip, 1979.

— 'Under Siege and Under Fire' (review of André Brink's *Mapmakers*), in 'Tonight' section, *The Star*, Johannesburg, 9 April 1984:9.

Gullón, Ricardo, 'On Space in the Novel', in *Critical Inquiry*, Autumn 1975: 11-28.

Harari, Josué V., *Textual Strategies: Perspectives in Post-Structuralist Criticism*, Cornell University Press, 1979.

Harmsen, Freda, 'The South African Landscape in Painting and Literature', unpublished M.A. thesis, University of the Witwatersrand, 1958.

Harris, Ann, 'My last hours . . . and my life with John Harris' (as told to Margaret Smith), *Sunday Times*, Johannesburg, 4 April 1965.

— 'Life with Harris – by his wife', *The Rand Daily Mail*, 7 November 1964.

Haugh, Robert, *Nadine Gordimer* (Twayne's World Authors Series, 315), New York: Twayne Publishers, 1974.

Heywood, C., *Nadine Gordimer*, Windsor, Berkshire: Profile Books, 1983.

Holland, Roy, 'The Critical Writing of Nadine Gordimer', in *Communiqué* 7(2), September 1982: 7-37.

Hope, Christopher, *My Chocolate Redeemer*, London: Heinemann, 1989.

— 'Language as Home: Colonisation by Words'; review of J.M. Coetzee, *White Writing* in *The Weekly Mail*, 22-28 July 1988: 15.

— Review of André Brink's *Chain of Voices*, in *The London Magazine* 22 (4), July 1982; 78-80.

Horn, Peter, 'Men Talk Women Talk', in *PreTexts* 1(1), Winter 1989: 64-72.

Horrell, Muriel (ed.), *A Survey of Race Relations in South Africa, 1964,* Johannesburg: South African Institute of Race Relations, 1965.

Hussey, Christopher, *The Life of Sir Edwin Lutyens*, London: Country Life Limited, 1950.

Iser, Wolfgang, *The Act of Reading: A Theory of Aesthetic Response* (1976), Baltimore and London: Johns Hopkins University Press, 1978.

JanMohamed, Abdul R., 'The Economy of Manichean Allegory: The Function of Racial Difference in Colonialist Literature', in *Critical Inquiry* 12, Autumn 1985: 59-87.
— *Manichean Aesthetics: The Politics of Literature in Colonial Africa,* Amherst: University of Massachusetts Press, 1983.
Jefferson, Ann, and David Robey (eds.), *Modern Literary Theory,* London: Batsford, 1982.

Karis, Thomas and Gwendolen M. Carter, *From Protest to Challenge: A Documentary History of Politics in South Africa 1882-1964* (vol. 3: *Challenge and Violence),* Stanford, California: Hoover Institution Press, 1977.
Karl, F.R., *American Fictions 1940-1980*, New York: Harper and Row, 1983.
Kedourie, Elie, 'The Limitations of Liberalism', in *The American Scholar*, Spring 1989.
Killam, G.D. (ed.), *African Writers on African Writing*, London: Heinemann, 1973.
Kolodny, Annette, *The Lay of the Land: Metaphor as Experience and History in American Life and Letters,* Chapel Hill: University of North Carolina Press, 1975.
Kuzwayo, Ellen, 'Introduction' to *Women in South Africa: From the Heart: An Anthology* (eds. Seageng Tsikeng and Dinah Lefakane), Johannesburg: Seriti Se Sechaba, 1988.

Lazar, Karen, 'Feminism as "piffling"? Ambiguities in some of Nadine Gordimer's Short Stories', in *Current Writing* 2(1), 1990: 101-116.
— 'The Personal and the Political in some of Nadine Gordimer's Short Stories', unpublished M.A. thesis, University of the Witwatersrand, 1988.
Le Guin, Ursula, *Dancing at the Edge of the World,* London: Victor Gollancz, 1989.
Lessing, Doris, *African Stories*, New York: Simon and Schuster, 1981.
— *The Grass is Singing*, Harmondsworth: Penguin, 1961.
Lockett, Cecily, 'Feminism(s) and Writing in the South African Context', in *Current Writing* 2(1), 1990: 1-21.
Lukacs, Georg, *The Meaning of Contemporary Realism* (translated by John and Necke Mander), London: Merlin Press, 1963 (originally composed 1955; originally published in German, 1957).

Maclennan, Don, 'The Vacuum Pump: The Fiction of Nadine Gordimer', in *Upstream* 7 (1), Summer 1989: 30-33.

Maclennan, John, Article on editorial page, *Sunday Star*, Johannesburg, 10 July 1988.

Malan, Rian, *My Traitor's Heart*, London: The Bodley Head, 1990.

Marquard, Jean, 'Some Racial Stereotypes in South African Writing', unpublished paper, read at the 'Conference on Literature and Society in Southern Africa', organised by the Centre for Southern African Studies, University of York, England, 8-11 September 1981 (and listed in *SA Literature/Literatuur 1981*, Annual Literary Survey Series 21, compiled by Francis Galloway, Censal Publication No. 9, Johannesburg: Ad. Donker, 1983).

Marx, Leo, *The Machine in the Garden: Technology and the Pastoral Ideal in America* (1964), Oxford University Press, 1967.

Maughan-Brown, David, 'The Noble Savage in Anglo-Saxon Colonial Ideology 1950-1980: "Masai" and "Bushman" in Popular Fiction', in *English in Africa* 10(2), October 1983: 55-77.

Mazrui, Ali A., 'The Patriot as Artist' (1966), in G.D. Killam (ed.), *African Writers on African Writing*, London: Heinemann, 1973: 73-90.

McEwan, Neil, *Africa and the Novel*, London: Macmillan, 1983.

Milbury-Steen, S., *European and African Stereotypes in Twentieth-Century Fiction*, New York University Press, 1981.

Milosz, Czeslaw, letter to the editor, *The New York Review of Books*, 21 July 1988.

Morphet, Tony, 'Two Interviews with J.M. Coetzee, 1983 and 1987', in *Triquarterly 69: From South Africa: New Writing, Photographs and Art* (Spring/Summer 1987), Northwestern University.

— '*Something Out There*: Nadine Gordimer', unpublished short paper offered at book launch of this title by Ravan Press in Johannesburg, 1984.

Mphahlele, Es'kia, 'South African Literature versus the Political Morality', unpublished opening address to the Annual Conference of The Association of English Teachers of South Africa, July 1983.

— *The African Image,* London: Faber and Faber, 1962.

Newman, Judie, *Nadine Gordimer* (Contemporary Writers Series), London: Routledge, 1988.

— 'Prospero's Complex: Race and Sex in Nadine Gordimer's *Burger's Daughter*', in *Journal of Commonwealth Literature* 20 (1), 1985: 81-99.

— 'Gordimer's *The Conservationist*: "That Book of Unknown Signs" ' in, *Critique* 22(3), 1981: 31-44.

Nkosi, Lewis, 'Crisis and Conflict in the New Literatures in English: A Keynote Address', in G. Davis (ed.), *Crisis and Conflict*, Essen: Verlag die Blaue Eule, 1990: 19-26.

Olson, Tilly, *Silences*, London: Virago, 1980.

The Oxford Dictionary of Quotations (3rd edition), Oxford and New York: Oxford University Press, 1980.

Panofsky, Erwin, *Meaning in the Visual Arts: Papers in and on Art History* (1957), London: Macmillan, 1978.

Parker, Kenneth (ed.), *The South African Novel in English: Essays in Criticism and Society*, London: Macmillan, 1978.

— ' "Imagined Revolution": Nadine Gordimer's *A Sport of Nature*', in C. Clayton (ed.), *Women and Writing in South Africa*, Johannesburg: Heinemann, 1989: 209-223; this paper is an expanded version of one read at the 'Conference on South African Literature' held at the University of Montpellier – Paul Valéry, May 1987.

Perrick, Penny, 'The Truth about the Lies' (review of Nadine Gordimer, *My Son's Story*), in *The Sunday Times*, London, 16 September 1990.

Pieterse, Cosmo, and Donald Munro, *Protest and Conflict in African Literature*, London: Heinemann, 1969.

Rhys, Jean, *The Wide Sargasso Sea*, Harmondsworth: Penguin, 1968.

Ricci, Digby (ed.), *Reef of Time: Johannesburg in Writing*, Johannesburg: Ad. Donker, 1986.

Rich, Paul, 'Tradition and Revolt in South African Fiction: The Novels of André Brink, Nadine Gordimer, and J.M. Coetzee', in *Journal of Southern African Studies* 9 (1), October 1982: 54-73.

Rive, Richard (ed.), *Olive Schreiner: Letters, 1871-1988*, Cape Town: David Philip, 1987.

Schreiner, Olive, *The Story of an African Farm* (1883), (Introduction by Richard Rive), Johannesburg: Ad. Donker, 1975.

Schwartz, Pat, 'Changing Words in the Short Story of South Africa' (profile of Nadine Gordimer), in Book Mail, *The Weekly Mail*, 1984.

Smith, Henry Nash, *Virgin Land: The American West as Symbol and Myth* (1950), Cambridge, Massachusetts: Harvard University Press, 1970 (with new preface by author, October 1969, for 20th anniversary printing).

Sontag, Susan, *Against Interpretation*, London: Eyre and Spottiswoode, 1967.

Stevick, Philip (ed.), *The Theory of the Novel*, New York: The Free Press, 1967.

Suhrkamp, Peter (ed.), *Bertolt Brechts Gedichte und Lieder*, Berlin und Frankfurt am Main: Suhrkamp Verlag, 1958.

Symons, Julian, 'Gordimer – South Africa's Conscience' (review of *Something Out There*), in *The Star*, Johannesburg, 5 April 1984.

Tolomeo, Diane, Review of M.A. Singleton, *The City and the Veld: The Fiction of Doris Lessing* (1977), in *World Literature Written in English* 17(1), 1978: 51-53.

Tomaselli, Keyan, *The Cinema of Apartheid: Race and Class in South African Film*, London: Routledge, 1989.

Tompkins, Jane P. (ed.), *Reader-Response Criticism: from Formalism to Post-Structuralism*, Baltimore and London: Johns Hopkins University Press, 1980.

Toolan, Michael, 'Taking hold of reality: politics and style in Nadine Gordimer' in ACLALS Bulletin, 7th Series No. 1, Commonwealth Fiction (1), (eds.) John Kwan-Terry and Koh Tai Ann, Singapore, 1985.

Trump, Martin, (ed.), *Rendering Things Visible, Essays on South African Literary Culture*, Johannesburg: Ravan, 1990.

— 'The Short Fiction of Nadine Gordimer', in *Research in African Literature*, 17 (3), Fall 1986: 341-69.

— Review article on *Narrating the Crisis: Hegemony and the South African Press* (eds. K. Tomaselli, R. Tomaselli and J. Muller, Johannesburg: Richard Lyon, 1987), in *English Academy Review 6*, December 1989: 162-64.

Tucker, Martin, *Africa in Modern Literature: A Survey of Contemporary Writing in English*, New York: Frederick Ungar, 1967.

Turner, Jenny, "A Lifestyle Rich in Black Ignorance" (review of Elleke Boehmer, *An Immaculate Figure*) and "Too much of a Good Thing" (review of Stephen Clingman, *The Novels of Nadine Gordimer*) in *The Guardian Weekly*, 6 June 1993: 28.

Van den Heever, C.M., *Somer*, Pretoria: J.L. van Schaik, 1953.

Van Wyk Smith, Malvern and Don Maclennan (eds.), *Olive Schreiner and After: Essays in Southern African Literature*, Cape Town: David Philip, 1983.

Viljoen, Deon, 'Identity and Commitment', in *Catalogue: Cape Town Triennial 1985*.

Visser, Nick, 'The Novel as Liberal Narrative: The Possibilities of Radical Fiction', in *Works and Days* 3 (2), 1985: 7-28.

Wade, Michael, *Nadine Gordimer* (Modern African Writers Series), London: Evans Brothers, 1978.

— "The 'Conspiracy Against Keeping Apart': Some Images of Blacks in Nadine Gordimer's Novels", *The African Past and Contemporary Culture*, (eds.) Erhard Reckwitz, Lucia Vennarini, Cornelia Wegener (Series African Literatures in English No. 8), Essen, Germany: Verlag die Blaue Eule, 1993: 81-94.

— "Landscape Iconography in 'The Novels of Nadine Gordimer', (ed.) Bruce King, London: Macmillan, 1993: 74-88.

— " 'Both as a Citizen and as a Woman?' Women and politics in Some Gordimer Novels", *From Commonwealth to Post-Colonial*, (ed.) Anna Rutherford, Mundelstrup, Denmark: Dangaroo Press, 1992: 276-291.

Wagner, Kathrin, "Credentials for Interpreting the Struggle" (review of Nadine Gordimer, *My Son's Story)*, in *Die Suid-Afrikaan* 31, February-March 1991: 44-45.

— ' "History from the Inside"?: Text and Subtext in Some Gordimer Novels', in G. Davis (ed.), *Crisis and Conflict: Essays on Southern African Literature*, Essen, Germany: Verlag die Blaue Eule, 1990: 89-107.

— ' "Dichter" and "Dichtung": Susan Barton and the "Truth" of Autobiography' in *English Studies in Africa* 32(1), 1989: 1-11.

— Review article on J.M.Coetzee, *Foe* 1986, in *The English Academy Review* 4, January 1987: 276-80.

— 'Joseph Conrad: *Heart of Darkness*', in C. Muller (ed.); *Explorations in the Novel*, Johannesburg: Macmillan, 1984: 61-73.

Ward, David, *Chronicles of Darkness*, London: Routledge, 1989.

Waters, H., 'Introduction' to *Race and Class* 31(1), July-September, 1989.

Watson, Stephen, *Selected Essays: 1980-1990*, Cape Town: The Carrefour Press, 1990.

Webster's Third New International Dictionary of the English Language, with Seven Language Dictionary (Encyclopaedia Britannica), Chicago and London: William Benton, 1966.

Weedon, Chris, *Feminist Practice and Post-Structuralist Theory*, Oxford: Blackwell, 1987.

Welty, Eudora, 'Place in Fiction', in *South Atlantic Quarterly,* January 1956: 57-72.

Welz, Dieter, *Writing Against Apartheid: South African Authors interviewed by Dieter Welz* (NELM Interview Series No. 2), Grahamstown: National English Literary Museum, 1987.

Williams, Raymond, *Keywords*, Glasgow: Fontana Books, 1976.

Woodward, Anthony, 'Nadine Gordimer', in *Theoria* 16, 1961: 1-12.

Wright, Derek, 'Requiems for Revolution: Race-Sex Archetypes in Two African Novels', in *Modern Fiction Studies* 35(1), Spring 1989: 55-67.

Wright, Ronald, *Stolen Continents*, London: Viking, 1991.

Yélin, Louise, 'Exiled In and Exiled From: The Politics and Poetics of *Burger's Daughter*', in Mary Lynn Broe and Angela Ingram (eds.), *Women's Writing in Exile*, Chapel Hill: University of North Carolina Press, 1989: 395-411.

Zwi, Rose, 'Prologue', in *The Purple Renoster* 8, Winter 1968; (special edition by Lionel Abrahams on 'The Idea of Johannesburg').

Works Consulted

Abrahams, Lionel, 'The Idea of Johannesburg' (editorial), in *The Purple Renoster* 8, Winter 1968: 2-4.

— 'Nadine Gordimer: The Transparent Ego', in *English Studies in Africa* 3(2), September 1960: 156-57.

Achebe, Chinua, *Morning Yet On Creation Day*, London: Heinemann, 1975.

— *Hopes and Impediments: Selected Essays 1965-1987*, London: Heinemann, 1988.

Aidoo, Ama Ata, 'No Saviours' (1969), in G.D. Killam (ed.) *AfricanWriters on African Writing*, London: Heinemann, 1973: 14-18.

Anonymous ("X"), 'Fall of a House' (review of *July's People*), in *The New York Review of Books*, 13 August 1981.

Appiah, Kwame Anthony, *In My Father's House: Africa in the Philosophy of Culture*, Oxford University Press, 1992.

Attwell, David, 'The "Labyrinth of My History": The Struggle with Filiation in J.M. Coetzee's *Dusklands*', unpublished paper presented at The History Workshop, University of the Witwatersrand, 6-10 February 1990.

— 'The Problem of History in the Fiction of J.M. Coetzee' in M. Trump (ed.), *Rendering Things Visible*, Johannesburg: Ravan, 1990: 94-133.

Bagley, Shona, 'Shawn Slovo; A World Apart' (interview with Shawn Slovo), in *Cosmopolitan*, December, 1988.

Baldwin, James, *Notes of a Native Son* (1964), London: Corgi Books, 1965.

Barrett, Michele, *Women's Oppression Today: Problems in Marxist Feminist Analysis*, London: Verso Press, 1980.

Barsby, Christine, 'Review Article: White Women Writers', in *English in Africa* 16 (l), May 1989: 97-104.

Berkman, Joyce A., *Olive Schreiner: Feminism on the Frontier* (Monographs in Women's Studies), St Alban's, Vermont: Eden Press, 1979.

Bertelsen, Eve, ' "*Veldtanschauung*": Doris Lessing's Savage Africa', unpublished paper, University of Cape Town, 1982.

Bowie, Malcolm, 'Jacques Lacan', in J. Sturrock (ed.), *Structuralism and Since: from Levi-Strauss to Derrida*, Oxford; Oxford University Press, 1979.

Boyers, Robert, 'Public and Private: on *Burger's Daughter*', in *Salmagundi* 62, Winter 1984: 62-92.

— *Atrocity and Amnesia: The Political Novel since 1945,* Oxford: Oxford University Press, 1985.

Bozzoli, Belinda, 'Marxism, Feminism, and South African Studies', in *Journal of Southern African Studies*, 9(2), April 1983.

Brantlinger, P., 'Victorians and Africans: The Genealogy of the Myth of the Dark Continent', in *Critical Inquiry* 12, Autumn 1985: 166-203.

Brink, André, 'Nadine Gordimer' (review of Robert F. Haugh, *Nadine Gordimer*, 1974), in *Books Abroad II* 4, Autumn 1975; 840.

Broe, Mary Lynn and Angela Ingram (eds.), *Women's Writing in Exile*, Chapel Hill: University of North Carolina Press, 1989.

Brooks, Peter, *Reading for the Plot: Design and Intention in Narrative*, Oxford: Oxford University Press, 1984.

Brown, Lloyd W., *Women Writers in Black Africa* (Contributions in Women's Studies 21), Connecticut; Greenwood Press, 1981.

Brydon, Diana, 'New Approaches to the New Literatures in English: Are We in Danger of Incorporating Disparity?', in H. Maes-Jelinek, Kirsten Holst Petersen and Anna Rutherford (eds.), *A Shaping of Connections*, Sydney: Dangaroo Press, 1989.

Bunn, D. and Taylor, J., 'Editor's Introduction' to *Triquarterly 69: From South Africa: New Writing, Photographs and Art* (Spring/Summer 1987), Northwestern University, 1987.

Canby, Vincent, 'Film: 7 Stories by Nadine Gordimer', *The New York Times*, 18 May 1983.

Case, Frederick I., Review of Nadine Gordimer's *Selected Stories* (1976), in *World Literature Written in English* 17(1), 1978: 54-55.

Chinweizu, Jemie O. and I. Madubuike, *Toward the Decolonisation of African Literature* (1980), London: K.P.I. Ltd., 1985 (distributed by Routledge and Kegan Paul).

Clayton, Cherry, 'Olive Schreiner and Katherine Mansfield: Artistic Transformations of the Outcast Figure by Two Colonial Women Writers in Exile', in *English Studies in Africa* 32(2), 1989: 109-120.

Clingman, Stephen, 'Revolution and Reality: South African Fiction in the 1980s', in M. Trump (ed.), *Rendering Things Visible,* Johannesburg: Ravan, 1990: 41-60.

— 'Nadine Gordimer and the Boundaries of Fiction,' unpublished paper read at the Annual Convention of The Modern Languages Association, Washington D.C., December 1989.

— 'Reading *Something Out There*', unpublished paper presented at the book launch arranged by Ravan Press for this title, Johannesburg, 1984.

— 'Multi-racialism, or *A World of Strangers*', in *Salmagundi* 62, Winter 1984: 32-61.

Coetzee, Ampie and James Polley (eds.), *Crossing Borders: Writers Meet the* ANC, Johannesburg: Taurus, 1990.

Coetzee, J.M. *Doubling the Point: Essays and Interviews* (ed. David Attwell), Cambridge, Mass.: Harvard University Press, 1992.

— *Age of Iron*, New York: Random House, 1990.

— 'Review of S. Rosen: *Hermeneutics as Politics*', in *Upstream* 6(4), Spring 1988: 61-63.

— 'The Novel Today', in *Upstream* 6(1), Summer 1988: 2-5; text of a talk given at *The Weekly Mail* Book Week, Cape Town, 13-l9 November 1987.

— 'Waiting for Mandela' (review article), in *The New York Review of Books*, 8 May 1986: 3, 6, 8.

— *Foe*: Johannesburg: Ravan, 1986.

— 'Truth in Autobiography', Inaugural Lecture, 3 October 1984, University of Cape Town, New Series No. 94, 1984.

— 'Idleness in South Africa', in *Social Dynamics* 8 (1), 1982; revised version reprinted in *White Writing*, 1988.

— *Waiting for the Barbarians*, Johannesburg: Ravan, 1981.

— 'Triangular Structures in Advertising', in *Critical Arts* 1 (2), June 1980: 34-41.

— Review of *The Guest*, in *Speak* 1(1), December, 1977.

— 'Achterberg's "Ballade van de Gasfitter": The Mystery of I and You', in *P.M.L.A.* 92(2), 1977: 285-96.

— 'The First Sentence of Yvonne Burgess's *The Strike*', in *English in Africa* 3(1), March 1976.

— *Dusklands*, Johannesburg: Ravan, 1974.

Conrad, Peter, 'Footholds in the Sunburnt Country', in a special section on Australian Literature, *The Times Literary Supplement*, 19 December 1986: 1421-23.

Cook, David, *African Literature: A Critical View*, London: Longman, 1977.

Cooke, John, *The Novels of Nadine Gordimer: Private Lives/Public Landscapes*, Baton Rouge: Louisiana State University Press, 1985.

— 'African Landscapes: The World of Nadine Gordimer', in *World Literature Today* 52(4), 1978: 533-38.

Culler, Jonathan, *On Deconstruction: Theory and Criticism after Structuralism*, London: Routledge and Kegan Paul, 1983.

Dangarembga, Tsitsi, *Nervous Conditions: A Novel* (1988), Seattle: The Seal Press, 1989.

Davidoff, L., J. L'Esperance, and H. Newby, 'Landscape with Figures: Home and Community in English Society', in J. Mitchell and A. Oakley (eds.), *The Rights and Wrongs of Women*, Harmondsworth: Penguin, 1976.

Davis, Gayle, 'Coetzee and the Cockroach Which Can't be Killed' (a report on Coetzee's address to *The Weekly Mail* Book Week), in *The Weekly Mail*, 13-19 November 1987: 13-19.

Davis, Lennard J., *Resisting Novels: Ideology and Fiction*, New York: Methuen, 1987.

Daymond, Margaret, '*Burger's Daughter*: A Novel's Reliance on History', in M. Daymond, J. Jacobs and M. Lenta (eds.), *Momentum,* Pietermaritzburg: Natal University Press, 1984.

Donaghy, Mary, 'Double Exposure: Narrative Perspective in Gordimer's *A Guest of Honour*', in *Ariel* 19(4), October 1988: 19-32.

Dovey, Teresa, *The Novels of J.M. Coetzee: Lacanian Allegories*, Johannesburg: Ad. Donker, 1988.

— 'Coetzee and his Critics: the Case of *Dusklands*', in *English in Africa* 14(2), October 1987: 15-30.

Driver, Dorothy, Introduction to 'Appendix II: South Africa' (a bibliography) in *The Journal of Commonwealth Literature* 24(2), 1989: 133-42.

— 'Olive Schreiner', (review of *Olive Schreiner: Letters 1981-1899*, (ed.) Richard Rive, 1987; and *Facets of Olive Schreiner*, Ridley Beeton, 1987) in *Upstream* 6 (1), Summer 1988- 33-37.

Du Plessis, Ménan, 'Towards a True Materialism' (review of J.M. Coetzee, *Waiting for the Barbarians*, 1980) in *Contrast 52* 13(4), December 1981.

Eagleton, Terry, *Criticism and Ideology: A Case Study in Marxist Literary Theory*, London: Verso Editions, NLB, 1976.

Eckstein, Barbara, 'The Body, the Word, and the State: J.M. Coetzee's *Waiting for the Barbarians*', in *Novel* 22(2), Winter 1989: 175-98.

Enright, D.J. 'The Thing Itself' (review of J.M. Coetzee, *Life and Times of Michael K., 1983*), in *The Times Literary Supplement*, 30 September 1983: 1037.

Finnegan, William, *Dateline Soweto: Travels with Black South African Reporters*, New York: Harper and Row, 1988.

Furbank, P.N., 'Mistress, Muse, and Begetter' (review of J.M. Coetzee, *Foe*, 1986), in *The Times Literary Supplement*, 12 September 1986: 995.

Gardiner, Judith, 'The Exhilaration of Exile: Rhys, Stead, and Lessing', in Mary Lynn Broe and Angela Ingram (eds.), *Women's Writing in Exile,* Chapel Hill: University of North Carolina Press, 1989.

Gallagher, Susan Van Zanten, *A Story of South Africa: J.M. Coetzee's Fiction in Context*, Cambridge, Mass.: Harvard University Press, 1991.

Gilbert, Sandra M. and Gubar, Susan, 'Sexual Linguistics: Gender, Language, Sexuality', in *New Literary Theory* 16(3), Spring 1985: 515-43.

Goodheart, Eugene, 'The Claustral World of Nadine Gordimer' (on *July's People*), in *Salmagundi* 62, Winter 1984: 108-177.

Gordon, Mary, 'A Moral Choice', in *The Atlantic Monthly*, April 1990: 78-84.

Gray, Paul, 'Life in the Territory of Exile' (review of *A Sport of Nature*), in *Time* magazine, 6 April 1987.

— 'Tales of Privacy and Politics: *Something Out There*', in *Time* magazine, 23 July 1984.

Gray, Stephen, 'Gordimer's *A World of Strangers* as Memory', in *Ariel* 19(4), October 1988: 11-16.

— Review of J.M. Coetzee's *White Writing: On the Culture of Letters in South Africa* (1988), in *Research in African Literatures* 20(2), Summer 1989: 304-306.

Green, Robert J., 'Politics and Literature in Africa: The Drama of Athol Fugard', in C. Heywood (ed.), *Aspects of South African Literature*, London: Heinemann, 1976: 163-173.

Greenblatt, Stephen and Giles Gunn (eds.), *Redrawing the Boundaries: The Transformation of English and American Literary Studies*, New York: The Modern Language Association of America, 1992.

Hacker, Andrew, 'Women at Work', in *The New York Review of Books*, 14 August 1986: 26-32.

Hagena, Antje, '"Liberal Realism" and "Protest Literature" as Concepts in South African Literary History', in G. Davis (ed.), *Crisis and Conflict*, Essen: Verlag die Blaue Eule, 1990: 73-88.

Hewson, Kelly, 'Making the "Revolutionary Gesture": Nadine Gordimer, J.M. Coetzee, and some Variations on the Writer's Responsibility', in *Ariel* 19(4), October 1988: 55-72.

Heywood, C. (ed.), *Aspects of South African Literature* (with an introduction by C. Heywood, 'The Quest for Identity'), London: Heinemann, 1976.

Higgins, John, *Criticism in Society* (review of *Criticism in Society*, Methuen, 1987), in *Upstream* 6(2), Autumn 1988: 41.

Hirsch, David H., *The Deconstruction of Literature: Criticism After Auschwitz*, Hanover NH: University Press of New England, 1991.

Hirsch, E.D., *Cultural Literacy*, Boston: Houghton Mifflin, 1987.

Hirson, Denis, *The House Next Door to Africa*, Africa South Paperbacks, Cape Town: David Philip, 1986.

Hofmeyr, Isabel, 'A Bewildering Parable' (review of J.M. Coetzee, *Foe*, 1986), in *The Star* Johannesburg, 22 September 1986.

Hulme, Keri, *The Bone People* (1985) (Picador) London: Pan Books, 1986.

Jacobson, Dan, *Adult Pleasures: Essays on Writers and Readers*, London: Andre Deutsch, 1988.

Jacobus, Mary (ed.), *Women Writing About Women*, London: Croom Helm, 1979.

Jahn, Janheinz, *A History of Neo-African Literature: Writing in Two Continents* (translated from the German by Oliver Coburn and Ursula Lehrburger), London: Faber and Faber, 1966.

Jelinek, H. Maes, Kirsten Holst Petersen, and Anna Rutherford, (eds.), *A Shaping of Connections: Commonwealth Literature Studies – Then and Now* (Essays in honour of A.N. Jeffares), Sydney: Dangaroo Press, 1989.

Jussawalla, Feroza and Reed Way Dasenbrock (eds.) *Interviews with Writers of the Post-Colonial World*, Jackson, Miss.: University Press of Mississippi, 1992.

Kanfer, Stefan, 'Friday Night' (review of J.M. Coetzee, *Foe*, 1986), in *Time* magazine, 23 March 1987: 67.

Katrak, K.H., 'Decolonising Culture: Toward a Theory for Post-Colonial Women's Texts', in *Modern Fiction Studies* 35(1), Spring 1989: 157-79.

Keegan, Tim, *Facing the Storm: Portraits of Black Lives in Rural South Africa*, Johannesburg: David Philip, 1988.

King, Bruce, " Towards Post-Colonial Literatures" in *Subjects Worthy Fame: Essays on Commonwealth Literature in Honour of H.H. Anniah Gowda* (ed. A.L. McLeod), New Delhi: Sterling Publishers, 1989: 53-61.

— *The New English Literatures*, London: Macmillan, 1980.

Klopper, Dirk, 'Ideology and the Study of White South African English Poetry', in M. Trump (ed.), *Rendering Things Visible*, Johannesburg: Ravan, 1990: 256-94.

Knox-Shaw, Peter, '*Dusklands*: A Metaphysics of Violence', in *Contrast 53* 14(1), September 1982: 26-37.

Lazarus, Neil, *Resistance in Post-Colonial African Fiction*, New Haven and London: Yale University Press, 1990.

Lenta, Margaret, 'Narrators and Readers: 1902 and 1975', in *Ariel*, 20(3), July 1989: 19-36.

Lessing, Doris, *African Laughter: Four Visits to Zimbabwe*, London: Harper Collins, 1992.

Leveson, Marcia, 'The Millionaire and the Shopkeeper – A Preliminary Investigation into the Jewish Stereotype in Early South African Literature', unpublished paper, University of the Witwatersrand, 1984.

Lockett, Cecily, 'The Men's Club', in *Upstream* 6(4), Spring 1988: 44-51.

— 'The Black Woman in South African English Literature', in *Journal of Literary Studies* 4 (1), March 1988: 21-37.

Lomberg, Alan, 'Withering into the Truth: The Romantic Realism of Nadine Gordimer', in *English in Africa* 3(1), March 1976: 1-12.

Macherey, Pierre, *A Theory of Literary Production* (1966), (translated by Geoffrey Wall), London: Routledge and Kegan Paul, 1978.

Marais, Michael, 'Interpretative Authoritarianism: Reading/Colonising Coetzee's *Foe*', in *English in Africa* 16(1), May 1989: 9-16.

— 'Language of Power: A Story of Reading Coetzee's *Michael K*', in *English in Africa* 16(2), October 1989: 31-48.

Mariani, Philomena (ed.), *Critical Fictions: The Politics of Imaginative Writing*, Seattle: Bay Press, 1991.

Marien, Wim, 'White Commitment in Africa: Decision-making in some of Gordimer's Novels', in G. Davis (ed.), *Crisis and Conflict*, Essen: Verlag die Blaue Eule, 1990: 109-116.

Martin, Richard G., 'Narrative, History, Ideology: A Study of *Waiting for the Barbarians* and *Burger's Daughter*', in *Ariel* 17(3), July 1986: 3-21.

McLeod, A. (ed.), *Subjects Worthy Fame: Essays on Commonwealth Literature in Honour of H.H. Anniah Gowda*, New Delhi: Sterling Publishers, 1989.

Milton, Edith, Review of *July's People*, et al., in *The Yale Review* 71, 1982: 258-59.

Moorhouse, Earl, 'Death in a Suitcase', in 'Sunday Magazine' section, *Sunday Times*, Johannesburg, 22 July 1984: 8-12.

Naidoo, Indres, *Robben Island: Ten Years as a Political Prisoner in South Africa's Most Notorious Penitentiary* (as told to Albie Sachs), (Vintage Books) New York: Random House, 1982.

Naipaul, Shiva, *North of South: An African Journey*, London: André Deutsch, 1978.

Nash, Roderick, *Wilderness and the American Mind* (1967) (revised version), New Haven and London: Yale University Press, 1973.

Ndebele, Njabulo, 'Redefining Relevance', in *PreTexts* 1(1), Winter 1989: 40-51.

— 'The Rediscovery of the Ordinary: Some New Writings in South Africa', in *Journal of Southern African Studies* 12(2), April 1986: 143-57.

— 'The English Language and Social Change in South Africa' (keynote address at the Jubilee Conference of the English Academy of Southern Africa, 4-6 September 1986), in *Triquarterly 69* (ed. D. Bunn *et al.*), Northwestern University, Spring/Summer 1987.

Neill, Michael, '"Groping Behind a Mirror": Some Images of the Other in South African Writing', in G. Davis (ed.), *Crisis and Conflict*, Essen: Verlag die Blaue Eule, 1990 157-82.

Nicol, Mike, "Too Black and White for Fiction", in *The Guardian Weekly*, June 21, 1992.

Nixon, Rob, *London Calling: V.S. Naipaul, Post-Colonial Mandarin*, Oxford University Press, 1992.

Nkosi, Lewis, 'Resistance and the Crisis of Representation', 39-51, unknown source: paper mailed to me in printed form by Lewis Nkosi, early 1989.

— 'Fiction by Black South Africans' (1966), and 'Relating Literature to Life: Lewis Nkosi and David Rubadiri, in Conversation' (1966), in G.D. Killam (ed.), *African Writers on African Writing*, London: Heinemann, 1973: 109-77, and 118-26.

Nourbese Philip, M., *Frontiers: Essays and Writings on Racism and Culture*, Stratford, Ontario: The Mercury Press, 1992.

Noyes, J.K., review of Michel Foucault: *The History of Sexuality* vol. 3: *The Care of the Self* (translated R. Hurley), in *Upstream* 7(1).

O'Brien, Conor Cruise, *Passion and Cunning: Essays on Nationalism, Terrorism and Revolution*, New York: Simon and Schuster, 1988.

Ozick, Cynthia, 'A Tale of Heroic Anonymity' (review of *Life and Times of Michael K*), in *The New York Times Literary Supplement*, 11 December 1983.

Patel, Essop (ed.), *The World of Nat Nakasa*, Johannesburg: Ravan Press, 1975.

Peck, Richard, 'What's a Poor White to Do? White South African Options in *A Sport of Nature*', in *Ariel* 19(4), October 1988: 75-93.

Podbrey, Joe, 'Kafka of the Karoo' (review of *Life and Times of Michael K*), in *The Financial Mail*, 9 December 1983: 62.

Povey, John, 'Landscape in Early South African Poetry', in Malvern van Wyk Smith and Don Maclennan (eds.), *Olive Schreiner and After,* Cape Town: David Philip, 1983: 116-28.

Prescott, Peter S., 'The Reluctant Revolutionary' (review of *Burger's Daughter*), in *Newsweek*, 27 August 1979: 53.

Rich, Paul, *White Power and the Liberal Conscience: Racial Segregation and South African Liberalism*, Johannesburg: Ravan Press, 1984.

— 'Liberal Realism in South African Fiction, 1948-1966', unpublished paper, University of London, 1983.

— 'Landscape, Social Darwinism, and the Cultural Roots of South African Racial Ideology', unpublished paper, University of London, 1982.

Roberts, Sheila, 'South African Censorship and the Case of *Burger's Daughter*', in *World Literature Written in English* 20(1), Spring 1981: 41-48.

— 'Character and Meaning in Four Contemporary South African Novels', in *World Literature Written in English* 19(1), Spring 1980: 19-36.

Ross, Robert L. (ed.), *International Literature in English: Essays on the Major Writers*, New York: Garland, 1991.

Rushdie, Salman, *Imaginary Homelands: Essays and Criticism 1981-1991*, London: Penguin, 1991.

Ryan, Pamela, 'Introduction', in *Journal of Literary Studies* 4(1), March 1988: 1-2.

Said, Edward W., *The World, The Text, and the Critic*, Cambridge, Mass.; Harvard University Press, 1983.

— *Orientalism* (Vintage Books), New York: Random House, 1979.

Salmagundi 62, Winter 1984; special edition on Nadine Gordimer entitled *Nadine Gordimer: Politics and the Order of Art*.

Sharpe, Jenny, 'Figures of Colonial Resistance', in *Modern Fiction Studies* 35(1), Spring 1989: 137-55.

Shava, Piniel Viriri, *A People's Voice: Black South African Writing in the Twentieth Century*, London: Zed Books, and Athens, Ohio: Ohio University Press, 1989.

Smith, Alan Huw, 'Three Pairs of Eyes' (includes review of *Life and Times of Michael K*), in 'Frontline Books' supplement, *Frontline* magazine, December 1983: 28-9.

Smith, Rowland, 'Inside and Outside: Nadine Gordimer and the Critics', in *Ariel* 19 (4), October 1988: 3-9.

— 'Masters and Servants: Nadine Gordimer's *July's People* and the Themes of her Fiction', in *Salmagundi* 62, Winter 1984: 93-107.

— 'Allan Quatermain to Rosa Burger: Violence in South African Fiction', in *World Literature Written in English* 22(2), Autumn 1983: 171-82.

— 'Living for the Future: Nadine Gordimer's *Burger's Daughter*', in *World Literature Written in English* 19(2), Autumn 1980: 163-73.

— (ed.) *Exile and Tradition*, London: Longmans, 1976.

Smyer, Richard I., 'Risk, Frontier, and Interregnum in the Fiction of Nadine Gordimer', in *Journal of Commonwealth Literature* 20 (1), 1985: 68-79.

Sparks, Allistair, 'J.M. Coetzee Reaches into the Heart of Darkness' (interview with J.M. Coetzee), in 'Today' section, *The Star*. Johannesburg, 2 November 1983: 17.

Spivak, Gayatri Chakravorty, *In Other Worlds: Essays in Cultural Politics*, London: Methuen, 1987; foreword by Colin MacCabe, 14 February 1987.

Suleiman, Susan Rubin, *Subversive Intent: Gender, Politics and the Avant-Garde*, Cambridge, Mass.: Harvard University Press, 1990.

Theoria 68: Literature in South Africa Today (special edition), (eds.) M. Chapman and M. Daymond, Pietermaritzburg: University of Natal Press, December 1986.

Torgovnik, Marianna, *Gone Primitive: Savage Intellects, Modern Lives*, University of Chicago Press, 1990.

Trump, Martin, 'Introduction', and 'Part of the Struggle: Black Writing and the South African Liberation Movement', in M. Trump (ed.), *Rendering Things Visible: Essays on South African Literary Culture*, Johannesburg: Ravan, 1990; x-xiii, 161-185.

— 'Debates in Southern African Literature of Liberation', in *Staffrider* 9(2), 1990: 37-49.

Van Donge, Jan Kees, 'Nadine Gordimer's *A Guest of Honour*: A Failure to Understand Zambian Society', in *Journal of Southern African Studies* 9(1), 1982: 74-92.

Van Staden, Gary, 'Azapo Plays a New Tune', in *Sunday Star*, Johannesburg, 7 October 1984.

Van Wyk Smith, M., *Grounds of Contest: A Survey of South African English Literature*, Kenwyn, Cape: Jutalit, 1990.

Vaughan, Michael, 'Storytelling and Politics in Fiction', in G. Davis (ed.), *Crisis and Conflict*, Essen: Verlag die Blaue Eule, 1990: 183-203.

— 'Literature and Politics: Currents in South African Writing in the Seventies', in *Journal of Southern African Studies* 9(1), October 1982: 118-38.

Viola, André, 'The Irony of Tenses in Nadine Gordimer's *The Conservationist*', in *Ariel* 19(4), October 1988: 45-54.

Visel, Robin, 'Othering the Self: Nadine Gordimer's Colonial Heroines', in *Ariel* 19 (4), October 1988: 33-42.

Visser, Nick, 'A Note on the Ending of *July's People*', in M. Trump, (ed.), *Rendering Things Visible*, Johannesburg: Ravan, 1990: 61-67.

Walcott, Derek, 'Leaving School – VII', in *The London Magazine*, September 1965: 4-14.

Walker, Alice, *Living by the Word: Selected Writings 1973-1987*, New York: Harcourt, Brace, Jovanovich, 1988.

— *In Search of Our Mothers' Gardens: Womanist Prose*, London: The Women's Press, 1984.

Wieseltier, Leon, 'Afterword', in *Salmagundi* 62, Winter 1984: 193-96.

Wilhelm, Peter, Review of J.M. Coetzee, *Life and Times of Michael K* (1983), in *Leadership S.A.*, Summer 1983.

— 'Savage Fiction' (review of *Burger's Daughter*), in *The Bloody Horse* 2, November/December 1980.

Williams, Raymond, 'Country and City in the Modern Novel', in *PreTexts* 2(1), Winter 1990: 3-13.

Woodward, Wendy, 'Radical Feminism, Feminine Creativity, and Modernist Gossip' (review article on Lesley Saunders (ed.), *Glancing Fires*, 1987; and G. Hanscombe and Virginia Smyers, *Writing for Their Lives*, 1987), in *Upstream* 6(2), Autumn 1988.

Index